Second Edition

Working with Families

An Integrative Model by Level of Need

Allie C. Kilpatrick
Professor Emerita, The University of Georgia

Thomas P. Holland
The University of Georgia

Allyn and Bacon
Boston • London • Toronto • Sydney • Tokyo • Singapore

Editor-in-Chief, Social Sciences: Karen Hanson
Series Editor, Social Work and Family Therapy: Judy Fifer
Series Editorial Assistant: Jennifer Muroff
Marketing Manager: Susan E. Brown
Composition and Prepress Buyer: Linda Cox
Manufacturing Buyer: Suzanne Lareau
Cover Administrator: Brian Gogolin
Production Administrator: Deborah Brown
Editorial-Production Service: P. M. Gordon Associates, Inc.

Copyright © 1999, 1995 by Allyn and Bacon
A Viacom Company
160 Gould Street
Needham Heights, MA 02194

Internet: www.abacon.com
America Online: keyword: College Online

Library of Congress Cataloging-in-Publication Data

Kilpatrick, Allie C.
    Working with families : an integrative model by level of need /
Allie C. Kilpatrick, Thomas P. Holland.—2nd ed.
        p.   cm.
    Includes bibliographical references and index.
    ISBN 0-205-27307-6 (pbk. : alk. paper)
    1. Family psychotherapy.   2. Family social work.   I. Holland,
Thomas P.   II. Title.
RC488.5.K55   1999
616.89'156—dc21   97-44973
                                                              CIP

Printed in the United States of America

10   9   8   7   6   5   4   3   2   02   01   00   99   98

This book is dedicated to our families—past, present, and future.

Contents

Foreword   ix

Preface   xi

Acknowledgments   xv

Authors   xvii

Contributors   xix

Outline of Approaches   xxiii

PART I   *Theory Base and Contextual Issues: Metatheories for Working with Families at Four Levels of Need*   **1**

1   **Levels of Family Need**   **3**
Allie C. Kilpatrick, Ph.D.
Level I   *4*
Level II   *6*
Level III   *8*
Level IV   *10*
Intervention Criteria   *10*
Summary   *13*

2   **An Ecological Systems–Social Constructionism Approach to Family Practice**   **16**
Thomas P. Holland, Ph.D., and Allie C. Kilpatrick, Ph.D.
Ecological Systems Perspective   *16*
Applications to Family Practice   *20*

Caveats in Using the Ecosystems Metatheory   22
Social Constructionist Perspective   23
Applications to Family Practice   27
Caveats in Using the Social Constructionist Metatheory   29
Comparing and Integrating the Metatheories   30
Summary   32

3 Contexts of Helping: Commonalities and Diversities   37
Allie C. Kilpatrick, Ph.D.
The Helping Relationship/Therapeutic Alliance   37
Diversity Issues   40
Summary   46

4 Ethical Issues and Spiritual Dimensions   50
Allie C. Kilpatrick, Ph.D.
Ethical Issues, Guides, and Codes   50
Spiritual Dimensions of Practice   57
Summary   60

PART II   *First Level of Family Need: Basic Survival Issues*   65

**5 Interventions to Meet Basic Needs in High-Risk Families
with Children   67**
R. Kevin Grigsby, D.S.W.
Typical Problems of Level I Families   68
Assessing the Level I Family: The Case of Mrs. G   68
Treatment   70
Treatment Approach   71
Evaluation of Effectiveness   76
Application to Families on Levels II, III, and IV   77
Summary   78

**6 A Family Case Management Approach
for Level I Needs   82**
Roberta R. Greene, Ph.D., and Nancy P. Kropf, Ph.D.
Family Problems   82
Family Case Assessment   83
Treatment Goals   84
Treatment Approach: A Generalist Model of Case Management   85
Evaluation   94
Application to Families at Other Levels of Need   95
Summary   95

PART III *Second Level of Family Need: Structure, Limits, and Safety Issues*   **101**

   7 Structural Family Interventions   **103**
     Peggy H. Cleveland, Ph.D.
     Typical Problems of Level II Families   *104*
     Family Case Assessment   *104*
     Treatment Goals and Interventions   *108*
     Interventions   *110*
     Evaluation   *117*
     Application to Families on Levels I, III, and IV   *118*
     Summary   *118*

   8 Social Learning Family Interventions   **122**
     Arthur M. Horne, Ph.D., and Thomas V. Sayger, Ph.D.
     Family Problems   *122*
     Assessment and Treatment Goals   *124*
     Social Learning Family Interventions   *126*
     Evaluation of Effectiveness   *132*
     Application to Families Functioning at Levels I, III, and IV   *133*
     Summary   *133*

PART IV *Third Level of Family Need: Problem-Focused Issues*   *137*

   9 Solution-Focused Family Interventions   **139**
     Peggy H. Cleveland, Ph.D., and Elizabeth W. Lindsey, Ph.D.
     Assumptions   *139*
     Typical Problems of Level III Families   *140*
     Family Case Assessment   *141*
     Theory Base and Basic Tenets   *141*
     Treatment Goals and Interventions   *143*
     Evaluation   *150*
     Application to Families on Levels I, II, and IV   *152*
     Summary   *152*

   10 Family Systems Interventions   **155**
     James A. Pippin, Ed.D., and Janice T. Callaway, M.S.W.
     Typical Problems of Level III Families   *155*
     Assessing the Level III Family: The Case of the Callahan Family   *156*
     Treatment Goals   *158*
     Treatment Approaches   *159*
     Evaluation of Effectiveness   *165*
     Application to Families on Levels I, II, and IV   *166*
     Summary   *166*

PART V   *Fourth Level of Family Need: Family and Personal*
             Growth Issues   **169**

    11 Narrative Family Interventions   171
        P. David Kurtz, Ph.D., Cynthia C. Tandy, M.S.W.,
           and John P. Shields, M.S.W.
        Family Problems   171
        Family Case Assessment   174
        Treatment Goals   174
        Intervention Approach   175
        Evaluation of Effectiveness   185
        Application to Families Functioning on Other Levels   186
        Summary   186

    12 Object Relations Family Interventions   192
        Allie C. Kilpatrick, Ph.D., and Ebb G. Kilpatrick, Jr., S.T.M.
        Family Problems   193
        Family Case Assessment   194
        Treatment Goals   195
        Intervention Approach: Theory Base and Major Tenets   195
        Application to Families on Level IV   199
        Interventions and Techniques   200
        Evaluation of Effectiveness   200
        Application to Families Functioning on Other Levels   203
        Summary   204

PART VI   *The Family in the Community: Ecosystem Implications*   **209**

    13 The Family in the Community   211
        Ray H. MacNair, Ph.D.
        The Ecological Perspective on Communities   211
        The Basics of the Community Ecosystem   213
        Assessment of Families in Community   214
        The Community as a Source of Pessimism or Optimism:
           A Sense of Collective Efficacy   218
        A Model of a Community Human Services Networking System   224
        Summary   226

    Glossary   231

    Author Index   239

    Subject Index   242

Foreword

As both a family practitioner and an educator for almost 40 years, I have been aware of the need to formulate a theoretical base for family practice that explains family dynamics and provides clear guidelines for effective interventions. Putting practice and theory together is not an easy task. In this book, the goal of bringing together family levels of need and practice models is accomplished in a manner that is both comprehensive and easy to grasp.

For me, some of the most valuable material in this book relates to the use of the practitioner's self in the helping process. Clearly, as in all helping endeavors, the person of the practitioner is the vital factor for facilitating change. Murray Bowen, in my opinion, accurately addressed the essence of family practice in his insistence that practitioners can progress with a family only as far as they have progressed in their own family relationships. My work with families over the years has confirmed over and over the pivotal role the maturity level of the practitioner plays in the helping process. Linking the self of the practitioner to the overall conditions of the problem context captures a powerful dynamic in the helping process.

In the second edition of *Working with Families*, Kilpatrick and Holland outline ways to approach the diversity of family dynamics, family need levels and lifestyles, and the many commonalities shared by all human aggregates throughout the life cycle. In this text, the emphasis on diversity and difference has not obscured the common human needs, capacities, and coping styles of people. Clearly, humans and human families have far more in common than is usually recognized by many theories of human behavior.

Some of the most cogent and thought-provoking parts of *Working with Families* are to be found in the constant emphasis on family strengths and coping capacities. While the authors assert that no single theory is adequate to deal with all family styles, the theories presented here all contain a basic strategy that focuses on levels of need rather than on levels of pathology.

The attention to the domains of family spirituality and professional ethics is especially relevant for the present period of rapid cultural change. The importance of the spiritual dimension cuts across all levels of family need. For some families, the spiritual dimension is crucial for their moral and behavioral guidelines. For other families, moral guidelines for behavior are sought from such nonspiritual sources as culture, society, and ethics. How can family practitioners understand family needs if they are unaware of the specific moral underpinnings for particular families?

Professional ethics serve as fundamental guidelines for social work practice. Family spiritual considerations and professional ethics form a critical part of the ecology of the treatment process for each family with whom we work. The attention *Working with Families* gives to spiritual and ethical considerations deserves careful reading.

Finally, this book contains a vast arsenal of ideas and directions for family practice. It responds to the need for a source that directs practitioners and students to different family problems, styles, and strengths, and provides specific directions for addressing the uniqueness of the family. It provides the basis for reflective consideration of the meaning of the spiritual and ethical dimensions of family work.

D. Ray Bardill
Professor, School of Social Work
The Florida State University
Past President,
American Association for Marriage and Family Therapy

Preface

The purpose of the first edition of *Working with Families* was to fill the need in social work and family therapy literature for an appropriately relevant textbook on family interventions, addressing the needs of families that students and practitioners typically see. Previous texts had focused on overviews of different models of family therapy, primarily emphasizing one model, a special population, or a problem group. Some have been geared toward middle-class, private-practice clients. Most have presented the therapist as the expert within a family systems context. What was needed was an integrative model for practice, one based on an assessment of the level of need in the family, and the particular problem(s) clients are facing within a wider ecological context. Once this assessment is done, then different interventions can be selected that are appropriate for that family's particular level of need at that point in time, around their specific problem area. The authors' goal was to meet the need for such a selective approach.

When students are given a broad overview of all the different models of working with families, they often come away from the course not knowing which specific approach to use in what particular situations. On the other hand, when only one model is taught, students are tempted to use that model with every family, even when it may not be suitable. When the focus is on a special population or problem group, students have difficulty generalizing appropriately to other populations or problem groups. Many family therapy texts are geared toward middle-class, walking-wounded, private-practice clients. These are *not* the families that students or practitioners typically see in agency settings.

The second edition of this book presents an updated integrative model to help students and practitioners make the fit between therapeutic style and family need. An overall ecosystems/social constructionism metatheory serves as the philosophical and theoretical base for working with families on all four levels of family need. Examples are given of specific approaches to intervention that would be relevant to use on each level of family need.

This book is useful as a text for students in social work, marriage and family therapy, counseling, psychology, and human service graduate courses, and for practitioners in any of these disciplines. It is especially geared toward applications with families typically seen in social service and family agencies, but it also addresses family needs at higher levels.

In this new edition the concept of family level of functioning is referred to as the level of family *need*. Some readers had difficulty making the transition from family *need* to family *functioning*. The way a family functions is, of course, based on their level of need. This edition is updated throughout with current content and methods. The concepts of resilience and family strengths are emphasized as the base upon which to build with families. The theory base of ecological systems and social constructionism is strengthened. Much attention is given to diversity issues. In fact, most of Chapter 3 is devoted to these crucial issues, and attention is given to diversity throughout the book as it relates to families at different levels of need. At a recent international social work conference, Lyons (1996) stated:

> *Approaching the millennium, political events, technological change, and socio-economic conditions suggest an increasing need for social workers to work cross-culturally (possibly within national boundaries), cross-nationally, or at a global level in international organizations. (p. 189)*

We seek to address this need by focusing on ethnic-sensitive practice. Most of the examples given in the practice models are generalizable across racial/ethnic groups and are relevant to the level of need experienced. The material on ethical issues has been revised to focus more attention to practice and professional codes of ethics. The content on spiritual dimensions of practice has been lengthened and strengthened. This added emphasis reflects the current state of knowledge, interest, and attention surrounding this subject area. Students are requesting more information on spirituality in order to meet expressed needs of clients as well as their own felt needs.

Part I covers the theory base and contextual issues that are utilized with families at any level of need. Chapter 1 presents a framework of the four levels of family need. It serves as a priority-setting guide, determining which approach one would use with a specific family. As such, the chapter is a beginning assessment tool grounded in the therapeutic assumption that interventions must begin addressing the level of the most basic need before moving on to higher-level interventions. In Chapter 2, the theory that undergirds this integrative approach is discussed. The metatheories of ecosystems and social constructionism form the philosophical and theoretical foundations.

Chapter 3 discusses the importance of the therapeutic alliance and the contextual issues of commonalities and diversities that must be addressed on any level of need; the focus on diversity and multiculturalism gives a global perspective to students and practitioners. The cross-cultural practice presented in this chapter guides ethnically sensitive practice and internationalizes work with families. Whether practiced in the United States or elsewhere, this perspective on diversity is crucial as our world becomes one community. Although the focus is on diversity issues, the emphasis is on commonalities that unite us rather than on differences that divide us.

Chapter 4 deals with ethical issues involved when working with families, and the spiritual dimensions that family members express. These spiritual dimensions have been sadly neglected by most practitioners and educators. Both ethical issues and spiritual dimensions must be addressed by family practitioners.

Parts II through V focus on interventions that are appropriate for families on each of the four levels of family need. Each chapter includes examples of interventions that would be relevant, but which are not the only ones that could be used on that level. With a shift in emphasis, some of the approaches could be used on more than one level of family need. Each chapter discusses how a specific approach could be applied to families that have needs on levels other than the one that we focus on in that chapter.

Each chapter in Parts II through V follows a similar format, addressing the following subjects:

- problem(s) presented by the family
- assessment, especially determining the level of need of the family
- goals of the intervention
- intervention approach used that would include the basic tenets of the approach, application to a family, specific interventions, and how the interventions are evaluated for effectiveness
- application to families on other levels of need
- summary
- discussion questions
- suggested readings
- references

Page numbers indicating where each of these subjects can be found in each chapter are given in the "Outline of Approaches" on p. xxiii.

Part II (Chapters 5 and 6) presents two approaches to family practice that are appropriate for families on the first level of need. These are family preservation, which is designed to address basic needs in high-risk families with children, and family case management, a more general approach for such families. In Part III, structural family interventions (Chapter 7) and social learning family interventions (Chapter 8) are applied to family need on Level II. Part IV addresses the third level of family need. It presents the models of solution-focused interventions that are representative of brief treatment approaches (Chapter 9) and family systems interventions (Chapter 10). We address interventions at the fourth level of family need in Part V, with the approaches of narrative family practice (Chapter 11) and object relations family interventions (Chapter 12).

In Part VI, the final chapter looks at the larger issues of the family in the community context. Chapter 13 discusses the ecosystem implications of working with families at the macrosystem level, thus integrating the previous chapters on intervention models with the theoretical and philosophical foundations presented earlier.

Reference

Lyons, K. (1996). Education for international social work. *Proceedings, Joint World Congress of the International Federation of Social Workers and the International Association of Schools of Social Work.* Hong Kong, pp. 189–191.

Acknowledgments

Our great appreciation goes to all the contributors to the second edition. They are experts in their fields, and we are grateful for the time and energy they have given. A special thank-you goes to the doctoral students at the University of Georgia who contributed their enthusiasm, attention to detail, and analyses.

The reviewers of the first edition—Carol Jabs, Concordia University; Sharon C. Shelton, University of Alabama; and Gail B. Werrbach, University of Maine—made some very valuable suggestions that made the book more relevant, readable, and user-friendly. Faculty and students who used the first edition in courses also gave us some useful and constructive ideas. These suggestions and ideas were helpful and have been incorporated into this edition.

Dr. Ray Bardill kindly agreed to rewrite the foreword for this edition. Many thanks go to him for taking time out of his busy schedule, and also for the many contributions and insights as well as inspiration he has provided the senior author in working with families. He has been a role model in having the courage to write and speak about spirituality while receiving criticism for doing so.

Thanks are due to the reviewers of the second edition: Joseph Richardson, Shaw University; Maureen Braun Scalera, Rutgers University; and Gary Villereal, Arizona State University. We are very grateful to Judy Fifer and the editorial staff of Allyn and Bacon. They have been most supportive and cooperative even while gently pushing to get this new edition into production. Their contributions have been helpful, timely, and professional. Thank you!

A final and most heartfelt note of appreciation goes to our families. They have been very patient and loving during this process, and contributed in unique ways to our ideas about families. The arrival of Allie's new granddaughter, Jessica Rose, and the addition of Tom's son-in-law, Thomas, are very special gifts.

Authors

Allie C. Kilpatrick, M.S.W., M.C.E., Ph.D., is Professor Emerita of the University of Georgia School of Social Work, where she taught for almost 25 years. She has published extensively in areas of family and social work practice and was instrumental in the development of the interdisciplinary certificate program in marriage and family therapy (MFT) at the University of Georgia, where she served as its coordinator. She is a Diplomate in Clinical Social Work, member of the Academy of Certified Social Workers, and Clinical Member and Approved Supervisor for AAMFT, and is licensed in Georgia as a Clinical Social Worker and as a Marriage and Family Therapist.

Thomas P. Holland, Ph.D., is Professor and Director of the Center for Social Services Research and Development, School of Social Work, University of Georgia. He also has been Associate Dean and Chairman of the doctoral program at the Mandel School of Applied Social Sciences, Case Western Reserve University, Cleveland, Ohio. Dr. Holland has published extensively on management and governance of nonprofit organizations. He was recently recognized by the University of Georgia as Outstanding Teacher of the Year and by his school as Outstanding Scholar of the Year.

Contributors

Janice T. Callaway, Pharm.D., M.S.W., is a doctoral student at the University of Georgia School of Social Work. Her research interests include family well-being, spirituality, and issues in higher education. She is currently completing a clinical internship with the McPhaul Marriage and Family Therapy Clinic at the University of Georgia.

Peggy H. Cleveland, Ph.D., is Director of the Division of Social Work at Valdosta State University, Valdosta, Georgia. She is a licensed Clinical Social Worker and Marriage and Family Therapist, and is a member of the Academy of Certified Social Workers. Her practice experience includes work with individuals of all ages, and marriage and family counseling. Her research has been in the areas of licensing and clinical practice with diverse populations, including people with AIDS.

Roberta R. Greene, M.S.W., Ph.D., is Professor and Dean, School of Social Work, Indiana University. Dr. Green is a leading author in the areas of gerontology and geriatric social work and multicultural issues. Her works include *Human Behavior Theory: A Diversity Framework, Social Work Case Management* (with B. S. Vourlekis), *Human Behavior Theory and Social Work Practice* (with P. Ephross), and *Social Work with the Aged and Their Families.*

R. Kevin Grigsby, D.S.W., is Director of Research and Development, Medical College of Georgia Telemedicine Center. A former faculty member at the Yale Child Study Center, he has published extensively, including *Advancing Family Preservation Practice* with S. Morton. His area of research is in the evaluation of innovative service delivery in underserved areas, and his practice includes outreach to families with children at imminent risk of out-of-home placement.

Arthur M. Horne, Ph.D., is Professor and Director of Training in Counseling Psychology and Coordinator of the Certificate Program in Marriage and Family Therapy at the University of Georgia. He is coauthor/coeditor of *Troubled Families, Group Counseling, Family Counseling and Therapy, Treating Conduct and Oppositional*

Defiant Disorders in Children, and other publications that draw from his research focus on at-risk children and professional practice with families.

Ebb G. Kilpatrick, Jr., M.Div., S.T.M., has worked with families in agencies and private practice for over 30 years. He supervised marriage and family therapy students and taught courses at Mercer University School of Medicine and the University of Georgia School of Social Work as a Clinical Member and Approved Supervisor of AAMFT and a Georgia licensed MFT. He is a member of the American Association of Pastoral Counselors, and is a retired Chaplain/Lieutenant Colonel in the Army Reserve.

Nancy P. Kropf, M.S.W., Ph.D., is Associate Professor and Associate Dean of the School of Social Work, University of Georgia. Her areas of research include caregiving relationships of older families and older people who have lifelong disabilities. Her extensive publications include *Developmental Disabilities: Handbook of Interdisciplinary Practice* (with B. A. Thyer) and *Gerontological Social Work: Knowledge, Service Settings, and Special Populations* (with R. L. Schneider).

P. David Kurtz, Ph.D., is Professor of Social Work and Education at the University of Georgia and Director of the Doctoral Program in Social Work. He is a licensed Clinical Social Worker, specializing in practice with families having troubled children or adolescents. Dr. Kurtz is the author of numerous publications on family treatment and social work practice and is especially interested in the professional applications of social constructivism.

Elizabeth W. Lindsey, Ph.D., is Assistant Professor of Social Work at the University of North Carolina at Greensboro. She was previously at the University of Georgia, where she taught marriage and family therapy courses. Her current research focuses on families and youth, and especially how they are able to emerge from homelessness successfully. She coordinates the UNCG social work exchange program with the University of Strathclyde, Glasgow, Scotland.

Ray H. MacNair, Ph.D., is Associate Professor at the University of Georgia School of Social Work. He served for 18 years as a public service consultant in the field of community development for human services. His research and publications are in the fields of community development, agency management, consumer participation, integration of services, and patterns of community planning. He is past president of the Association for Community Organization and Social Administration, which is for social work educators.

James A. Pippin, Ed.D., is Associate Professor at the University of Georgia School of Social Work. His practice experience includes serving as Executive Director and practitioner of a family service agency and director of a youth diversion center. He has taught courses and workshops in marriage and family therapy and has a private practice for couples in distress. He is a licensed Clinical Social Worker and Marriage and Family Therapist in the state of Georgia.

Thomas V. Sayger, Ph.D., is Associate Professor and Director of Training in Counseling Psychology at the University of Memphis. He conducts research on multifamily group prevention programs to strengthen home–school–community connections for families at risk for substance abuse, school failure, and behavioral problems. He is coauthor of *Treating Conduct and Oppositional Defiant Disorders in Children.*

John Shields, M.S.W., is a former alternative school teacher whose social work practice has focused on working with juvenile offenders and their families. He is currently a doctoral student in the School of Social Work at the University of Georgia and is working as a Research Consultant to the Northeast Georgia Board for Mental Health, Mental Retardation, and Substance Abuse Services.

Cynthia C. Tandy, M.S.W., is a licensed Clinical Social Worker who specializes in Family Practice. She has extensive experience in rural community mental health programs and is a candidate for a Ph.D. in social work at the University of Georgia.

Outline of Approaches

Level of Need	I		II		III		IV	
Authors	Grigsby	Greene & Kropf	Cleveland	Horne & Sayger	Cleveland & Lindsey	Pippin & Callaway	Kurtz, Tandy, & Shields	Kilpatrick & Kilpatrick
Approach	Family Preservation	Case Management	Structural Family Interventions	Social Learning Family Interventions	Solution-Focused Interventions	Family Systems Interventions	Narrative Family Interventions	Object Relations Family Interventions
Problem(s)	68*	82	104	122	140	155	171	193
Assessments	68	83	104	124	141	156	174	194
Goals	70	84	108	124	143	158	174	195
Intervention approach	71	85	108	126	143	159	175	195
Basic tenets	71	86	111	126	141	159	175	195
Application	72	91	109	127	144	161	178	199
Interventions	73	91	110	127	148	161	178	200
Evaluation	76	94	117	132	150	165	185	200
Other levels	77	95	118	133	152	166	186	203
Summary	78	95	118	133	152	166	186	204
Discussion questions	78	96	119	134	152	166	186	204
Suggested readings	79	96	119	134	153	167	187	205
References	80	97	120	135	153	167	189	205

Note: Numbers in the table body are page references.

Theory Base and Contextual Issues: Metatheories for Working with Families at Four Levels of Need

Working with families is so important that a family focus is now a major priority for the helping professions. Yet, existing approaches to this field tend to emphasize only one model for practice, assuming that this one model fits all types of family problems. But the differences in types of family issues and problems are extensive. These differences indicate a need for multiple methods from which the family practitioner may select and apply an approach on the basis of how well it fits with the needs and issues that a specific family is currently facing.

This section begins with an analysis of types, or levels, of family needs and functioning. To start where the family is, it is essential that the practitioner first assess the family's needs. The theoretical framework of an ecosystems and social constructionism perspective utilized in this book is set forth in Chapter 2. In Chapter 3, the context of helping is explored, focusing on the helping relationship, diversity and ethnically sensitive practice, gender issues, oppression, poverty, and family structures. Chapter 4 deals with ethical issues and the spiritual dimensions of practice when working with families.

The chapters in this first section set the stage for the ones that follow. The specific approaches to working with families at various levels of need flow from this theoretical and philosophical base and build on it.

Levels of Family Need

ALLIE C. KILPATRICK, Ph.D.

Helping professionals see families that are on many different levels of need. Their circumstances, problems, and skills are varied. For a practitioner to use only one model of assessment and intervention is like the saying, "If the only tool you have is a hammer, everything looks like a nail." The situation, is required to fit the helper's model even when there is no workable fit. Thus, the helper's need is met, rather than the clients' needs. This chapter describes four levels of family need and explores various methods of assessment and interventions that are relevant at each level.

In her 1945 social work classic, *Common Human Needs*, Charlotte Towle wrote about needs in relation to factors that affect human development. She contended that the following elements are essential if persons are to develop into maturity and be motivated toward social goals: physical welfare such as food, shelter, and health care; opportunity for emotional and intellectual growth; relationships with others; and provision for spiritual needs. She points out that needs are relative to a person's age and life situation. Most human needs are typically met within a family structure or in relationship with others.

Abraham Maslow (1970) developed a hierarchy of needs that supports Towle's thinking and expands our understanding of human development. According to his hierarchy, a person must satisfy primary physiological needs before social needs can be considered. He included five levels of need: physical and life-sustaining needs—the need for food, water, air, warmth, sexual gratification, elimination of bodily wastes, etc.; physical safety—the need for protection from physical attack and disease; love—the need to be cherished, supported, and aided by others; self-esteem—the need to have a sense of personal worth and value, to respect and value one's self; and self-realization—the need to be creative and productive, and to attain worthwhile objectives. We must remember, however, that often a lower-level need cannot be satisfied without a relationship with another person, as, for example, a young child's need for food.

Building upon these two formulations of needs, family problems encountered in helping situations may be seen as clustered around various levels of need based on the primary need at that time. These range from the basic survival needs to concerns about the self-actualization of family members and spiritual needs. Weltner (1985, 1986) views functional levels of families' needs from the analogy of building a house, which draws our attention to the necessity of addressing the most basic level of needs before moving to higher levels of need. Figure 1.1 illustrates the four levels of family need that will be utilized in this book.

Level I

The most basic level of family need has to do with the essential requisites for survival and well-being. These include the family's needs for food, shelter, protection from danger, health care, and minimums of nurturance. Referring to the house analogy, Level I would be the basement, and refers to life and death issues (see Figure 1.1).

Some families experience crises such as a job loss or major illness that leave them destitute. Other families that do not adequately meet these challenges are often considered neglectful and underorganized. These families lack a leadership and control structure that is needed in order to meet basic nurturing and protection needs of members. In other words, there is insufficient parenting capacity. According to the Beavers Family Competence Scale (Beavers, Hulgus, & Hampson, 1988), these families are leaderless; no one has enough power to structure interactions. This situation was more descriptive of neglectful families in lower socioeconomic circumstances than of nonneglectful families in similar circumstances (Gaudin, Polansky, Kilpatrick, & Shilton, 1991).

Sometimes, families struggling with Level I problems show evidence that the parental coalition is weakened or undermined by a parent–child coalition; family closeness is amorphous and vague, with indistinct boundaries among members. Faced with such basic resource deprivations as food, shelter, protection, education, clothing, transportation, and medical care, these families are rarely able to provide one another with the necessary emotional nurturance (Epstein, Bishop, & Baldwin, 1982). Examples of typical problems may include an overwhelmed single mother (as is the case in most neglectful families); the incapacitation or dysfunction of the strongest family member by illness, alcohol, or drugs; and natural or emotional catastrophes and pervasive life stresses that have depleted physical and emotional resources.

Work with these families must build on basic strengths and resiliencies—as is true at all levels—and focus on resources. For Level I families, Weltner (1985) suggests that the intervention should center on mobilizing support for the ineffective executive or parental system. Intervention could begin with a survey of potential resources from the community, including church groups or extended family (geno-

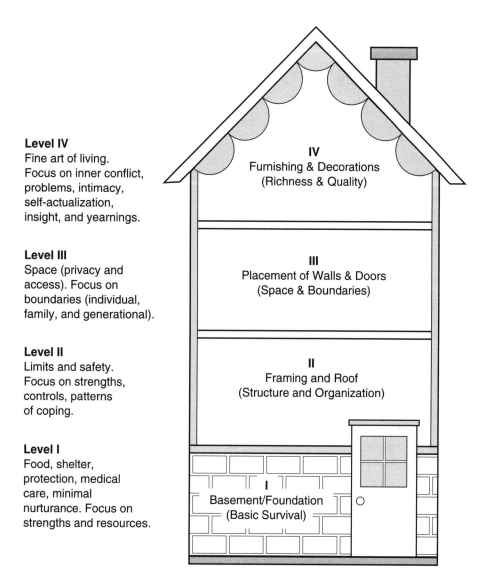

Level IV
Fine art of living.
Focus on inner conflict,
problems, intimacy,
self-actualization,
insight, and yearnings.

Level III
Space (privacy and
access). Focus on
boundaries (individual,
family, and generational).

Level II
Limits and safety.
Focus on strengths,
controls, patterns
of coping.

Level I
Food, shelter,
protection, medical
care, minimal
nurturance. Focus on
strengths and resources.

IV
Furnishing & Decorations
(Richness & Quality)

III
Placement of Walls & Doors
(Space & Boundaries)

II
Framing and Roof
(Structure and Organization)

I
Basement/Foundation
(Basic Survival)

FIGURE 1.1   Levels of family needs: issues and relevant interventions.

(From Kilpatrick & Cleveland, 1993.)

grams and ecomaps are helpful; see Hartman & Laird, 1983), and assess and build on family resilience and family strengths. Resilience, or the ability to withstand and rebound from crises and adversities, can be strengthened. Helping families to discover positive meanings to stress and distress is an important ingredient in strength-based interventions. Wolin and Wolin (1993), for example, highlight the "survivor's pride" (p. 8). This help could be offered to families demonstrating resilience in some area. Case management and referral to medical, income maintenance, and legal resources; protective services and family preservation programs; and hospitalization in crises may be necessary. Advocacy and guidance may be indicated, depending on the situation. Guidance on the use of respite care, referral to substance-abuse counseling, child development and child care information, and budget and time management may be necessary. Often, an advocacy role with school, welfare, and correctional or juvenile justice systems is necessary. Table 1.1 illustrates some of the issues, relevant intervention strategies, and possible intervention techniques that could be applicable on this level.

A case study presented by Paquin and Bushorn (1991) is illustrative of a family with needs on Level I and typical interventions. It demonstrates the mobilization of resources through case management skills, and the building on strengths to meet family needs.

> *Mrs. R. and her two children, aged 12 and 2, came to the clinic because Mrs. R. was dependent on diazepam and her supplier had retired from medical practice. During her first session, she discussed her difficulties with welfare and how she was concerned about losing her apartment, having the utilities turned off, or being attacked by her upstairs neighbors with whom she was having a feud. She was placed on a drug-withdrawal program by the clinic psychiatrist, and the clinic worker assisted her in contacting her welfare worker to resolve misunderstandings dealing with obtaining benefits on a continued basis. As Mrs. R. began assuming a measure of control over her life, welfare helped her find suitable day care so she could return to school to become a hairdresser. With education and support, her position in the family as parent with leadership responsibilities and capabilities was reinforced. She was encouraged to attend a parents' support group at the clinic. (p. 357)*

Level II

With Level II families, the basic needs of minimal safety, stability, and nurturance have been met, *and* maintaining authority and setting limits are the prominent issues. In the house analogy in Figure 1.1, Level II refers to the framing and roof of the house, and represents the family's structure and organization. The parental system is unable to set and maintain sufficient limits for one or more family members, and this inability threatens the stability of the whole family system. This failure could involve either a lack of clear expectations or a lack of power to enforce the expectations.

Other examples could include families where the children are out of control, acting-out teenagers, and parents who are involved in substance abuse or excessive gambling, or are otherwise failing to maintain key structures for the family. Marital conflict may appear to be out of control and threaten dissolution of the family unit. Violence in the family may be a threat, but members are not seen as needing immediate protection.

TABLE 1.1   Family Assessment and Intervention

Level	Issue	Intervention Strategy	Intervention Technique
I	• Is executive capacity sufficient to manage all basic nurturant needs? • Food, shelter, protection, medical care, minimal nurturance. • Resilience of individual and family.	• Focus on strengths, not problems. • Survey and mobilize available support to bolster executive capacity. • Family resilience building. • Positive response to stress.	• Family Preservation. • Case Management. • Marshal more troops from: A. Nuclear Family. B. Extended Family. C. Community. • Professional as convener, advocate, teacher, role model.
II	• Is there sufficient authority to provide minimal structure, limits, and safety?	• Focus on strengths. • Develop a coalition of those in charge against those needing control. • Increase clarity of expectation.	• Parental coalitions. • Set limits. • Clear communication. • Social learning skills. Written contracts. Behavioral reinforcers. Task assignments.
III	• Are there clear and appropriate boundaries? A. Family B. Individual C. Generational	• Focus on problems. • Clarify the "ideal" family structure in conformity with ethnic or family expectations. • Generational clarity.	• Defend family and individual boundaries. • Balance triangles. • Rebuild alliances. • Develop generational boundaries. • Communication skills.
IV	• Are there problems of inner conflict or problems with intimacy? • Are family members self-actualizing?	• Focus on problems. • Clarification and resolution of legacies and historical trauma. • Insight. • Focus on yearnings and spiritual needs.	• Narrative interventions. • Family sculpture. • Object relations interventions. • Resolution of three-generational issues. • Spiritual growth.

Adapted from Weltner, 1985, p. 49.

Again, interventions would begin with a survey of strengths, resiliences, and resources. In order to have the authority to deal with the situation and to offer sufficient hope, the practitioner must be in charge of structuring the sessions. Structural interventions enable the spouses to develop a coalition strong enough to demonstrate sufficient authority for the family to gain control of threatening or destructive behaviors.

Weltner (1986) points out that the focus of treatment in such situations must be to "develop a coalition of those in charge against those needing control" (p. 53). Family mapping of coalitions (Minuchin, 1974; Hartman & Laird, 1983) could be helpful with these families. Social learning and behavioral techniques with structural considerations may prove empowering to family members. Paquin and Bushorn (1991) show how behavioral techniques can help clarify the family's expectations for the behavior of each of its members and help them recognize their potential for modifying the behaviors of other family members.

A case study presented by Weltner (1985) illustrates a family functioning on Level II and typical interventions.

> *Ken Friendless was referred at 13 for school failure, lack of friends, and bizarre behavior including shooting at a neighbor's window with his shotgun. He was seclusive, awake until 3:00 A.M. reading science fiction, then sleeping past school time. His mother, drained by the stormy adolescences of three older girls, struggled to maintain herself and her job, upon which the family depended. She had no reserves to marshal on behalf of Ken, her last child.*
>
> *When it became clear that she could not single-handedly confront her determinedly eccentric son, two meetings were called with mother and her three daughters, two of whom were living at college, the third working in the same community. They ran through their concerns about Ken's lack of discipline and his sarcastic, withdrawn style. All agreed on the need for a bedtime, study times, school attendance, chores around the house, and regular mealtimes.*
>
> *In a third meeting, all four confronted him and laid down the law. Ken accepted with surprising ease. A long period of treatment of mother and son ensued, but the basic restructuring begun in this meeting was critical to Ken's emergence as an enjoyable, and now popular human being. (p. 45)*

While a wide variety of techniques may be used, both Level I and Level II interventions are essentially structural (Weltner, 1985) and ecosystems oriented. The goal is to mobilize all of the resources available, to modify the organizational patterns of the family, and to increase and test the strength of the parental or executive system. It is important to remember that children such as Ken have a readiness to fall in line. They are often aware of how much their own and their family's lives suffer as a result of their lack of discipline and control.

Level III

Level III focuses on space, with privacy and access as the issues. Using the house analogy in Figure 1.1, this level is concerned with the inner architecture. While the foundation, walls, and roof are satisfactory, the arrangements of inner space, or the placement of walls and doors, are not. Level III families are complicated, and they have a structure and style that is often perceived as working. They may draw upon and express a three-generational legacy, not a set of inherited deficiencies (Weltner, 1985). As pointed out by Aponte (1976), underorganized families (Levels I and II) generally do not transmit adequate patterns of coping. By contrast, Level III and IV families have a rich mixture of coping mechanisms. Weltner (1985) describes these coping mechanisms as their characteristic defenses, the culture to which they are committed and which they attempt to pass on to and through their children.

If work with such families involves changing ingrained patterns, we can anticipate some struggle. Therefore, our techniques need to encompass and adapt to such struggles. The Beavers Interactional Competence Scale (Beavers et al., 1988) rates these families as having marked or moderate dominance (control is close to absolute, with little or no negotiation; dominance and submission are the rule) while family members are isolated and distanced from each other.

Level III interventions involve processes of reshaping the internal architecture of the family so that everyone has appropriate space, access, and privacy. Interventions with these families must challenge the existing family structure and confront the family's tendency to remain in current patterns of behavior. Examination of the communication and power structures around the presenting problem may be useful. Differentiation and individuation of family members from each other and the emotional system, flexibility, and clear generational boundaries are essential.

Weltner (1985) presents a case study that is illustrative of Level III families.

> *Maria Fireworks was a 16-year-old whose unending episodes of drinking and defiance locked her into an endless struggle with her father. Coming from generations of Italian patriarchs, he would not step away from her daily provocations. He responded with increasing verbal and physical abuse, and with groundings which Maria ignored. Given the roar of this battle, Mrs. Fireworks was not audible. She had submissively adapted to her husband's control years ago. Her daughter also easily overwhelmed her feeble attempts at parental authority.*
>
> *Despite her temptation to tackle father and quiet him down, the therapist instead sympathized with his plight and with the lack of respect shown him by Maria. She admired his persistence and offered to help in bringing Maria under control. However, she defined control of teenage girls as a mother's responsibility and requested that Mr. Fireworks help the therapist to teach his wife to deal with such a difficult teenager. Tasks like keeping track of her hours, checking her room for drugs, and calling the school were now delegated to mother, who reported to father. Mr. Fireworks, an "expert in confrontation," was asked to coach his wife in this fine art. Her manner became more assertive. The therapist praised father for this growth in his second-in-command. And, as a consequence, Maria's acting up diminished. (p. 46)*

The "second-in-command" designation was an increase in status for the wife. Depending upon her own cultural orientation and values, she may or may not be content with this position. She may at some time be ready to move to Level IV and have as her goal the achievement of equality of status with her husband. Her empowerment to be more assertive is a first step.

Level IV

In Level IV families, basic needs are met and structural boundaries are relatively clear and satisfactory. Presenting problems often focus on a desire for greater intimacy, greater sense of self, or more autonomy. The concern of Level IV families is the fine art of living fully and growing toward actualization of each member's potentials. In relation to the house analogy, this level of functioning represents decorations, pictures, rugs, and lamps. Here the richness and quality of individuals and family life become the focus of interventions. Although some of these issues may have been discussed at earlier levels, it is on Level IV that such issues as inner conflicts, intimacy, self-realization, insight, and spiritual yearnings become the primary focus and are explored in depth.

Genograms extending over three or four or more generations are useful on this level in showing transgenerational patterns. Family sculpting may also be used. A focus on narrative interventions and rewriting one's own story are especially applicable on this level of family functioning. Object relations family interventions may be particularly helpful with these families, who desire insight into patterns and intergenerational functioning. Some families or individuals may want to focus on clarifying personal values, meanings, and spirituality, or they may wish to deal with existential issues. Helping professionals must be open to pursuing such issues, be comfortable in discussing them, and be able to assist families in clarifying their values and discovering the transcendent aspects of their beings without imposing personal conclusions on them. Referrals to church-related counseling centers may be indicated.

Following is a family situation that may be a typical example for Level IV families.

A middle-class couple with several children entered treatment with the complaint by the wife of vague feelings of depression and loneliness. She and her husband began to do extended family work with some emphasis on object relations. Working through some of their earlier relationships and projection processes and contacts with family made the wife feel more connected and less lonely. The couple were able to weather the terminal illness of her mother in a relatively calm fashion, without the wife becoming too depressed during the grief-work period. The loss of her mother opened up desires of both the couple to focus more on inner awareness and spiritual growth. Building upon insights gained and ongoing contacts with extended family, both were able to rewrite their own life stories to some degree.

Intervention Criteria

Once the primary, current level of need is assessed, then an opening for intervention must be determined. Do you start with the family, the couple, or an individual? Do you deal with what people do, what they think and feel, or what has happened in the past? Do you assume health or pathology? Is the primary need for maintenance of functioning or problem resolution? These questions are addressed by an intervention choice points grid developed by Pinsof (1995, 1991), shown in Figure 1.2.

The context columns in the table refer to the people who are involved in the problem-maintenance structure. This could be the family (including the extended family and the community), the couple in the same generation (allowing for alternate lifestyles), or an individual. The orientations headings refer to three intervention choices.

The behavioral/interactional choice has to do with what people do, their actions, and changing it. It involves surface behavior, and is visual. Social-learning, strategic, functional and structural techniques may be used here.

The experiential choice makes use of cognition, affect, communication, and interpersonal relationships—what people think and feel. It involves meaning and uses auditory senses—listening. Both these first two choices focus on the here and now.

The historical choice is the third intervention. It adds the dimension of time and addresses what has happened in the past. Family-of-origin work and psychodynamic or psychoanalytic methods may be used.

This model assumes that the people involved are healthy and that the problem can be resolved at a direct behavioral level. Therefore, in order to choose how to intervene, your decision points should progress from upper left to lower right, as shown in Figure 1.2. In other words, begin with the context of the family and the behavioral orientation. If the approach in this cell does not work, proceed down the cells diagonally to working with the couple experientially. If this approach does not work, then go to the individual and work with historical material. The

Orientations	Contexts		
	Family/ Community	Couple Dyadic	Individual
Behavioral/Interactional	*Start Here If Fails Go*		
Experiential			
Historical			

FIGURE 1.2　Intervention Choice Points

Adapted from Pinsof, 1991.

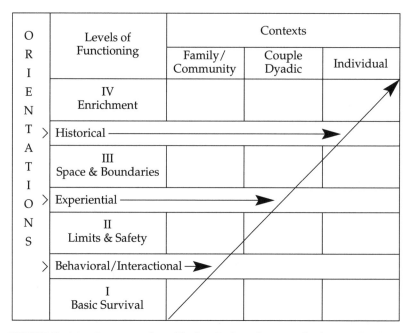

FIGURE 1.3   Intervention Choice Points by Level of Functioning

progression is problem- or failure-driven in that if a more direct approach is not successful, you proceed to another, less direct approach. It is also circular in that you continue to deal with meaning and behavior, and link what you are doing to the presenting problem. There is an explicit contract between the practitioner and the family to address the problem, so there must be a link between the presenting problem and what the practitioner does. This helps to keep the practitioner honest.

The essence of the choice framework is that working with families is a process of discovery, a "peeling of the onion." Is the problem simple and superficial, or deep and complex? The family is assumed to be healthy and to have a simple, superficial problem that can be addressed at the family-unit level with behavioral interventions until it is proven that the problem exists at deeper levels. Therefore, practice begins with simple, cost-effective interventions. The goal is to teach the family to learn from the practitioner how to solve problems for themselves. This process may involve internalizing the approach of the practitioner so the family can assume what the practitioner would say or do and thus work things out for themselves.

Once a family's basic survival needs are met, this choice framework can provide a guide for work at the four levels of need within the house metaphor. The three orientations of the Pinsof choice points grid are then applicable at the intersection of the levels of the family need, as shown in Figure 1.3. The overlay of these two grids provides a practical guide for choosing the most applicable treatment model and the individual, couple, or family focus based on the assessment of family need.

A caveat is that these guidelines are rough frameworks into which families may not easily fit. There may be characteristics of several levels of need, as well as orientations. Professional judgment is required to decide the more relevant point of entry and intervention. The key question for the family practitioner is "What specific therapeutic intervention produces specific change in specific families under specific conditions?"

Summary

Needs and problems of families are quite varied. It is helpful to view families through the lenses of their particular level of need in order to assess strengths and resiliences and provide relevant interventions. Problems encountered in practice with families tend to cluster into four levels of need, from very basic to very high. Lower-level needs must be met before higher-level needs are addressed. Four levels of family need are described, ranging from basic survival to self-actualization. An analogy of building a house is used to illustrate the basic assumptions. In the first two levels, strengths are emphasized. On the higher two levels, problem areas are addressed directly. Working with these types of problems requires purposive selection among methods of practice and the application of appropriate interventions according to situation and needs of the specific family. Issues on each level, relevant intervention strategies, and possible techniques are identified.

Remember that these levels are not discrete. Family need is a continuum and rarely shows categorical typologies. Some characteristics are found in several levels. In the assessment process, the level that is most characteristic of the needs experienced by a particular family at that point in time must be assessed. In Levels III and IV particularly, the most crucially felt need of a given family could vary between the two levels, depending upon whether there is a specific problem or crisis that needs to be addressed at that time, or if the need is more toward growth.

Interventions that are particularly appropriate at a given level may also be used at some other levels, given certain conditions. An intervention choice point grid provides a guide that can be used in connection with the levels of need to decide the context and orientation for intervention. The application of specific methods of interventions with other levels of need is discussed in each chapter in Parts II through V with discussion and caveats.

Discussion Questions

1. Describe the four levels for assessing family needs, and give some relevant intervention strategies and techniques that may be useful for each of these levels.
2. On which level would families involved with addiction issues likely be found, and where would be the most likely point for intervention?

3. What are some challenges or obstacles that would keep families' basic needs at a low level? What are some strengths, skills, or actions that would raise families' basic needs to a higher level?
4. What do the decorations in Weltner's "house" represent? At what level of need are the families who are concerned with these decorations? How would a therapist help them?
5. Formulate a case study to illustrate Level IV families.
6. Is the determination of family need level the responsibility of the clinician, or is it a joint effort involving the client(s)? What happens in the event of a disagreement of levels of need?
7. Apply all concepts discussed in this chapter to the choice point grid (Figure 1.2), utilizing families with whom you are working or know.
8. Select an incident from your childhood. Identify and describe the level of need of your family at that time. Choose a point of intervention in terms of context and orientation, and explain your rationale.

Suggested Readings

Beavers, W. R., & Hampson, R. B. (1990). *Successful families.* New York: W. W. Norton & Co.

Family competence is seen as ranging from healthy family functioning to severely dysfunctional, and is viewed along a progressive continuum. The approach focuses on assessment and intervention and stems from years of clinical, observational, and empirical work.

Minuchin, S., & Montalvo, B. (1967). Techniques for working with disorganized low socioeconomic families. *American Journal of Orthopsychiatry, 37,* 380–387.

Minuchin, S., Montalvo, B., Guerney, B. G., Rosman, B. L., & Schumer, F. (1967). *Families of the slums.* New York: Basic Books.

These two books focus on the structure and dynamics of poor and disorganized families, and give specific techniques for working with them. They are based on a research study of families with more than one delinquent child, and are especially helpful when working with Level I families.

Towle, C. (1945). *Common human needs.* Washington, DC: National Association of Social Workers.

This book is one of the classics in social work. It discusses in more detail the human needs that are common to all. It is one of the few books that urge provision for spiritual needs.

Weltner, J. S. (1986). A matchmaker's guide to family therapy. *Family Therapy Networker, 10*(2), 51–55.

This is an easy-to-read summary of the levels of functioning as seen by Weltner. It will give more detail than is given in this chapter for those who wish to explore the concept further.

References

Aponte, H. (1976). Underorganization in the poor family. In P. Guerin (Ed.), *Family therapy, Theory and practice.* New York: Gardner Press.

Beavers, W. R., Hulgus, Y. F., & Hampson, R. B. (1988). *Beavers system model of family functioning: Family competence and family style evaluation manual.* Dallas: University of Texas Health Science Center.

Epstein, N. B., Bishop, D. S., & Baldwin, L. M. (1982). McMaster model of family functioning: A view of the normal family. In F. Walsh (Ed.), *Normal family processes.* New York: Guilford.

Gaudin, J., Polansky, N. A., Kilpatrick, A. C., & Shilton, P. (1991). Structure and functioning in neglectful families. Presented to the Ninth National Conference on Child Abuse and Neglect, Denver, Colorado.

Hartman, A., & Laird, J. (1983). *Family-centered social work practice.* New York: Free Press.

Kilpatrick, A., & Cleveland, P. (1993). Unpublished course material. University of Georgia School of Social Work.

Maslow, A. (1970). *Motivation and personality.* New York: Harper and Row.

Minuchin, S. (1974). *Families and family therapy.* Cambridge, MA: Harvard University Press.

Paquin, G. W., & Bushorn, R. J. (1991). Family treatment assessment for novices. Milwaukee, WI: Families International, Inc. *Families in Society: The Journal of Contemporary Human Services, 72*(6), 353–359.

Pinsof, W. (1991). An integrated approach to chronic marital conflict. *The Learning Edge Series* (Video). Washington, DC: American Association for Marriage and Family Therapy.

Pinsof, W. (1995). *Integrative problem centered therapy: A synthesis of biological, individual, and family therapies.* New York: Basic Books.

Towle, C. (1945). *Common human needs.* Washington, DC: National Association of Social Workers.

Weltner, J. S. (1985). Matchmaking: Choosing the appropriate therapy for families at various levels of pathology. In M. P. Mirkin & S. L. Koman (Eds.), *Handbook of adolescents and family therapy* (pp. 39–50). New York: Gardner Press.

Weltner, J. S. (1986). A matchmaker's guide to family therapy. *Family Therapy Networker, 10*(2), 51–55.

Wolin, S. J., & Wolin, S. (1993) *The resilient self.* New York: Villard Books.

Chapter 2

An Ecological Systems–Social Constructionism Approach to Family Practice

THOMAS P. HOLLAND, Ph.D., and ALLIE C. KILPATRICK, Ph.D.

This chapter presents an overall framework within which the integrative model to family practice by level of need takes place. For family practice to be more applicable to the families served by helping professionals, we are adapting the comprehensive theories or metatheories of ecological systems and social constructionism for this framework. Each meta- or comprehensive theory offers a way of looking at the world, and each is inclusive of other methods (Breunlin, Schwartz, & Kune-Karrer, 1992; Payne, 1991). The description of these metatheories, their divergences and convergences, and how they blend to form a firm foundation for an integrated approach to family practice is now presented.

Ecological Systems Perspective

The ecological systems (ecosystems) perspective is a framework for assessment and interventions. It has been a dominant theoretical approach for viewing human behavior in the social environment. The environment is all-inclusive of micro- to macro-level systems and resources required for meeting family needs. The interface between people and their environment is seen as bidirectional and interactional, meaning that people affect the environment and in turn the environment affects people. The focus for the practitioner is to assess and intervene in all relevant factors at all levels of systems. This allows the practitioner to view situations holistically in assessment and interventions. It also stimulates the use of a broad repertoire of interventions that are suitable for the varying needs of particular family situations. Because it can encompass any relevant treatment model, the ecosystems approach can serve as a unifying perspective in family practice (Long & Holle, 1997; Meyer, 1988). It makes clear the need to see people and their environments within their historic and cultural contexts, in relationships to each other, and as continually influencing one another.

The Ecological View

The ecological perspective is based in the metaphor of biological organisms that live and adapt in a complex network of environmental forces. Von Bertalanffy (1968) believed that living organisms are organized wholes, not just the sum of their separate parts, and that they are essentially open systems, maintaining themselves with continuous inputs from, and outputs to, their environments.

The ecological perspective rests on an evolutionary, adaptive view of human beings in continuous transaction with their environment, with both the person and the environment continuously changing and accommodating each other (Brower, 1988). The key assumptions of an ecological perspective emphasize that people and environments are holistic and transactional. This approach makes clear the need to see people and their environments within their historic and cultural contexts, in relationships to each other, and as continually influencing one another, as described by Germain and Gitterman (1995).

Because ecologists were among the first systems thinkers, the perspective is also systemic. Germain and Gitterman give seven major concepts of the ecosystems perspective that are applicable to working with families. These are reciprocal exchanges, life stress, coping, habitat, niche, relatedness, and adaptations.

   1. Transactions are understood as continuous **reciprocal exchanges** in the person–environment system. Through these exchanges, each shapes, changes, or otherwise influences the other over time. People's needs and predicaments are viewed as outcomes of person–environment exchanges, not just the products of personality or environment alone (except in those cases where a specific problem may be an outcome of environmental or societal processes alone).
   2. The concept of **life stress** can refer to either a positive or a negative person–environment relationship (Lazarus, 1980). Germain and Gitterman (1987) cite Cox's explanation that stress can be seen as positive when an environmental demand, process, or event is experienced as a challenge, and is therefore associated with positive feelings, a higher level of self-esteem, and the anticipation of mastery. Stress can be seen as negative when "actual or perceived environmental demands, harms, losses, or conflicts (or the future threat of any of these) exceed the actual or perceived capacity for dealing with them" (p. 488). They state that life stress and challenge express forms of person–environment relationships because they include both the external demand and the accompanying physiological or emotional stress at a subjective level.

3. The concept of **coping** refers to the special adaptations that are made in response to internal stress. Lazarus (1980) states that two major functions of coping are problem solving and managing negative feelings, and that these are interdependent. Each of these coping adaptations needs personal, familial, and environmental resources and relationships. When coping efforts are working, the demand or threat that causes the stress may be reduced or eliminated, and thus a crisis is avoided. If coping efforts are not successful, disruption in social functioning may result in various areas. Stress and coping are both transactional. Therefore, they help the practitioner to maintain a focus on both people and environments.

4. **Habitat** refers to the place where a person or family lives. Germain (1985) states:

> *In the case of human beings, the physical and social settings within a cultural context are the habitat. Physical settings such as dwellings, buildings, rural villages and urban layouts must support the social settings of family life, social life, work life, religious life, and so on, in ways that fit with life styles, age, gender, and culture. Habitats that do not support the health and social functioning of individuals and families are likely to produce or to contribute to feelings of isolation, disorientation, and despair. Such stressful feelings may interfere further with the basic functions of family and community life. (p. 41)*

Here again, many impoverished rural and urban communities around the world do not have the resources of habitats that support healthy social functioning and overall human well-being.

5. A **niche** is perceived as the result of one's accommodation to the environment. It refers to the status that is occupied by a member of the community. Niches are defined differently in different societies and in different historical eras. In our society today, one aspect of a good niche is a set of rights, including the rights of equal opportunity to educational and economic resources. However, devalued personal or cultural characteristics such as color, ethnicity, gender, age, affinity/sexual orientation, disability, poverty, or other types of oppression force millions of people to occupy niches that are incongruent with human needs and well-being (Germain, 1985).

6. The concept of **relatedness,** based on attachment theory (Bowlby, 1973), incorporates ideas about emotional and social loneliness and isolation (Weiss, 1973). Many research studies demonstrate the important influences of supportive networks of relatives, friends, neighbors, work colleagues, and pets in helping people cope with painful life stresses (Cobb, 1976; Gaudin & Polansky, 1986). This aspect of the ecological perspective suggests the entry points in social networks for professionals to help people work out adaptive social arrangements in family, group, community, and institutional life.

7. It is important to remember that **adaptations,** as used in the ecological perspective, are active, dynamic, and often creative processes. People and their environments create an ecosystem in which each shapes the other. Thus, people are not mere reactors to environmental forces. Sometimes they change environments to allow themselves to meet their physical and psychological needs. An example is a recent sit-in by handicapped students at a major university for better accessibility to buildings. They must then adapt to the changes they have induced. At other times, people change themselves to conform or adjust to environmental imperatives or to satisfy needs and reach goals (Germain & Gitterman, 1980, 1995).

The Family Systems View

Systems theory was developed to go beyond mechanistic biology to include the interfunctioning of parts that make up whole systems. It goes beyond static concepts to take account of the temporal quality of life and the omnipresence of change. Among the key assumptions of this theory that are particularly relevant to family systems are wholeness, feedback, equifinality, and circular causality (Watzlawick, Beavin, & Jackson, 1967).

Wholeness

Because systems behave as wholes, change in any one part will cause change in other parts and throughout the entire system. When this assumption is applied to family systems, it means that a family is not simply a collection of individuals, but a coherent composite whose components behave as an irreducible unit. Therefore, the behavior of each individual in the family is related to and dependent upon the behavior of all the others. For this reason, improvements or regressions in one family member prompt repercussions—positive and negative—in other family members (Goldenberg & Goldenberg, 1991; Nichols & Schwartz, 1991; Watzlawick et al., 1967).

Feedback

Open systems are regulated by feedback loops or inputs from family members and from the environment. These inputs are acted upon and modified by the family system. Feedback can be either positive or negative. Negative feedback contributes to homeostasis by the process of self-regulation and plays an important role in maintaining the stability of relationships. It reduces the tendency toward deviation from the family norms. On the other hand, positive feedback leads to change when it is used by the family system to amplify a pattern. For learning and growth to occur, families must incorporate positive feedback. All families together must use some degree of both forms of feedback in order to adapt while maintaining their equilibrium in the face of developmental and environmental stresses (Goldenberg & Goldenberg, 1991; Simon, Stierlin, & Wynne, 1985; Watzlawick et al., 1967).

Equifinality

Equifinality means that the same result may be reached from different beginnings (Von Bertalanffy, 1968). In open systems, different initial conditions may lead to the same final result, and different outcomes may be produced from the same causes. The primary principle here is that in order to understand families, it is more important to consider the ongoing organization of their interactions, not just the genesis or the product of these interactions (Simon et al., 1985; Watzlawick et al., 1967).

Circular Causality

Circular causality means that systems are constantly modified by recursive circular feedback from multiple sources within and outside the system. Events are related through a series of interacting loops or repeating cycles. In other words, there is no simple linear cause and effect; events and behaviors interacting with each other over a period of time produce the effects (Nichols & Schwartz, 1991).

Applications to Family Practice

The use of the ecosystems metatheory in working with families supports adherence to certain principles that are consistent with this perspective.

1. This perspective requires professionals to carry out their practice according to the needs of a particular family, rather than viewing all family needs in terms of a single preferred treatment.

2. This perspective supports a variety of practice roles and tasks. It can serve as a base for internal and external changes, legislative advocacy, policy and planning, program development, primary prevention activities, research, and administration.

3. The practitioner's attention must encompass three interdependent realms or contexts in which human growth, development, and social functioning take place: **Life transitions** encompass developmental changes such as puberty, aging, role changes, loss, or other crises events faced by families. **Interpersonal processes** include patterns of relationship and communication in dyads, families, groups, social networks, communities or neighborhoods, and organizations. **Environmental properties** include the aspects of social and physical settings—their formal and informal resources and deficits—as they affect families (Germain & Gitterman, 1987). The use of genograms and ecomaps (Hartman & Laird, 1983; Mattaini, 1997) can facilitate the focus on these contents.

4. The focus is on strengths, not deficits, on solutions, not problems, and on the potential for continued family and individual growth and needed social change.

5. Assessment and intervention from an ecological systems perspective require knowledge of the diverse systems involved in interactions between people and their environments (Hefferman, Shuttlesworth, & Ambrosina, 1988). The different levels of systems, shown in Figure 2.1, are helpful in the assessment process around a given problem situation.

- In this model, the **microsystem** represents the individual in family and group settings that incorporate the day-to-day environment.
- The **mesosystem** incorporates the interactions of individuals, families, and groups within the person's microsystem.
- The **exosystem** represents the social structures, both formal and informal, that influence, delimit, or constrain what goes on there. It also includes community-level factors that have an impact on the way the person functions.
- The **macrosystem** involves societal forces and subsumes cultural and societal values, attitudes, and beliefs that influence the micro- and exosystems.

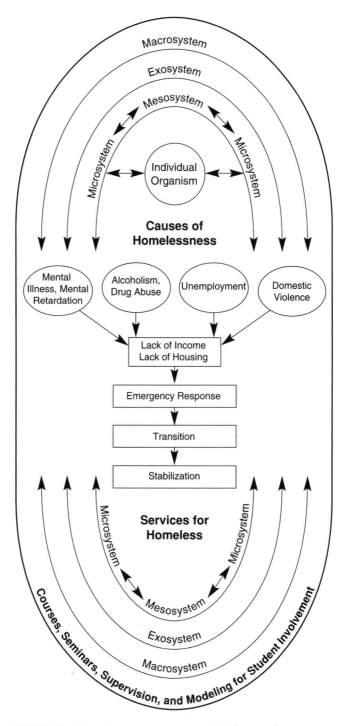

FIGURE 2.1 An ecosystems model for student involvement with homeless families.

(From Cleveland & Kilpatrick, 1990.)

The example of homelessness shown in Figure 2.1 illustrates the use of the figure in helping students learn the ecosystems model. First, we look at the courses of
homelessness, which may be apparent in several levels of systems. For example,
mental illness, alcoholism, unemployment, and/or domestic violence may have
precipitated the loss of income and housing. Any of these causes could be interrelated at micro-, meso-, exo-, or macrosystem levels. Services for homeless families
must also be provided at several system levels. Individual/family counseling at
the micro- and mesosystem levels is indicated in the emergency and transition levels. Resources at the exosystem level for temporary shelter and other transition services are needed. Changes in public attitudes and policy concerning employment
opportunities, emergency responses, and causes of homelessness may take place
at the macrosystem level.

The key assumptions in family systems theory of wholeness, feedback, equifinality, and circular causality are applied at the micro- and mesosystem levels. The
ecosystems perspectives of reciprocal exchanges, life stress, coping, habitat, niche,
and relatedness are applicable at the exo- and macrosystem levels.

Consideration should be given to the interplay of influences on all four levels
during the assessment and intervention processes with families. This interplay
helps in understanding the causes of a particular problem situation and also in the
provision of services for such problems. Information concerning other problem
areas can be used to fill in the blanks in the model to make the ecosystems theory
more visible. Effective case management skills are important to applying this
framework with some families.

By utilizing knowledge of all levels of the ecosystems perspective, the practitioner is better equipped to assess and provide services for families in accordance
with the presenting problems and the family's current level of need. This application requires flexibility, creativity, and mobility outside the office and into the
home and community.

A summary of how practitioners can implement this ecosystems perspective
in their work is offered by Greene and Ephross (1991, p. 293).

- View the person/family/environment as inseparable.
- See the family practitioner as an equal partner in the helping process.
- Examine transactions between the person/family/environment by assessing
  all levels of systems affecting adaptiveness.
- Assess life situations and transitions that induce high stress levels.
- Attempt to enhance a person/family's personal and interpersonal competence
  through positive relationships and life experiences.
- Seek interventions that extend the goodness of fit among the person/family
  and the environment at all system levels.
- Focus on mutually sought solutions and person/family empowerment.

Caveats in Using the Ecosystems Metatheory

While ecosystems theory offers a wealth of ideas about families and family practice, the family practitioner must be aware of some possible pitfalls in its use. One

issue is that this perspective may lead to a conservative stance of valuing the status quo and avoiding real change. Influences that upset the homeostasis of a system may be framed as problems or forms of deviance, leading to responses that do not assess them on their own merits, but in terms of reducing or limiting their threats to existing relational patterns. Conflict may be seen as a negative influence, disrupting systemic balance; conformity may be assumed to be good. The underlying concern of treatment can be upon ways to reduce tensions in the system and return it to stability as soon as possible.

A second issue is that ecosystems theory emphasizes how people adapt to environmental structures that exercise social control. Existing circumstances tend to be accepted as givens, and the focus may become how to adjust participants within those limits, rather than questioning the limits or valuing disruptions positively. Professionals may be in the role of experts in diagnosing sources of tension and in finding ways to enable participants to adapt in order to return to equilibrium. Thus, reducing tensions and reestablishing harmony may become goals of intervention. Successful adjustment of individuals within existing social norms may be assumed to be the highest good, and individuality, creativity, and autonomy become subordinate to the needs of the system.

Third, one may conclude that use of this metatheory requires many different interventive skills that practitioners are required to master in order to address the entire range of needs on all system levels. This conclusion, of course, is unrealistic. Metatheories provide a comprehensive theoretical framework within which the domain-specific theories and interventions are integrated and planfully utilized to meet specific needs in a specific situation with specific persons. We support Wakefield's (1996) belief that ecosystems theory is not sufficient in itself, and that practitioners should have skills in domain-specific interventions like those presented in this book. We disagree, however, with his contention that an ecosystems theory base is not clinically useful. Myriads of professionals have attested to the usefulness of the metatheory as presented here and supplemented by specific interventive methods to meet varying levels of need.

If family practitioners can avoid such pitfalls and heed these caveats, then effective applications of ecosystems theory may be made to practice. The key points of this section on ecosystems theory are summarized in Table 2.1.

Social Constructionist Perspective

A more recent arrival on the family practice scene, the social constructionist approach is based upon the metaphor of literature. Human actions and relationships are seen in terms of organized efforts to create meaning out of personal experiences. These efforts are like composing narratives, stories that people write about themselves. Experiences of the objective and the subjective realms are selectively arranged on the basis of assumed themes, which organize, structure, and give meaningfulness to the person or family (Berger & Luckmann, 1966; Hoffman, 1988, 1990; Sarbin, 1986; Von Glasersfeld, 1987).

Stories are crucial means that people in every culture use to create meaning and purpose in life. In all communities and families, stories appear in a variety of forms,

TABLE 2.1   Key Principles of Ecological Systems Perspective

Ecological View

Transactions are continuous, reciprocal exchanges.
Life stresses are either positive or negative person–environment relationships.
Coping refers to problem solving and managing negative feelings.
Habitat is the physical and social setting within cultural contexts.
Niche is the result of one's accommodation to the environment.
Relatedness involves supportive networks and attachments.

Systems View

Wholeness—change in one part causes changes throughout system.
Feedback—regulates system by inputs from family and environment.
Equifinality—there is more than one way to get to a final goal.
Circular causality—not linear cause and effect but interactions.

Practice Focus

Recognize diverse needs of families on varying levels.
Explore various practice roles involved in ecosystems dual focus.
Attend to life cycle transitions, interpersonal processes, and environmental settings.
Focus on strengths not deficits, solutions not problems.
Assess ecosystems at four levels (micro, meso, exo, macro).

Pitfalls

Focusing on personal adaptations to the exclusion of social change.
Valuing homeostasis as the goal.
Individuality, creativity, and autonomy becoming subordinate to the system.

including anecdotes, myths and fables, plays and movies, novels and poems, histories and biographies, case studies, and others. Much of our development as social beings occurs through listening to and understanding narratives, the stories that people around us tell about their own and others' lives. Reminiscences by the elderly represent important efforts to articulate meanings in their lives, and encouraging such reflections has been recognized as an important component of practice with the aged. Stories constitute the basic structures all persons use in order to make sense of their lives, and hence understanding narratives is fundamental to the practice of social work with families (Goldstein, 1988; Scott, 1989).

The social constructionism perspective on human behavior emphasizes the textual structure of everyday life, especially how people develop meaning in the diverse events of their day-to-day experience. Behavior is seen through the analogy of a story that a person is creating and telling about what that person is doing and how such tasks and experiences are organized into a meaningful whole (O'Hanlon & Weiner-Davis, 1988; Holland, 1991). One's present, dominant story can be empowering, or it can undermine meaningful relationships and effective social functioning (Polkinghorne, 1988).

A fundamental assumption of social constructionism is that reality is constructed or generated by participants, rather than being objective, external, or given. Our efforts to make sense of inner and outer experience involve trying to formulate some coherence and meaning from streams of events (Ricoeur, 1981). In order to create this formulation, we draw upon our culture's storehouse of themes and attributions, handed down by our relatives and community leaders. Persons interpret events and experiences on the basis of cultural patterns, preformulated clusters of meaning that serve to enable the person to make sense of perceptions. All of these constructed meanings depend for their existence upon the minds of the persons carrying and using them. No one's beliefs or conclusions are more "real" than another's, and all participate in editing, revising, and continuing the stories of meaning that they share.

Such contexts of meaning take on a narrative form, linking past, present, and anticipated future, involving movement toward or away from goals. Or the form may emphasize blockage or no change (Gergen, 1982). Story patterns involving interrupted movement toward a desired goal, followed by an inescapable defeat, constitute the theme of tragedy, while patterns involving movement away from a desired goal, followed by unexpected success, constitute the romantic theme. Other themes in many cultures include the use of a journey as a metaphor for life experiences, eventual retribution for injustices, and struggles between light and darkness or hope and despair.

Stories and Personal Meaning

The human practice of storytelling is a basic method that people use to create, sustain, and transmit meaning in their lives. The act of creating stories, as well as the stories themselves, links the particular events of human experience together and gives them sense or meaning. Whether the resulting narratives are intended to be true or fictional accounts, their creation involves the formulation of coherent sequences that draw the events of people's lives into meaningful wholes that have structure, purpose, and direction.

Drawing from cultural and familial storehouses of anecdotes, legends, tales, and myths, individuals and families construct personal narratives about their own lives that help them understand who they are, where they are headed, and how they cope with success and failure, pain and joy (Geertz, 1973; Gelber & Specter, 1987). These stories organize actions and events around certain values and explain choices in terms of unique histories, intentions, and goals. People also draw upon others' stories as models to copy or avoid, and they offer their own stories to others for similar purposes. Everyone brings stories from his or her own past as well as an interest in the stories of others, thus providing a ready opening for reflection on the function of constructed meanings as a key ingredient in practice with families.

Stories are organized by means of plots and themes that reflect some values adapted from the culture. The plot of a story shows the listener or reader how the participants struggle to make sense of their experiences. As the story progresses, the characters attempt to understand the significance of their experiences and to express the values underlying their roles. Rather than a simple sequence of cause leading to effect, participants typically make use of later experiences in reflecting upon earlier ones, deriving meaning about them retrospectively, and thus coming to understand their point or value—the theme of their unique stories.

Meaning emerges from our efforts to understand the values underlying our own and others' experiences. We assess alternative interpretations and choose one that seems to provide the most sensible interpretation available. Another person encountering these events in another time or situation or cultural context may draw a different conclusion about them (Derrida, 1986; Gadamer, 1982). The naive listener may assume that his or her individual interpretation is the only one that makes sense or is acceptable, while a listener who has a wider acquaintance with alternative themes and interpretations may compare the teller's implicit assumptions about experiences and their meanings with other interpretations of the same events (Polkinghorne, 1988).

Family functioning is dependent upon coherent and integrated patterns of meaning, shared by all the members. Our families of origin transmit the previous generations' themes through telling stories about family members; these socialize the children into the available themes and interpretations of experience (Gergen & Davis, 1988). Members bring themes and values that may diverge, thus introducing conflicts or inconsistencies in the merged story.

While each person develops an integrative framework of meaning, all of us draw upon basic values, themes, and plots offered by our culture and subculture. Some persons have been socialized into very restrictive and stereotyped subcultures and, once they leave the limited environment of their youth, find the acceptable plots inadequate for coping with the complexities of their lives. The skilled professional can help clients recognize the values, themes, and plots they have used as well as their sources and their limitations. Through dialogue, professionals can then help clients as they begin to understand that past events are not meaningful in and of themselves, but rather gain significance by the overall choices and directions of life choices. Then professional and client together can consider alternative approaches to interpreting and understanding events, including times when the dominant theme did not account satisfactorily for an experience. Thus, the relationship can release the client from the sense of being controlled by past assumptions, value judgments, or interpretations attached to events, and open the possibility of change.

A further component of social constructionism is the assumption that themes and clusters of assumed reality (cultures) cannot be controlled from the outside. They are not amenable to reconstruction through objective or instrumental manipulation by any outside technical expert because they are formulations of the participants themselves. Participants may observe their own patterns and explore alternatives for themselves, allowing them to understand their experiences in new ways and hence respond differently from the past. All that an outsider can do is to reflect themes in use and offer participants alternative themes for making meaning out of their experiences for their consideration of them. Outsiders (including practitioners) can attempt to create a context that invites participants to pursue such observations, reflections, and developments for themselves, but they cannot directly change the participants' themes or actions.

The Australian family therapist Michael White (1991) tells the story of a client, Elizabeth, who consulted him with regard to persistent domestic conflicts with her children and her own despair of ever resolving the family's tensions. His questions led to discussion of how the situation influenced her thoughts about herself as a parent. Elizabeth's reflections revealed the private story of failure that had come to be the way she understood herself and her experiences as a parent. She examined the ways in which she had come to view herself as a failure and the extensive costs of such a perspective on her self-esteem and her relationships.

With White's encouraging questioning, Elizabeth began to identify some of the ways in which the tyranny of this view of herself had not been effective, ways in which she had been able to resist the failure theme. Stepping away from such a perspective and the accompanying guilt was a crucial step for Elizabeth. Attention to ways that she had, in the past, asserted initiative and effectiveness led to a realization of another version of who she was. This reclaimed self was characterized by abilities to seize the initiative, to make decisions, and to resist others' negative evaluations of her. Elizabeth began feeling more confident and began taking greater initiative and control with her children.

Applications to Family Practice

The social constructionist approach has extensive applicability for practice with families and for the role of the practitioner.

1. It is assumed that all interpretations and meanings are created by the participants, so there is no outside, "right" standard by which to diagnose or modify. Since everyone, including the professional, is engaged in developing meanings in order to deal with experience, the helping relationship is essentially a process of joint work on the themes brought by the family and the professional. In this shared work, the relationship is between equals and is nonhierarchical, and the power or right to assert interpretations is equally shared (Gergen & McNamee, 1992; Simon et al., 1985; Whitaker & Bumberry, 1988).

2. The professional respects the family's right to make use of its own themes and seeks to understand their origin and application. Together, the family and the professional explore the implications of the assumptions, directions, and anticipated ends of the family's dominant story.

3. Often, families seeking help bring stories that involve a problem-saturated description of themselves. Alternative themes or ones describing their strengths are not expressed, as they do not fit with the dominant story (White, 1991). The inconsistencies among family members' interpretations are examined respectfully, as are any incompatibilities between the interpretations of the family and the community. The practitioner offers alternative themes for the family to consider as ways to make relationships more satisfying. The treatment process involves inviting the family to step back from its dominant story and the constraints imposed upon them by that story's assumptions. New meanings and assumptions are offered for reconstructing the family's experiences into more satisfying patterns. Then the professional supports the family's efforts to experiment with acting upon its new theme of strengths (White & Epston, 1990).

4. The process of family practice can be understood as based in an interpretive relationship: The practitioner assists a family by listening carefully to its story, and bringing to awareness the themes and values that its members are using to give meaning to the events of personal experience. Assumed themes are brought out for reflective examination, thus externalizing problems and diminishing their hidden power. Through providing space for joint reflections and explorations of new possibilities, the practitioner invites the family to construct more coherent and satisfying ways of coping than previous approaches have provided.

5. By listening to the family's story, identifying underlying themes, and drawing attention to ways that it has acted effectively instead of being controlled by a problem, the professional becomes a collaborator with the family, a coeditor of a living story that is in process of being rewritten. The resulting product is an interwoven text, a jointly authored story of these lives coming into temporary intersection and then diverging (Goldstein, 1988; Whitaker & Bumberry, 1988).

6. We can nurture the development of such supportive, rather than paternalistic, relationships with families by reminding ourselves of the importance of trying to understand what a particular person's experiences seem like from the person's own perspective, and by attempting to appreciate life and its problems as they are construed in the person's subjective experience (Goldstein, 1988). What families often need is not so much expert advice, technical fixes, or precise data as it is a responsive listener to their efforts to make sense out of their experiences, and overt, caring encouragement to resume their roles as the capable authors of their own stories (Gergen & McNamee, 1992).

7. Effective practice involves sensitivity in listening to stories, understanding their meanings, assessing alternate themes, and assisting families in their efforts to reconstruct personal stories in ways that empower them to return to active authorship of their own lives. The social constructionism approach to family practice emphasizes the client's *strengths,* rather than pathology or deficits, emphasizes *exceptions* or times when the problem was not present, and builds upon those times when something the client tried *did* work effectively. Questions and comments are used to create an expectancy for change and progress, building upon the themes of stories of success. Drawing on previous strengths, solutions, and positive trends in the family's experience, the practitioner emphasizes new realities in which the family is empowered to solve the difficulty or see that it is already solving the problem (O'Hanlon & Weiner-Davis, 1988). The relationship between family and professional is one of joint exploration and coauthorship, not a hierarchy in which one person has solutions to the other's deficits (Link & Sullivan, 1989).

Caveats in Using the Social Constructionist Metatheory

Social constructionism has prompted a shift in the attention of family practitioners from actions to meanings, from expertise to collaboration, and from diagnosis of problems to mutual creation of solutions. However, the spread of interest in social constructionism ought not be accepted as an unmixed blessing. Implications of its own story about how families and family interventions operate should be examined critically.

The first caveat regarding social constructionism is its assumption of relativism regarding all meanings. The theory holds that there is no reality "out there," and that meanings are strictly constructed by participants. If that is the case, then any interpretation would be as good as any other, from inclusive themes to destructive ones. The theory provides no explicit grounds for precluding various interpretations of experience, including illusions or sadism. Families trying to deny their pain would have legitimate base for doing so with the maximum possible comfort, a condition about which the theory provides no evident guidance (Becvar & Becvar, 1988; Nichols & Schwartz, 1991). While social constructionism does not necessarily lead to coauthorship of denials or destructive interpretations, nothing within the theory clearly precludes such possibilities.

A related problem with social constructionism is its inattention to the evident differences in power among family members, and between families and communities. Dominant members of a family may impose their preferred interpretations upon subordinate members, denying them the legitimacy of their own meanings and undermining their well-being. Likewise, community prejudice and discrimination may lead to denial of basic resources and opportunities for some families, particularly minorities, thus limiting their life chances and well-being regardless of the family's constructions or reconstructions. Again, nothing in social constructionism necessarily supports such abuses of power, but nothing in the theory draws explicit attention to them or provides explicit ways of dealing with them.

Underneath these problems lies a logical dilemma that confronts social constructionism: If there is no external reality, then that principle would preclude the assertion that the components of constructionism itself are true representations of anything, including its descriptions of how people deal with problems, develop meaning, undergo change, or do therapy (Held, 1990). In short, if we cannot know reality, then we cannot assert anything about it. Social constructionism can't have it both ways.

A likely response of advocates of social constructionism to such concerns may be that all of our perceptions of reality are incomplete. The theory is intended to be a metamodel for practice, rather than an assertion about ontological reality. Such defenses are hardly sufficient, since any theory would hasten to take refuge inside such permissiveness. So while social constructionism suggests many useful ideas for family practice, it continues to face difficult challenges in its formulation and refinement. The concern for family practitioners is to emphasize the strengths of this metamodel and avoid its pitfalls. The key points of this section on social constructionism are summarized in Table 2.2.

TABLE 2.2   **Key Principles of the Social Constructionist Perspective**

Stories and Personal Meaning

Stories transmit meaning.
Their creation formulates coherent sequences.
They shape one's identity.
They organize values and explain choices.
They are organized by plots and themes.
They involve choosing from alternative interpretations.
Family functioning depends upon shared meanings.
Meanings cannot be controlled from outside.
Emphasis shifts from actions to meanings, from expertise to collaboration, from diagnosis to problems to mutual creation of solutions.

Practice Focus

Nonhierarchical relationship.
Shared explorations.
Offer new meanings and assumptions.
Bring their themes and values to awareness.
Be coauthor of a living story with them.
Nurture supportive, not paternalistic, relationships.

Pitfalls

Seeing any interpretation as being as good as any other.
Inattention to power differences in family and community regarding interpretations.
Assuming that social constructionism has all the answers and that they are the best.

Comparing and Integrating the Metatheories

Both of these approaches to family practice are comprehensive theories or metatheories, and both offer ways of looking at the world, particularly with regard to individual and social change (Payne, 1991). Each is inclusive in the sense that it accepts perspectives and methods drawn from other theories. We now look at a comparison of the two metatheories.

Both ecosystems and constructionism assume that a family is a group of persons involved in sustained, intimate interaction with one another. The interaction among these members becomes patterned or regularized on the basis of mutually shared expectations, meanings, and responses. Similarity or congruences among the meanings and expectations of members are the basis for stability and satisfaction, while incongruences lead to dissatisfaction and conflict. Creative explorations of alternative, more congruent shared meanings are the main concern of practice.

The two metatheories converge on a number of aspects and dimensions of family practice. The time focus of both is upon the present and the anticipated

TABLE 2.3 Convergences in Ecosystems and Constructionism

Dimension	Comment
Time	Both are focused on the present and the anticipated future, rather than upon the past.
Goals	Both seek to identify and develop creative alternatives, rather than to correct past deficits.
Style of intervention	Both are exploratory, nondirective, less structured, seek exceptions to problems; not corrective, analytical, or educational.
Context	Both focus upon the family as a system, not upon individuals.
Role of practitioner	A peer as much as possible in the process of mutual reflection and exploration of alternatives; not analytical, instructive, or prescriptive.
Interpretation of experience	Symbolic or metaphorical; not literal or in terms of problems to be controlled.
Understanding of "resistance"	Protective of the core meanings and relationships among members; not lack of motivation or dysfunction.
Criteria for success	Mutual acceptability, satisfaction, and meaningfulness to participants; not logical, objective, or behavioral.

future, rather than upon the past. The context of each is the family as a group, not upon individuals. The goals emphasized by both perspectives involve enabling the family to identify and develop creative alternatives to unsatisfying patterns, rather than correcting past deficits. The role of the practitioner called for by both is to be a peer as much as possible in the process of mutual reflection and exploration of alternatives and change, not to be analytical, instructive, or prescriptive. The style of intervention emphasized by each is exploratory, nondirective, less structured, seeking exceptions to problems, not corrective, analytical, or educational.

Both metatheories interpret experience in symbolic or metaphorical terms, not as literal, or as problems to be controlled. Their treatment of "resistance" is one protective of the core meanings and relationships among family members, not one that works in terms of lack of motivation or dysfunction. The criteria for success of intervention emphasized by both are mutual acceptability, satisfaction, and meaningfulness among family members, not logical, objective, or behavioral measures. The key similarities between these perspectives are summarized in Table 2.3.

The two metatheories diverge somewhat in their emphases within the treatment process. The ecosystems perspective focuses attention upon breakdowns in family equilibrium needing negotiation to reestablish homeostasis or mutually satisfactory exchanges. Constructionism treats family issues in terms of breakdowns in shared meaning that need reconstruction into new and more satisfying shared meanings.

Both the ecosystems and social constructionism approaches to family practice provide broad perspectives on how to understand and deal with family issues. The ecosystems model focuses primarily on the transactions of the family within the

TABLE 2.4   Comparisons in Ecosystems and Constructionism

Criteria

1. Explicit knowledge base: how clear and extensive is the grounding of the approach in theory and research?
2. Focus of attention: how are family issues defined?
3. Change process: does the approach explain how family change occurs?
4. Guidelines for intervention: does approach delineate actions of the practitioner?
5. Values: what values are emphasized?

Ecosystems	Social Constructionism
1. Moderate	Limited
2. Disruption of equilibrium	Meaninglessness
3. Negotiation of new homeostasis	Construction of new meanings
4. As expert	As coauthor
5. Harmony	Meaningfulness

larger social environment, while the social constructionist model emphasizes the meanings that families and their members formulate out of those streams of events.

Both approaches are based on specialized bodies of knowledge. The ecosystems theory emphasizes knowledge of the diverse transactions among people and their environments. Means of strengthening the effectiveness of those interactions are major concerns of practice. Social constructionism focuses on how people find meaning in the diverse experiences of their daily lives; treatment involves the development of meanings that are more empowering for families. The key divergences between these perspectives are summarized in Table 2.4.

Although neither approach is a complete practice model in itself, both theories have spawned a variety of specific methods and techniques for application in professional practice with families (Meyer, 1988; Rosen, 1988). For example, the life model of social work practice is based in ecosystems theory (Germain & Gitterman, 1980), as is the family-centered approach (Hartman & Laird, 1983) and the competence approach (Maluccio, 1981). The narrative approach to family practice (White & Epston, 1990) and the solution-focused approach (O'Hanlon & Weiner-Davis, 1988) are based in social constructionism. These and other practice models provide the specificity needed in working directly with families.

Summary

This chapter offers a comprehensive framework for assessing and working with families at each of the four levels of family need presented in the previous chapter. The ecosystems–social constructionism approach to family practice is a combination of two metatheories that complement each other to form a broad theoretical base for family assessment and practice. This approach offers a way of looking at the world and particularly at personal and social change.

The two metatheories each have specific strengths that inform family practice. However, limits of each are discussed. The family practitioner should be aware of these limitations, as they have definite implications for practice. There are areas in which the two theories diverge that supplement each other and fill in particular gaps. There are more similarities that emerge as the theories are analyzed by specific dimensions. These convergences enable the practitioner to draw upon the two metatheories in creating a meaningful approach to assessing and working with families.

The following sections of this book provide specific practice methods that can be used in working with families. Each is applied to one of the four levels of family need within the overall framework of the linked ecosystems–social constructionism approach.

Discussion Questions

1. Discuss the key assumptions of the systems view and apply these to a family.
2. Select a presenting problem and design an intervention utilizing the social constructionist perspective on human behavior.
3. Why is it important for practitioners to view a client system holistically?
4. How could the combined ecosystems–social constructionist approach be utilized with lower functioning clients? Does the use of social constructionist theory imply that clients must be verbally skilled?
5. Discuss how the two metatheories diverge in their emphasis within the treatment process, and the ways in which the integration of these two metatheories could be helpful in working with families.
6. Discuss how the theories of social constructionism and ecosystems can be combined to address the problems of families in poverty.
7. Prepare a narrative about your life or an important episode in your life according to the concepts of the social constructionist approach.
8. What biases do you have that would limit your use of social constructionist theory in working with families?

Suggested Readings

Coles, R. (1989). *The call of stories: Teaching and the moral imagination.* Boston: Houghton Mifflin.

The training of child psychiatrists has been immensely enriched by the work of Robert Coles, whose volume leads the reader through the author's experiences of working with the learning from the children in his practice as well as the students in his classes. This book demonstrates the wide applicability of the narrative framework for practice and for education in the helping professions.

Greene, R. R., & Ephross, P. H. (1991). *Human behavior theory and social work practice.* New York: Aldine de Gruyter.

This book gives a good overview of the ecosystems perspective within a human behavior framework. Applications to practice are made.

Hoffman, L. (1990). Constructing realities: An art of lenses. *Family Process, 29*(1), 1–12.

> *Social construction theory is used to move toward a more collaborative and unconcealed therapeutic stance. This theory plus a second-order view and sensitivity to gender issues are the three "lenses" used for constructing realities.*

Polkinghorne, D. E. (1988). *Narrative knowing and the human sciences.* Albany: State University of New York Press.

> *Using literary criticism, philosophy, history, and recent developments in the social sciences, this volume shows how to use research information organized by the narrative form—such information as clinical case histories, biographies, and personal stories. The relationships between narrative formats and classical empirical research designs are examined, and suggestions for studying human behavior from a narrative framework are set forth.*

Sarup, M. (1989). *An introductory guide to poststructuralism and postmodernism.* Athens: University of Georgia Press.

> *Three of the most influential figures in recent literary criticism—Jacques Lacan, Jacques Derrida, and Michel Foucault—have had extensive influence upon the way we think about meaning in our experiences. This book traces the rise of narrative approaches to thought, radically opposed to the Enlightenment tenets of progress and scientific truth, and explores some implications of this perspective for the future of human social life.*

Wakefield, J. C. (1988). Psychotherapy, distributive justice, and social work, Parts 1 & 2. *Social Science Review, 62*(2,3), 187–210, 353–382.

> *Wakefield argues that social work's organizing value is minimal distributive justice where all people would have a minimally acceptable level of basic economic, social, and psychological goods. This concept seems to build on an ecosystems framework and then utilize varying methods and interventive skills for meeting specific levels of needs.*

References

Becvar, D. S., & Becvar, R. J. (1988). *Family therapy: A systemic integration.* Boston: Allyn & Bacon.

Berger, P., & Luckmann, T. (1966). *The social construction of reality.* Garden City, NY: Doubleday.

Bowlby, J. (1973). Affectional bonds: Their nature and origin. In R. S. Weiss (Ed.), *Loneliness: The experience of emotional and social isolation* (pp. 38–52). Cambridge, MA: MIT Press.

Breunlin, D. C., Schwartz, R. C., Kune-Karrer, B. M. (1992). *Metaframeworks: Transcending the models of family therapy.* San Francisco: Jossey Bass.

Brower, A. M. (September 1988). Can the ecological model guide social work practice? *Social Service Review, 62*(3), 411–429.

Cleveland, P. H., & Kilpatrick, A. C. (1990). Social work students involvement with the homeless: An international model. Paper presented to the International Congress of Schools of Social Work, Lima, Peru.

Cobb, S. (1976). Social support as a moderator of life stress. *Psychosomatic Medicine, 38*(5), 300–314.

Derrida, J. (1986). Difference. In M. C. Taylor (Ed.), *Deconstruction in context.* Chicago: University of Chicago Press.

Gadamer, H. G. (1982). *Truth and method.* New York: Continuum and Social Isolation. Cambridge, MA: MIT Press.

Gaudin, J. M., Jr., & Polansky, N. A. (1986). Social distancing of the neglectful family: Sex, race and social class differences. *Children and Youth Services Review, 8,* 1–12.

Geertz, C. (1973). *The interpretation of cultures.* New York: Basic Books.

Gelber, J., & Specter, P. D. (1987). *Psychotherapy: Portraits and fiction.* Northvale, NJ: Jason Aronson.

Gergen, K. J. (1982). *Toward transformation in social knowledge.* New York: Springer-Verlag.

Gergen, K. J., & Davis, K. E. (Eds.). (1988). *The social construction of the person.* New York: Springer-Verlag.

Gergen, K. J., & McNamee, S. (1992). *Social constructionism in therapeutic process.* London: Sage.

Germain, C. B. (1985). The place of community within an ecological approach to social work practice. In S. H. Taylor & R. W. Roberts (Eds.), *Theories and practice of community social work* (pp. 30–55). New York: Columbia University Press.

Germain, C. B., & Gitterman, A. (1980). *The life model of social work practice.* New York: Columbia University Press.

Germain, C. B., & Gitterman, A. (1987). Ecological perspective. In A. Minahan et al. (Eds.), *Encyclopedia of social work* (18th ed.) (pp. 488–499). Silver Spring, MD: National Association of Social Workers.

Germain, C. B. & Gitterman, A. (1995). Ecological perspective. In R. L. Edwards et al. (Eds.), *Encyclopedia of social work* (19th ed.) (pp. 816–824). Silver Spring, MD: National Association of Social Workers.

Goldenberg, I., & Goldenberg, H. (1991). *Family therapy: An overview* (p. 38). Monterey, CA: Brooks-Cole Publishing.

Goldstein, H. (1988). Humanistic alternatives to the limits of scientific knowledge. *Social Thought, 14*(1), 47–58.

Greene, R. R., & Ephross, P. H. (1991). *Human behavior theory and social work practice.* New York: Aldine de Gruyter.

Hartman, A., & Laird, J. (1983). *Family centered social work practice.* New York: Free Press.

Hefferman, J., Shuttlesworth, G., & Ambrosina, R. (1988). A systems/ecological perspective. In *Social work and social welfare: An introduction.* St. Paul, MN: West Publishing.

Held, B. S. (1990). What's in a name: Some confusions and concerns about Constructivism. *Journal of Marital and Family Therapy, 16,* 179–186.

Hoffman, L. (1988). A constructivist position for family therapy. *The Irish Journal of Psychology, 9,* 110–129.

Hoffman, L. (1990). Constructing realities: An art of lenses. *Family Process, 29*(1), 1–12.

Holland, T. P. (1991). Narrative, knowledge, and professional practice. *Social Thought, 17*(1), 32–40.

Lazarus, R. S. (1980). The stress and coping paradigm. In L. A. Bond & J. C. Rosen (Eds.), *Competence and coping during adulthood* (pp. 28–74). Hanover, NH: University Press of New England.

Link, R. J., & Sullivan, M. (1989). Vital connections: Using literature to illustrate social work issues. *Journal of Social Work Education. 25*(3), 192–230.

Long, D. D. & Holle, M. C. (1997). *Macro systems in the social environment.* Itasca, IL: Peacock.

Maluccio, A. N. (1981). *Promoting competence in clients.* New York: Free Press.

Mattaini, M. A. (1997). *Visual ecoscan for clinical practice.* Silver Spring, MD: NASW Press.

Meyer, C. H. (1988). The ecosystems perspective. In R. A. Dorfman (Ed.), *Paradigms of clinical social work.* New York: Brunner/Mazel.

Nichols, M. P., & Schwartz, R. C. (1991). *Family therapy: Concepts and methods,* 1st and 2nd eds. Boston: Allyn & Bacon.

O'Hanlon, W. H., & Weiner-Davis, M. (1988). *In search of solutions: A new direction in psychotherapy.* New York: Norton.

Payne, M. (1991). *Modern social work theory: A critical introduction.* Chicago: Lyceum.

Polkinghorne, D. E. (1988). *Narrative knowing and the human sciences.* Albany: State University of New York Press.

Ricoeur, P. (1981). *Hermeneutics and the human sciences.* Cambridge, UK: Cambridge University Press.

Rosen, H. (1988). The constructivist-developmental paradigm. In R. A. Dorfman (Ed.), *Paradigms of clinical social work* (pp. 317–355). New York: Brunner/Mazel.

Sarbin, T. R. (1986). *Narrative psychology: The storied nature of human conduct.* New York: Praeger.

Scott, D. (1989). Meaning construction and social work practice. *Social Service Review, 63*(1), 39–51.

Simon, F. B., Stierlin, H., & Wynne, L. (1985). *The language of family therapy.* New York: Family Process Press.

Von Bertalanffy, L. (1968). *General systems theory.* New York: Braziller.

Von Glasersfeld, E. (1987). The control of perception and the construction of reality. *Dialectica, 33,* 37–50.

Wakefield, J. C. (1996). Does social work need the ecosystems perspective? Parts 1 & 2. *Social Service Review, 70*(1,2), 1–32, 183–213.

Watzlawick, P., Beavin, J. H., & Jackson, D. D. (1967). *Pragmatics of human communication: A study of interactional patterns, pathologies and paradoxes.* New York: Norton.

Weiss, R. S. (Ed.) (1973). *Loneliness: The experience of emotional and social isolation.* Cambridge, MA: MIT Press.

Whitaker, C. A., & Bumberry, W. M. (1988). *Dancing with the family.* New York: Brunner/Mazel.

White, M. (1991). Deconstruction and therapy. *Dulwich Centre Newsletter, 3,* 21–40.

White, M., & Epston, D. (1990). *Narrative means to therapeutic ends.* New York: Norton.

Chapter 3

Contexts of Helping: Commonalities and Diversities

ALLIE C. KILPATRICK, Ph.D.

In assessing and working with families, four levels of family need have been presented. Following the assessment of the primary level of need, intervention procedures are planned, based on this information. The metatheories of ecological systems and social constructionism are utilized as comprehensive perspectives within which to undertake the assessment and interventions with each family.

Another important consideration in the context of family practice is the acknowledgment of commonalities and diversity. It is crucial that the family practitioner have knowledge, awareness, and skill in developing the necessary core and common conditions of the helping relationship or therapeutic alliance, and in dealing with diversity issues.

Practitioners share many more commonalities than differences with families. These commonalities can serve as the foundation for building the therapeutic alliance and also for exploring differences. Errors in professional judgment that should be avoided are the tendencies (a) to see differences or commonalities when they are *not* there, or (b) to not see differences or commonalities when they *are* present. This chapter seeks to explore and balance these two concepts of commonalities and differences.

The Helping Relationship/Therapeutic Alliance

The metatheories of ecosystems and social constructionism that provide the basis for the integrative approach to family practice emphasize the principles of respect, responsive listening, caring encouragement, nonhierarchical relationships, shared power, and equality of meanings as commonalities in working with families.

Closely related to these principles is the "I-Thou" relationship described by Buber (1958) where there is an emphasis upon what takes place between people, for our purposes, especially between the practitioner and the family. The goal is for each to relate to the other in a way that acknowledges the other's internal life, without any possibility of one being exploited by the other. The interaction is a dialogue. The focus or emphasis is upon the interchange between them and the experience of mutual confirmation that can occur.

Historically, the concept of the helping relationship has permeated work with people since the early days of social casework and psychoanalysis. Biestek (1957) traced the development of this concept in social casework from Mary Richmond in 1899 through 1951. He then developed his legendary seven principles of relationship, which started with the client's needs expressed to the practitioner as the first direction of the interaction, the response of the caseworker to the client's needs as the second direction, then the awareness of the client to the caseworker's responsiveness as the third direction. Based upon the needs of the client, the seven principles were then articulated as individualization, purposeful expression of feelings, controlled emotional involvement, acceptance, nonjudgmental attitude, self-determination, and confidentiality.

We have adapted Biestek's (1957) formulation to include terms relating his concepts to working with families (see Table 3.1). These principles are relevant today and applicable to the family as the client system, though none are absolute. For example, the principle of confidentiality is limited by rights of other individuals, the practitioner, the community, and society. Such behaviors as abuse are legally required to be reported.

The personal characteristics and behaviors displayed by practitioners are intrinsically related to the formation of working and maintenance relationships. The research of Rogers, Gendlin, Kiesler, and Truax (1969) and Truax and Carkhuff (1967) presented evidence suggesting that therapists' ability to function in three core emotional and interpersonal dimensions has a significant influence on effectiveness. These core characteristics are **empathy,** the ability to accurately perceive what people are experiencing and to communicate that perception to them; **respect,** positive regard and the indication of a deep and honest acceptance of the worth of persons apart from behaviors; and **genuineness,** the ability to be honest with him or herself and with others. A fourth core condition of **warmth** (treating people in a way that makes them feel safe, accepted, and understood) was added by Goldstein (1975), who observed that without warmth, the practitioner may be "technically correct but therapeutically impotent" (p. 31). These four core characteristics are necessary conditions for assuring that no harm is done, and for developing a therapeutic climate within which family work may be conducted.

Most family practitioners consider the relationship between the family and the practitioner to be an essential ingredient of the therapeutic process. However, little systematic attention has been given to examining the function of the therapeutic alliance in working with families. Minuchin (1974) has talked about the necessity for the therapist to "join" the family, and Davatz (1981) has emphasized the importance of "connecting" with family members. Pinsof and Catherall (1986) state that

TABLE 3.1   Seven Principles in the Helping Relationship

First Direction: The Need of the Family	Second Direction: The Response of the Practitioner	Third Direction: The Awareness of the Client/Family	The Name of the Principle
1. To be treated as individuals			**1.** Individualization
2. To express feelings	The practitioner is sensitive to, understands, and appropriately responds to these needs.	The client/family is somehow aware of the practitioner's sensitivity, understanding, and response.	**2.** Purposeful expres- sion of feelings
3. To get empathic responses to problems			**3.** Controlled emo- tional involvement
4. To be recognized as people of worth			**4.** Acceptance
5. Not to be judged			**5.** Nonjudgmental attitude
6. To make own choices and decisions			**6.** Self-determination
7. To keep secrets about self and family			**7.** Confidentiality

Adapted from Biestek, 1957, p. 17.

the therapeutic alliance may be the primary mediating variable that determines the outcome of discrete interventions. They assert that adding the alliance concept to the theoretical base of family therapy illuminates and brings into focus a critical aspect of therapy that has existed in a theoretical twilight (p. 138). Pinsof (1994) builds on previous definitions to define the alliance:

> *The therapeutic alliance consists of those aspects of the relationship between and within the therapist and patient systems that pertains to their capacity to mutu-ally invest in and collaborate on the tasks and goals of therapy. (p. 7)*

The major difference between this definition and preceding ones is that it tries to account for the social field in which the alliance occurs. There is an alliance between two systems—not just two people, regardless of the number of people directly involved in the sessions. The client system consists of all the human systems that are or may be involved in the maintenance or resolution of the presenting problem. The therapist system consists of all the people involved in treating the client system. In other words, the systems consist of all the people that can influence the change process. In working with families, the therapeutic alliance exists on at least three levels—the individual alliance with each family member, the subsystem alliance with each of the multiperson subsystems as parents and children, and the whole system alliance with the whole family system (Pinsof & Catherall, 1986). The alliance the practitioner has with one or two family members impacts the alliance with other family members in a circular, reciprocal fashion. Therefore, no single alliance with dyads or triads can be considered in isolation.

Any individual is affected by the way in which relevant members of his or her social field feel about the practitioner or interventions. If a spouse is resentful of the therapeutic process, then this resentment may be a significant mediating factor in the outcome. On the other hand, a supportive spouse or family system may greatly facilitate the outcome of the process.

A significant contribution to understanding the therapeutic alliance has been the development of three systemically oriented scales to measure the alliance in individual, couple, and family work (Pinsof, 1994; Pinsof & Catherall, 1986). Each measures the content dimensions of tasks, goals, and bonds as they relate to the therapeutic alliance.

Diversity Issues

A second set of contextual issues has to do with diversity among clients and families. Within diversity issues are included cultures, ethnicity, race, social class, religious affiliations, regional identities, gender, age, disability, affinity orientation, and other factors that may significantly affect and define our lives. Some of those that are most relevant to practice with families are now more specifically addressed. They include issues of ethnic sensitive practice, multiculturalism, gender, oppression, poverty, and family structures.

Ethnic Sensitive Practice

Ethnic sensitive practice must be in tune with the history, values, and perspectives of the family's ethnic group and social class position. An important component is giving attention to the oppression of members of racial and ethnic groups, and choosing relevant practice models for that family's needs at that point in time. Some assumptions of ethnic sensitive practice are that (1) history affects the generation and solution of problems, (2) the present is more important than the past or future, (3) nonconscious phenomena affect family functioning, and (4) although ethnicity can be a source of strain, discordance, and strife, it is also a source of cohesion, identity, and strength (Schlesinger & Devore, 1995).

A second important component to ethnic sensitive practice is multiculturalism, which is defined as learning to understand, appreciate, and value (not just tolerate) the unique aspects of cultures different from our own. The end product is learning to value others though they may be different from us. Multiculturalism is learning that "different from" does not mean "less than." It is getting in touch with our cultural conditioning, learning how we view the world through our own particular filters, and working toward inclusion rather than exclusion and conformity (Bennett-Alexander, 1993).

Efforts at problem resolution must be in tune with ethnically distinctive values and community customs. Such practice involves the concept of the "dual perspective"—a conscious and systematic process of perceiving, understanding, and comparing simultaneously the values, attitudes, and behavior of the larger societal system with those of the family's immediate community system. It recognizes that all clients are a part of two systems: the dominant or sustaining system, which is the source of power and economic resources; and the nurturing system, composed of the physical and social environment of the family and community. Ethnic and class history and traditions often involve institutional sources of oppression. Therefore, practice with families must pay simultaneous attention to family and community/systemic concerns.

Value patterns are constantly undergoing change according to McGoldrick, Giordano, & Pearce (1996). They earlier stated that it is very important for the family practitioner to keep track of four related issues:

1. the value patterns characteristic of the family's culture of origin;
2. where the family is in the acculturation process, and what values have been or are being changed at the time of the intervention;
3. the family's understanding or misunderstanding of mainstream values;
4. in cross-cultural marriages, what conflicts have occurred or what compromises are being made to compensate for the differences between the two background value patterns (McGoldrick, Pearce, & Giordano, 1982, pp. 45–46).

McGoldrick, Preto, Hines, and Lee (1991, pp. 579–580) state, "Ethnocentrism, clannishness, prejudice, fear, and distrust of outsiders can prevent cooperation, reinforce exclusivity, and deepen intergroup conflicts. The solution to these problems lies not in eradicating cultural differences, however, but in developing their potential to become a source of cultural enrichment."

A cross-cultural practice model has been developed by Chau (1990) to guide ethnically sensitive practice. The model consists of four quadrants defined by two axes as shown in Figure 3.1. One axis represents the ideological value continuum of "Ethnocentrism and Pluralism." The other axis defines the targets or goals of intervention and is arranged on a continuum of "Individual Change to Sociostructural Change." The resulting quadrants (A, B, C, D) specify the four practice processes of psychosocial adaptation, ethnic "conscientization," ethnic rights advocacy, and interethnic integration, which are defined in Figure 3.1.

Not only is this perspective applicable to a broad array of minority needs, but it also accommodates the use of different practice methods. It enables practitioners to learn about and apply ethnic sensitivity in their helping activities throughout the processes of problem identification, assessment, planning, intervention, and evaluation.

As we strive toward ethnically sensitive practice, it is helpful to see where we as part of society have been before and where it is we as part of society still need to go. The People of Color Leadership Institute (1993) defines cultural competence as a continuum:

Cultural Destructiveness: Attitudes, policies, and practices that are destructive to cultures and, consequently, to the individuals within the culture.

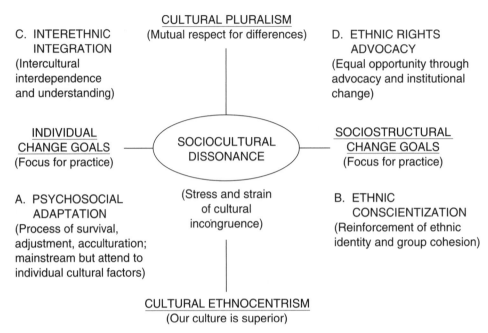

FIGURE 3.1   **A cross-cultural practice model.**

(Adapted from Chau, 1990.)

Cultural Incapacity: Unintentional cultural destructiveness characterized by the lack of capacity to help minority clients or communities and the belief in racial superiority.

Cultural Blindness: The belief that people are all the same and that services can be universally applied without consideration of and respect for differing needs and customs.

Cultural Precompetence: A system that realizes its weaknesses in serving minorities and actively attempts to improve some aspect of service to a specific population, such as recruiting ethnic-minority personnel, establishing community liaisons, and seeking cultural knowledge.

Basic Cultural Competency: Accepting and respecting differences, and conducting ongoing self-assessment regarding the continuous expansion of cultural knowledge and resources.

Advanced Cultural Competence: Seeking to add to the knowledge base of culturally competent practice, characterized by advocacy of cultural competence throughout the system and improved relations between cultures throughout society.

Critical tasks that have to be mastered before cultural competency can be achieved are outlined by Hardy (1997). He states that it is the synthesis of the various tasks that enables one to develop a self–other perspective, and that there are five steps for developing cultural competency: (1) challenge segregated thinking; (2) expand notions of culture; (3) challenge the myth of color blindness; (4) embrace race and gender as organizing principles; and (5) embrace the relativity of reality. He goes on to state:

> *Cultural competency empowers us to work with, understand and have compassion for those who fall outside the boundaries of primary groups with which we identify or derive our sense of self and belonging. It is only when we—as a civilized society—can accomplish this feat that we will begin to dismantle the constructs of racism, sexism, elitism and homophobia that weaken our spirit and threaten to destroy us as a people. (p. 19)*

Hardy (1995) advocates the use of the cultural genogram in training culturally competent family practitioners. A similar tool is the culturagram (Congress, 1997), which is used to assess and empower culturally diverse families. Our goal should be to develop advanced cultural competence in our own and students' family practice, and advocate for this level of competence in society.

Gender Issues

In the forefront of family practice today are issues of gender. Feminism has served to raise sensitivity to gender issues and shake the foundations of patriarchy. This consciousness-raising has had far-reaching implications for family practice.

It became evident in the 1970s that some of the assumptions of family practice were at odds with some of the basic tenets of the feminist movement. In 1978, Hare-Mustin shook the family therapy establishment with a paper in *Family Process*. Ongoing dialogue has continued in the journals and at professional meetings. The major points of conflict were identified concisely by Broderick and Schrader (1991, p. 36) who cite Libow, Raskin, and Caust (1982) and can be summarized in four points:

1. Most family therapists tend to focus on ongoing, reciprocal circular causation, while the feminist therapist focuses on the linear causation of historic sexism and structural inequities.
2. While family therapists intervene with the goal of improving relationships and patterns of interaction, the feminist therapist's goal is, rather, "to facilitate the growth of a strong competent woman who has enhanced control over resources" and "to increase the ability of women to work together politically to change society and its institutions" (Libow, Raskin, & Caust, 1982, p. 8).
3. The family therapist is seen as utilizing expert power while feminists are committed to utilizing referent power (which highlights the commonality of all women's experiences).
4. The family therapist works within the ethnic, social, and religious values of the client family whereas the feminist therapist challenges those norms and values that directly or indirectly support sexism and patriarchy.

In true systemic fashion, the women's movement has had an effect upon men. Many men are now seeing themselves in a different way, asking different questions, and exploring more mature masculine identities (Moore & Gillette, 1990). Feminists have articulated how male dominance in patriarchy has been oppressive and abusive of the feminine in everyone—of both the so-called feminine characteristics and virtues and actual women themselves. In their radical critique of patriarchy, some feminists conclude that masculinity is essentially abusive. They assert that connection with such characteristics as love, relatedness, and gentleness comes only from acknowledging the feminine aspects in all persons.

The men's movement has responded with the view that patriarchy is not the expression of deep and rooted masculinity, for truly deep and rooted masculinity is not abusive (Moore & Gillette, 1990). Rather, patriarchy is the expression of the immaturely masculine, the shadow or crazy side of masculinity. It expresses the stunted masculine, fixated at immature levels. They see patriarchy as an attack on masculinity in its fullness as well as femininity in its fullness. Those caught up in the structures and dynamics of patriarchy seek to dominate not only women but men as well. Patriarchy is thus seen as based on fear—of women as well as men. Moore and Gillette go on to say that what is missing is not adequate connection with the inner feminine, but an adequate connection to the deep and instinctual masculine energies, the potentials of mature masculinity. They were being blocked from connection to these potentials by patriarchy itself, by reaction to the feminist critique, and by the lack in their lives of meaningful and transformative initiatory process into manhood.

As men are now beginning to get more in touch with masculine potentials, it seems to be time for men and women to come together in their mutual explorations for fullness and maturity. As Keen (1991) states, "We are more profoundly united by our common humanity than separated by gender" (p. 10). As we explore the meaning of being persons from within the horizons of male and female experiences, the stories of pain and promise will be equally relevant for both sexes. The most hopeful thing we can do to end the gender battles is simply to share with each other, tell our stories, and listen quietly and respectfully. We can then begin to create new visions of manhood and womanhood together.

Social constructionism has underscored sensitivity to gender issues in working with families. Hoffman (1990) states that focus on gender exposes established assumptions and mores in psychological theory that have been taken for granted and that are detrimental not only to women but also to men. Gender stereotypes and prescriptions for behavior negatively influence both genders by restricting opportunity on all levels of family functioning. Thus it is important for family practitioners to regularly consider their own personal issues and social forces that impact on the therapeutic system.

Oppression

Some groups in society are oppressed because of their race and ethnicity, gender, sexual orientation, income, and age. Other client groups with mental, developmental, or physical disabilities may also be viewed as survivors of oppression. Shulman (1991) uses oppression theory to demonstrate how these types of oppression affect the client's motivation to use help, including the practitioner's interventions. He focuses on the socioeconomic factors of income, gender, and ethnicity as illustrative of the ways context and oppression can affect the lives of clients.

A major factor in oppression is lack of access to the basic economic resources necessary for the well-being of any family. Insufficient economic resources can lead to inadequate housing, limited medical services, inadequate diet, limited recreation, and an absence of necessary social supports. All of these stresses, and others resulting from economic dependency, can exacerbate the stresses associated with parenting and keeping a family together. Minority groups and people of color face oppression in discrimination in access to housing and economic opportunities (Ooms, 1992). In addition, racist attitudes can have a powerful impact on one's self-image. Institutional racism can also affect the attitudes of practitioners who are working with the economically oppressed. Because gender interacts with economic, housing, unemployment, and racial issues, it can be viewed as a thread throughout each of the other factors that the family practitioner needs to be aware of and sensitive to in working with families.

Another area that is impacted by oppression relates to Levels III and IV of family functioning, as discussed in Chapter 1. Because of societal attitudes and restrictions, some people are limited by these external boundaries in reaching their potential. Using a social constructionist approach within the consideration of the larger ecosystems dynamics could promote empowerment and thus more self-actualization with these families.

Poverty

In a 1992 Family Impact Seminar on "Families in Poverty," held in Washington, DC, Ooms (1992) stated that poverty in America has become primarily an issue for single-parent families with children. Child poverty rates have climbed back to the high levels of the 1960s and are higher than for any other age group. There are very large racial differences in poverty rates. Persistent poverty is primarily a minority issue. Whereas 10% of all children are persistently poor, 90% of all children poor for ten years or more are black.

According to a recent analysis of longitudinal data (Sawhill & Condon, 1992), income mobility has not been increasing in recent decades. In fact, because there is a growing gap between wages at the bottom and the top, lifetime income inequality appears to be growing. Sawhill and Condon outlined three major factors which most people agree have contributed to the rise in poverty among families with children since the 1970s. These are demography (the rise in single-parent families), the economy (growing inequality of earnings), and public policy (real welfare benefits fell about 40%).

The National Commission on Children, in a report of the National Opinion Research Project (1991), identified several groups of children and families for whom life is most difficult. When the population of children and parents is analyzed separately by income, race, and geography, significant stresses and threats to children's well-being are found for particular subgroups. Minority families, poor families generally, and especially poor families living in large cities indicated a variety of problems and stresses that directly affected their children's safety and well-being.

Poverty is a diversity issue that directly affects many families. Poverty and lack of housing have given rise to unprecedented rates of homelessness. Families with children are the fastest-growing homeless population. Practitioners must be acutely aware that these families in poverty have needs that are at Levels I and II of family functioning. These needs must be addressed before needs at Levels III and IV can be given adequate attention.

Family Structures

Another diversity issue influencing practice is that of varying family structures. Many different structures have replaced the traditional two-parent, mother-at-home, father-working image of bygone days. These new structures include single-parent families, childless families, blended families, same-sex families, multigenerational families, and others. Each has unique dynamics and issues that should be understood by the practitioner and taken into consideration when working with the family.

Some family structures are more vulnerable than others. For example, at any given time, one-quarter of American children are living with just one parent, usually a divorced or never-married mother. For many of these children, their father's physical absence from the home has enormous emotional and financial consequences (National Opinion Research Project, 1991). In many families, both fathers and mothers find it necessary to work long hours outside the home in order to support their families.

These changes within families and the stresses they often engender are exacerbated by changes in the larger society. For many families, close-knit communities and the ready support of nearby relatives and friends no longer exist. As families move in order to pursue employment, educational opportunities, and retirement relocations for older Americans, the geographic distance between extended family members has increased. In many cases, work and other demands further isolate families within communities, leaving them little time or opportunity for neighborhood, civic, or community involvement (Ooms, 1992). Not only do practitioners need to be sensitized to the different family structures, but also they must recognize the ecosystems factors that impact on these structures.

Summary

Within an ecosystems–social constructionism perspective, there exist many commonalities and differences of which we must be aware as we work with families who are functioning at various levels. Our common humanness unites us and is a foundation upon which to build a therapeutic alliance. Differences and diversity issues must be recognized with the goal of developing mutual respect and appreciation for differences. Thus the focus is on commonalities that unite us, not differences that divide us. *The helping relationship or therapeutic alliance* is a necessary condition for assuming that no harm is done and for developing a climate within which work can be done on problems that families bring to practitioners. The core needs of clients and the core conditions of the professional relationship of empathy, respect, genuineness, and warmth are commonalities for all our work with families: The therapeutic alliance consisting of the practitioner and client systems accounts for the social field in which the alliance occurs. *Diversity issues* include valuing multiculturalism and engaging in ethnically sensitive practice. A cross-cultural practice model and a cultural competence continuum are aides to developing ethnic sensitivity in a practitioner. Ways that diversity issues interfere with the provision of social justice and contribute to oppression must be addressed.

In the forefront of family practice today are issues of gender, not just women's issues. Consciousness-raising over the past few decades has served to focus our attention more on the oppressiveness of patriarchy, thus precipitating changes in both genders. However, oppression is felt by other groups as well, because of race, ethnicity, sexual preference, income, age, and the like. A major factor in oppression is access to the basic economic resources that are necessary for the well-being of any family. Practitioners must be especially sensitive to these families who are functioning at Levels I and II. Closely tied in with oppression is poverty, which is an especially crucial issue for minorities and single-parent families with children. These varying family structures—such as single-parent families but including also blended, childless, same-sex, multigenerational families and others—may be especially vulnerable. Family practitioners must be sensitive to the different family structures and also realize the impact of ecosystem factors upon them.

Discussion Questions

1. How does the addition of the concept **alliance** alter the previous understanding of the helping relationship?
2. How can the issue of gender impact the development of the therapeutic alliance on the three levels of individual, subsystem (parents or children), and whole family system?
3. Using a family from your practice, assess the manner in which you engaged or joined the client. Extend this discussion of the therapeutic alliance through all the contexts of helping.
4. What efforts can be made to show value and appreciation of the culture of the families with whom we work?
5. For each of the six points along the cultural competence continuum, give an action and/or attitude that might be representative of a person functioning at this point. Identify where you see yourself on this continuum. What could you do to become more culturally competent?

Suggested Readings

Biestek, F. P. (1957). *The casework relationship.* Chicago: Loyola University Press.

This is a classic on the therapeutic relationship and should be required reading for all helping professionals. A chapter is devoted to each of the seven principles of the helping relationship.

Boyd-Franklin, N. (1989). *Black families in therapy: A multisystems approach.* New York: The Guilford Press.

The author dispels myths, focuses on strengths, and sets African American families in context. She gives major treatment interventions in a multisystemic approach and discusses diversity of family structures.

Brown, L. S., & Ballou, M. (Eds.) (1992). *Personality and psychopathology: Feminist reappraisals.* New York: Guilford Press.

Synthesizing over 20 years of feminist thinking, this book gives original critiques of primary psychological theories and their accompanying definitions of pathology. The authors challenge previous theories of how healthy personalities develop, and points out the need to keep any theory of personality relevant to women's lives.

Edwards, R. L. (Ed. in Chief), 1995. *Encyclopedia of social work.* (19th ed.), Vol. I, II, & III. Washington, D.C.: National Association of Social Workers.

This most recent encyclopedia provides an objective overview of social work in the United States. It contains ten articles specifically on the family, another on marriage/partners, and many others on methods of practice and diversity issues. It is highly recommended as a state-of-the-art reference book.

Jordan, J. V., Kaplan, A. G., Miller, J. B., Stiver, I. P., & Surrey, J. L. (1991). *Women's growth in connection.* New York: Guilford Press.

This book offers a new perspective on women's development, and women's ways of being in the world. The authors are clinicians, supervisors, and teachers who have been searching for therapeutic models that are based upon and reflect the lives of women rather than male models. It discusses women's meaning systems, values, and their organization of experiences.

Pinsof, W. F., & Catherall, D. R. (1986). The integrative psychotherapy alliance: Family, couple and individual therapy scales. *Journal of Marital and Family Therapy, 12*(2), 137–151.

This article introduces the therapeutic alliance concept into the family and marital therapy domain. It conceptualizes individual, couple, and family therapy as occurring within the same systemic framework. Three new scales that measure the alliance in individual, couple, and family therapy are discussed.

References

Bennett-Alexander, D. (1993). Preparing for the reality of multiculturalism. *The University of Georgia Columns, 20*(13), 5.

Biestek, F. P. (1957). *The casework relationship.* Chicago: Loyola University Press.

Broderick, C. B., & Schrader, S. S. (1991). *The history of professional marriage and family therapy.* In A. S. Gurman & D. P. Kniskern (Eds.), *Handbook of family therapy* (Vol. II) (pp. 3–40). New York: Brunner/Mazel.

Buber, M. (1958). *I and thou* (2nd rev. ed.). New York: Charles Scribner's Sons.

Chau, K. L. (1990). A model for teaching cross-cultural practice in social work. *Journal of Social Work Education,* (2), 124–133.

Congress, E. P. (Ed.). (1997). *Multicultural perspectives in working with families.* New York: Springer.

Davatz, U. (1981). Establishing a therapeutic alliance in family systems therapy. In A. S. Gurman (Ed.), *Questions and answers in the practice of family therapy.* New York: Brunner/Mazel.

Goldstein, A. (1975). Relationship enhancement methods. In F. Kanfer & A. Goldstein (Eds.), *Helping people change: A textbook of methods.* New York: Pergamon Press.

Hardy, K. V. (1995). The cultural genogram: Key to training culturally competent family therapists. *Journal of Marital and Family Therapists, 21*(3), 227–237.

Hardy, K. V. (1997). Steps toward becoming culturally competent. *Family Therapy News, 28*(2), 13, 19.

Hoffman, L. (1990). Constructing realities: An art of lenses. *Family Process, 29*(1), 1–12.

Keen, S. (1991). *Fire in the belly: On being a man.* New York: Bantam Books.

Libow, J. A., Raskin, P. A., & Caust, B. L. (1982). Feminist and family systems therapy: Are they irreconcilable? *American Journal of Family Therapy, 10,* 3–12.

McGoldrick, M., Giordano, J., & Pearce, J. K. (1996). *Ethnicity and family therapy,* 2nd ed. New York: Guilford Press, pp. 45–46.

McGoldrick, M., Pearce, J. K., & Giordano, J. (1982). *Ethnicity and family therapy.* New York: Guilford Press, pp. 45–46.

McGoldrick, M., Preto, N. G., Hines, P. M., & Lee, E. (1991). Ethnicity and family therapy. In A. S. Gurman & D. P. Kniskern (Eds.), *Handbook of family therapy* (Vol. II) (pp. 546–582). New York: Brunner/Mazel.

Minuchin, S. (1974). *Families and family therapy.* Cambridge, MA: Harvard University Press.

Moore, R., & Gillette, D. (1990). *King, warrior, magician, lover: Rediscovering the archetypes of the mature masculine.* San Francisco: Harper San Francisco.

National Opinion Research Project (1991). *Speaking of kids: A national survey of children and parents.* Washington, DC: National Commission on Children.

Ooms, T. (1992). *Families in poverty: Patterns, contexts, and implications for policy.* Washington, DC: American Association for Marriage and Family Therapy Family Impact Seminar.

People of Color Leadership Institute. (Jan/Feb 1993). Cultural competence continuum, *NRCCSA News.* Washington, DC: POCLI.

Pinsof, W. F. (1994). An integrative systems perspective on the therapeutic alliance: Theoretical, clinical and research implications. In A. Horvath & L. Greenberg (Eds.), *The working alliance: Theory, research and practice.* New York: Wiley.

Pinsof, W. F., & Catherall, D. R. (1986). The integrative psychotherapy alliance: Family, couple and individual therapy scales. *Journal of Marital and Family Therapy, 12*(2), 137–151.

Rogers, C., Gendlin, E. T., Kiesler, D. L., & Truax, C. B. (1969). *The therapeutic relationship and its impact.* Madison: University of Wisconsin Press.

Sawhill, I. V., & Condon, M. (1992). Is U.S. income inequality really growing? Sorting out the fairness question. In *Policy Bites,* No. 13. Washington, DC: Urban Institute.

Schlesinger, E. G., & Devore, W. (1995). Ethnic-sensitive practice. In R. L. Edwards (Ed. in Chief), *Encyclopedia of social work* (19th ed.) (pp. 902–908). Silver Spring, MD: National Association of Social Workers.

Shulman, L. (1991). *Interactional social work practice: Toward an empirical theory.* Itasca, IL: Peacock.

Truax, C. B., & Carkhuff, R. R. (1967). *Toward effective counseling and psychotherapy: Training and practice.* Chicago: Aldine.

Chapter 4

Ethical Issues and Spiritual Dimensions

ALLIE C. KILPATRICK, Ph.D.

The entire therapeutic venture is fundamentally an exercise in ethics, involving the inventing, shaping, and reformulating of codes for living together (Efran, Lukens, & Lukens, 1988). Family interventions thus become a dialogue whose goal is the creation of a context in which accommodation of the needs and desires of all the participants is facilitated. Fundamental to this context is the dimension of spirituality. Although little recognized, some form of spirituality is a commonality in humanity. At varying times in a person's life, this aspect of being seeks expression. This chapter discusses the contexts of ethical issues and spiritual dimensions of practice with families.

Ethical Issues, Guides, and Codes

Most professional groups that work with families have their own codes of ethics by which members are expected to abide. It is essential that practitioners know and practice these codes. Issues discussed here are those which involve some of the larger difficulties that we confront in family practice. This section points out some of the ethical issues in working with families, and then presents several models for dealing with ethical issues.

Ethical Issues

Thorny issues arise when working with families. Some of the issues discussed here are separating interventions from the larger ecosystems, focusing on individual or family welfare, using informed consent, use of confidentiality, and avoiding deception and manipulation.

1. *Separating interventions from the larger social, cultural and political ecosystems.* For many years, family therapists have spoken of problems as symptoms of family system dysfunction, rather than as manifestations of individual illness. Interventions have been focused on first-order change (individual behavior change within an unchanged system) or second-order change (changes within the system itself and the rules governing it). However, as cited by Doherty and Boss (1991, p. 613), we do not always consider the wider implications of the community, social, cultural, and political systems in the cause of the problems or the ripples our interventions may cause in this wider pond on either level of change.

An illustration of how both society and the practitioner's interventions play roles in exacerbating problems for clients can be seen in abusive families. For many years, society tolerated abusive behavior toward women and children. Now, society has changed and practitioners label such behaviors as "bad" or "mad." If abusive behavior is part of a family's heritage, then their forebears are also seen as "bad." If practitioners tell them that the negative consequences will likely remain with them all their lives, then they probably will, inasmuch as people create their own reality based, at least in part, upon this perception (Becvar & Becvar, 1993).

Society does evolve appropriate rules of conduct, and practitioners contribute to defining acceptable and unacceptable behaviors and problems. We also define what constitutes an ethical issue. Perhaps the ethical imperatives here are to avoid narrowing the range of focus to the point where there is little we see that is not illness, thus limiting preventive interventions (Becvar & Becvar, 1993, p. 114), and ensuring that we do no harm. We must be careful that our interventions do not create more problems than they solve, but we must also be careful that we do not ignore ethical dilemmas that arise in our practice concerning such social justice issues as institutional racism, societal gender bias, or accessibility to resources.

2. *Individual welfare or family welfare.* In a survey of members of the American Association for Marriage and Family Therapy (Green & Hansen, 1989), the ethical dilemma rated as the second most frequently encountered and the second most important was the tension between "family versus individual needs" (second only to "reporting child abuse"). Practitioners are concerned with protecting the rights and promoting the welfare of all clients. When there are multiple clients, an intervention that serves one person's best interests may be counterproductive for another person. The ethical imperative here is to attempt to balance therapeutic responsibility toward individuals and the family as a unit (Doherty & Boss, 1991).

The basic philosophy of Western medicine and the medical code of ethics imply that a clinician's primary loyalty is to the patient as an individual; broader issues of public welfare are relegated to public health. In the Eastern European tradition, however, the clinician's first obligation is to the community and second to the individual. Society also defines the roles of men and women. Practitioners have been guilty of subordinating rights of women and children to the family good, even when it is to their detriment. It is not surprising that the issue of individual versus family rights was first raised by feminists, who have argued convincingly that balancing individual and family welfare requires practitioners to see beyond the therapy room to the family context (Doherty & Boss, 1991).

3. *Informed consent.* The idea of informed consent involves "a knowledgeable decision based on adequate information about the therapy, the available alternatives, and the collateral risks" (Bray, Shepherd, & Hays, 1985, p. 53). State laws and professional association codes of ethics have made informed consent procedures standard practice. Disclosure documents are often read by family members before they see the practitioner (Huber & Baruth, 1987). The information that clients should have in order to make informed choices includes the procedures, goals, and possible side effects of interventions; the qualifications, policies, and practices of the practitioner; and other available sources of help. Ethical issues arise around the coercion of reluctant adults or children in the family, especially when it violates the autonomy of a skeptical family member. Refusing to see the family unless all members are present could also be coercive to willing members, who may feel obligated to make successful efforts to engage the other members. Doherty and Boss (1991) assert that refusing treatment if all the family does not participate would be unethical in public mental health centers, which are often the last resort for troubled families.

4. *Confidentiality.* The client has the right to be protected from the disclosure of information discussed in sessions, unless permission, usually written, is given for this disclosure (Huber & Baruth, 1987). However, judicial decisions—as in the case of incest, child abuse, or other clear dangers to a client (such as that addressed by the Tarasoff decision) and third parties such as family courts and insurance companies—have compromised the ideal of full confidentiality for clients (Doherty & Boss, 1991).

The ethical challenge for practitioners also comes within the relationships of family members and how to deal with secrets. Whether the practitioner keeps full confidentiality of private revelations, no confidentiality among family members, or a balance between the two, the practitioner's position should be clearly communicated to the family. The ethical imperative is to disclose the practitioner's policy on confidentiality as part of initial informed consent for treatment (Doherty & Boss, 1991).

5. *Deception and manipulation.* According to Doherty and Boss (1991), the issue of deception is, along with gender bias, a central ethical issue in contemporary family treatment. According to some theories, manipulation should be avoided at all costs. Others state that all practitioners influence clients by sharing or withholding information about the practitioner's thoughts and feelings concerning the client.

Given the universality of the influence of practitioners on clients and the continual decisions made by the practitioner about what to disclose, the issue is not whether the intervention is paradoxical or straightforward (since neither is inherently deceptive), but whether any concealment involved is ethical, and whether the therapist remains trustworthy (Doherty & Boss, 1991). The ethical issue is that the practitioner does not deceive the family about the practitioner's beliefs or intentions or conceal family realities that the family deserves to know about.

Handling the ethical issues we have discussed builds upon the principles of relationship, ecosystems, and social constructionism that were discussed in earlier chapters. These principles consistently focus on the integrity of practitioners in respectful, genuine, and caring relationships with families and with themselves. We now turn to guides for understanding dimensions of ethical judgment and elements of intervention decisions, and codes of ethics.

Guides for Decision Making

The variety of ethical issues faced by family practitioners may be examined in terms of some underlying dimensions. Woody (1990, p. 135) proposes a pragmatic approach to dealing with ethical concerns in family practice, drawing upon theories of ethics, codes of professional conduct, practice theories, sociological context, and the professional identity. These components are outlined in Table 4.1. These components serve as five decision bases for practitioners to use for a comprehensive analysis in preventing ethical problems and in reaching defensible ethical decisions. The assumption is that practitioners draw from several bases in the process of weighing competing values and coming to a decision, and use both intuitive and critical thinking.

Another perspective on how family practitioners deal with ethical issues was drawn from qualitative research by Holland and Kilpatrick (1991). They developed a three-dimensional framework based on their findings from a grounded theory study of practitioners and how they defined and made ethical decisions. Their model of **dimensions of clinical judgment** consists of the three bipolar dimensions: the focus of decisions, ranging from means to ends; the interpersonal orientation, ranging from autonomy to mutuality; and the locus of authority, ranging from internalized to externalized.

The first dimension focuses directly on the practitioner's decisions and identifies a tension between pursuing solutions that maximize benefits regardless of risk versus complying with principles and procedures that are seen to reflect the values of the profession. The issue of deception and manipulation may be involved here.

The second dimension examines the interpersonal orientation in the decision-making process. It reflects practitioners' struggles between the protection of individual freedom and self-determination, and the responsibility of mutual caring that urges active intervention in the service of protection and improvement for the good of all. Here, the issues of separating interventions from the larger ecosystem and focusing on individual family welfare come into play.

The third dimension involves the source of authority in the decision-making process. It focuses on the grounds for making these decisions, and represents the conflict of allegiance to values that lie within the individual or the client/worker relationship and the obligation to comply with external sources such as agency policy or existing norms. Issues of informed consent and confidentiality are applicable here (see Figure 4.1).

Crossing these three dimensions permits examination of each area in relation to the other two, which yields a comprehensive look at one's ethical orientation. Such a perspective suggests looking for interactions across these three dimensions in specific practice situations. A professional or a family may have a pattern of dealing with ethical problems that emphasizes following standard policies and

**TABLE 4.1   Overview of the Decision Bases for Resolving Ethical Concerns
in Clinical Practice**

Theories of Ethics	Professional Codes of Ethics	Professional Theoretical Premises

Offer logical methods for ethical decision making based on universal principles.
 	
Intuitive thinking draws on contract theory: Honors natural duties stemming from the principle of justice and the special professional duty to promote client welfare, dignity, liberty, self-determination, privacy, etc.
 	
Critical thinking draws on contract theory of social justice and on utilitarian theory: The greatest good for the greatest number of persons involved.
	General rules, norms, and principles should become a second nature for the professional. Encompass therapist competence/integrity, confidentiality, and promoting client welfare, self-determination, dignity, etc. Many values stem from the tradition of individualism.
	
	Contain conflicting principles and obligations.
	
	Abstractions require definition and interpretation.
	
	Codes are evolving to interface with sociological interface.
		Different assumptions about and definitions of human nature, behavior, pathology, and health.
		
		These determine meanings for promoting "client welfare."
		
		Diverse concepts about right or effective therapist conduct relating to:
		  competence
		  integrity
		  therapeutic relationship
		  confidentiality
		  power
		  resistance
		  symptoms
		  role of strategy
		
		Compare family systems, psychoanalytic, behavioral, structural, strategic, feminist, etc.

Sociological Context	Therapist's Personal/Professional Identity
Sociocultural values and their evolution affect client and therapist values, societal priorities, and laws. Public policy guidelines derived from statutory law, state regulatory boards, and precedent cases create responsibilities for therapists. Organizational context, mission, roles, policies, etc. impact on the conduct of therapy.	A person is present in the helping relationship, does the intuitive or critical thinking, and ultimately makes choices based on beliefs integrated from the personal conscience, secular philosophy and/or religion, professional ethics, and theoretical concepts. Identifies and weighs information from all decision bases, including judging one's own knowledge, integrity, and personality needs. An ethical "character" plus professional values, knowledge, and skills make an integrated personal/professional identity.

J. D. Woody, Resolving ethical concerns in family practice: Toward a pragmatic model, reprinted from Volume 16, Number 2, of the *Journal of Marital and Family Therapy,* Copyright 1990, American Association for Marriage and Family Therapy. Reprinted with permission.

procedures, exercising centralized control, and protecting the security of his or her position or the internal stability of the family. Another's approach to ethical dilemmas may emphasize a pattern that seeks to distribute power more broadly, to emphasize attainment of ends at the expense of following standard procedural

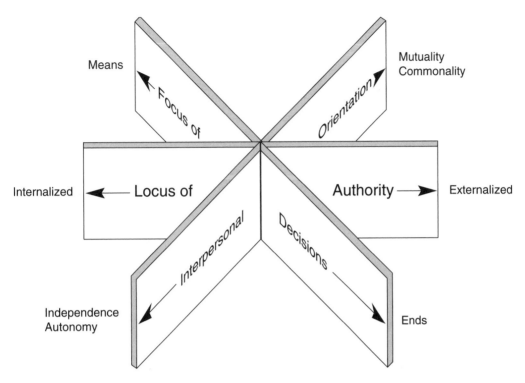

FIGURE 4.1   Dimensions of ethical judgment.

rules, and to advance individual autonomy. Posing these dimensions in terms of polar extremes does not entail their opposition or mutual exclusion. One may seek to balance them by seeking both group stability and individual flexibility, to encourage both productivity and cohesiveness, and to be both nurturing and powerful. *The importance of balance along each of the dimensions may be highlighted by the extreme forms that any of these values can take if unchecked.*

Codes of Ethics

Any profession has the responsibility to articulate its basic values and ethical principles and standards that are relevant to all professional functions, settings, and populations served. These codes of ethics serve to guide decision making and conduct when ethical issues arise. As discussed previously, ethical decision making is a process. Keeping in mind the guides for decision making and the dimensions for clinical judgment, we turn our attention now to codes of ethics. These codes are essential for guiding conduct and maintaining professional standards. All professions that include working with families have their own codes of ethics. For illustrative purposes, the codes of ethics for the National Association of Social Workers and for the American Association for Marriage and Family Therapy are discussed.

NASW Code of Ethics (1996)

The broad ethical principles in the code of ethics of the National Association of Social Workers are based on social work's core values of service, social justice, dignity and worth of the person, importance of human relationships, integrity, and competence. The updated code became effective on January 1, 1997, and serves the following six purposes: It identifies core values of social work; summarizes broad ethical principles reflecting these values and sets standards; identifies relevant considerations and conflicts; provides ethical standards for which the profession is accountable; socializes new practitioners to social work's mission, values, ethical principles, and ethical standards; and articulates standards used to assess unethical conduct.

The code sets forth standards to which all social workers should aspire and which are relevant to the professional activities of all social workers. The standards include the categories of social workers' ethical responsibilities to clients, to colleagues, in practice settings, as professionals, to the social work profession, and to the broader society.

The longest and most in-depth standard is the first one, the responsibility to clients, which is five pages in length. It covers the following: the commitment to clients, which is the primary obligation; self-determination of clients; the provision of valid informed consent to clients; competence in providing services; the understanding of cultural competence, oppression, and social diversity; conflicts of interest including dual relationships; privacy and confidentiality; access to records; sexual relationships with clients, which are strictly forbidden; physical contact; sexual harassment; derogatory language; payment for services; clients who lack decision-making capacity; interruption of services; and termination of services. Special attention must be paid to each of these as practitioners discharge their professional responsibilities to clients in a respectful, caring manner.

AAMFT Code of Ethics (1991)

The code of the American Association for Marriage and Family Therapy is binding on members in all categories, including students, clinical members, and supervisors. It is similar in many respects to the NASW code. Eight categories are addressed. These are responsibility to clients; confidentiality; professional competence and integrity; responsibility to students, employees, and supervisors; responsibility to research participants; responsibility to the profession; financial arrangements; and advertising.

The code urges marriage and family therapists to report any alleged unethical behavior of colleagues so that the profession can be self-regulating and uphold the standards. Reports should be made to appropriate professional associations and state regulatory bodies.

Other professions that work with families, such as psychologists, counselors, chaplains, and nurses, have their own codes of ethics. State licensing boards also have their own, sometimes as an umbrella code that covers several helping professions. All family practitioners are strongly encouraged to become very familiar with the relevant codes that govern their practice. A code of ethics cannot guarantee ethical behavior. Practitioners' ethical behavior must come from their personal commitment to engage in ethical practice.

Spiritual Dimensions of Practice

The 1996 Joint World Congress of the International Federation of Social Workers and the International Association of Schools of Social Work in Hong Kong heard the proclamation that there is a quiet revolution taking place in social work and other professions that is challenging the sole reliance on a traditional scientific-theory basis in favor of a more inclusive view of the human condition. The suggestion was made that social work's bio-psycho-social paradigm be expanded to a bio-psycho-social-spiritual-cosmic paradigm as the integral basis for all courses taught (Schwartz & McGehee, 1996).

Because the majority of the world's families adopt some identifiable form of expression for their spirituality (Campbell & Moyers, 1988), it seems logical that practitioners should attend to the spiritual belief systems of clients if they are to understand better the families with whom they work. As the globe shrinks, long-delayed encounters with other cultures have contributed to a widespread increase in spiritual pluralism. Fox (1983) describes what he sees happening as an "ecosystemic" revolution, a paradigmatic shift in our views of spirituality.

The Harvard Medical School held the international conference "Spirituality and Healing in Medicine" in 1996. Of the 900 M.D.'s in attendance, 200 acknowledged using spirituality as a healing tool in their practices. The focus of the conference was on the future role of prayer and religious experience in the healing process. The finding of Harvard medical researchers that spirituality is associated with fewer medical symptoms was shared with conferees (Smith, 1996).

Prominent attention is being given the subject of spirituality in other secular activities. These include bookstores, various professional conferences, *Time* and *Newsweek* magazines, countless non-church-related associations such as Celestine Prophecy, A Course in Miracles, Readings of Edgar Cayce, Angels, and so on. Spirituality is becoming part of the mental set of our times. The 25-volume *World Spirituality* series has released its 22nd volume, Peter Van Ness's (1996) *Spirituality and the Secular Quest* (outside the church). Secular spirituality is defined as "perceiving oneself to be connected to a larger whole through some unitive and transcending principle and living one's life accordingly" (Reed, 1997, p. 45).

Barriers

There are several barriers to addressing spiritual concerns of families. One is that in order to become more scientific, we think we must separate ourselves from nonscientific spiritual constructs. The spiritual dimension is seen as esoteric and unobservable (Cornett, 1992), allowing the entrance of bias and subjectivity. Subjective constructs such as spiritual power, psychic energy, or divine intervention are hard to observe and measure (Prest & Keller, 1993). Cornett's (1992) view is that the failure to integrate spirituality into our clinical thinking represents an impoverishment.

A second barrier concerns the imposition of a particular frame of reference on clients. Effective practice is predicated on a nonimposing, nonjudgmental practitioner stance. Our spiritual commitments are better expressed through caring behavior. However, rather than monitoring our own spiritual expression in clinical work as we monitor other areas, many practitioners have simply discounted the need to explore the spiritual aspects of clients' lives, often with the assumption that these aspects are conflict-free, functional, or comfortable (Cornett, 1992). Other barriers include rigid conceptions of spirituality and biases against formal institutions (Prest & Keeler, 1993).

Definition of Spirituality

A definition of spirituality would need to encompass the person's understanding of and response to meaning in life (Cornett, 1992). It would include faith and values as spiritual dimensions (Kilpatrick & Holland, 1990), and also include the process of conceptualizing the individual's connection with others, the world, and the Creator (Campbell & Moyers, 1988). Spiritual expression could also be defined as the individual's response to the events in life over which he or she has no control. Canda (1988) gives an encompassing definition as follows:

> *The gestalt of the total process of human life and development relates to the person's search for a sense of meaning and totally fulfilling relationships between oneself, other people and the encompassing universe and ontological ground of existence, whether a person understands this in terms that are theistic, atheistic, nontheistic, or any combination of these.*

Assagioli (1990) considers spiritual as referring to all states of awareness, all the human functions and activities that have as their common denominator the possession of higher values—values such as the ethical, the aesthetic, the heroic, the humanitarian, and the altruistic.

Implementation

Conflicts in values and the search for direction, meaning, integration, and faith in our lives underlie many of the problems we confront in practice. Despite the difficulties in dealing with such elusive and complex issues, in helping clients, few areas have more importance than these. Even in poor communities, according to Aponte (1995) in his book *Bread and Spirit*, the challenge to the family is not only about bread or basic resources, but as much about spirit. We must build a sense of dignity, purpose, and future in families that have given up hope, meaning, and self-worth and succumbed to a sense of despair. Here, optimism and hope are the core elements in building the resilience so necessary when working with Level I family needs.

It is important, however, that practitioners have an understanding and awareness of their own spirituality if they are to be helpful to family members in their pilgrimage of life. The practitioner's own spirituality can be an obstacle or an asset. Effective practice includes recognizing clients' desires and readiness to deal with spiritual concerns, accepting them, and being as comfortable with discussing this dimension as with discussing the physical, emotional, and intellectual dimensions of practice (May, 1982). Whatever clients may believe in, Becvar (1997) asserts that a spiritual orientation would help them to define meaning in life and achieve ultimate satisfaction, and may encourage deeper levels of healing. Bardill (1997) states that a failure to account for the spiritual reality in practice means that a powerful reality of life has been ignored.

The intentional use of spirituality in practice is unique, not because of words or actions, but because of our assumptions of how these words or actions interface with the transcendent dimension. According to Anderson and Worthen (1997), three assumptions are basic to a spiritual perspective. These are (1) an awareness that God or a Divine Being exists, (2) a recognition that humans have an innate yearning for a connection with this Being, and (3) a belief that this Being is actively interested in humans and acts upon our relationships to promote beneficial change. Working from these assumptions, practitioners share their own spiritual selves, and then the range of available resources and possibilities for change expands for all. Specific suggestions for incorporating the spiritual dimension into practice are given by Kilpatrick and Holland (1990) in their discussion on spiritual dimensions of practice. The transpersonal or spiritual dimension is one of empowerment by the energies and wisdom that flow from a greater wholeness. It is the bedrock of empowerment for the practitioner and families, and for national and international work.

Instead of relegating issues of value, meaning, and purpose of life to the private sphere, the Judeo-Christian tradition emphasizes that faith permeates all aspects of life, linking each individual with the community or public sphere. Such linkages often prompt people of faith into actions of concern for others, especially the poor and the vulnerable. While these persons may not have always spoken with one voice on every issue, they have affirmed in numerous ways their shared faith that the spiritual dimension of life leads to a transcendence of individualism, and to a life of commitment and service to others (Leiby, 1985; Peck, 1987).

The convenient popular dichotomy between public and private morality works against the integration of our communities as well as our personal and professional lives. Our shared public interests rely in large part upon the development of private virtue. Both private and public order depend upon the availability of material resources and fair systems for their allocation to all. Therefore, a commitment to values of social justice and to the difficult tasks of implementing such values in our economic and political systems is essential (Siporin, 1986). Our spiritual heritage further emphasizes that individual self-actualization is gained through committed relationships with others, through investing our own resources and our very selves in furthering the good of others (Kilpatrick & Holland, 1990).

Recognition of the spiritual foundations of our lives and our professional practice leads to a number of implications regarding the client, the practitioner, their relationship, and the social context of the profession. Consistent with our social constructionist framework, clients are our peers, human beings similar to us. Exploration of spiritual issues is undertaken with respect for the individual's, couple's, or family's spiritual frameworks, and with the understanding that their belief system represents their view of reality.

The spiritual, social, emotional, and material or physical dimensions of life are necessary for our growth; each should be considered in the therapeutic relationship. A biopsychosocial/spiritual model of human functioning makes spiritual issues a legitimate focus for practitioners and provides for a more complete understanding of the strengths, weaknesses, and problems of families. Policies and services that provide for the accessibility to resources in all of these areas are essential for human well-being. Increased openness to addressing relevant spiritual beliefs and metaphors could often provide the practitioner with an important avenue to effective intervention and with potential resources for support and change.

Summary

Ethics and spirituality are both involved in the inventing, shaping, and reformulating of the way we are with ourselves and others. They are at the same time very personal matters and also the blueprints that shape how we relate to others.

This chapter shows how ethical issues impact what we are able to do with families. Current ethical issues raised in this chapter are separating interventions from the larger ecosystems; focusing on individual or family welfare; using informed consent; use of confidentiality; and avoiding deception and manipulation. Guides for decision making are presented. These include an overview of decision bases, dimensions of clinical judgment, and codes of ethics. These provide guidelines for making ethical decisions in practice.

A final context to be considered in family practice is the spiritual dimension. This is an often neglected area, but one that is vital to many people. There are barriers to addressing families' spiritual concerns that must be overcome. Definitions of spirituality include faith, values, how a person understands and responds to meaning in life, and each person's connection with others and the world. Increased openness in dealing with families' relevant spiritual beliefs may enrich and enhance practice. Spirituality is a resource to draw upon not only from within the individual or family, but also in utilizing churches within the ecosystem and the values emphasized in social constructionism.

Discussion Questions

1. Describe and discuss ethical issues that may arise in an intervention with a family with a strong patriarchal tradition.
2. Regarding the ethical dilemma of meeting family versus individual needs, how would you balance the therapeutic responsibility toward both?

3. How do you effectively work with clients who present spiritual ideas that are different than, or even conflicting with, your own?
4. How could you be able to assess when a client/family is ready to or needs to discuss spiritual issues?

Suggested Readings

Assagioli, T. (1990). *Psychosynthesis: A manual of principles and techniques.* Wellingborough, UK: Crucible Press.

The author defines and maps the geography of spiritual transformation through psychosynthesis. Psychological disturbances may serve as precursors to a more ethically and spiritually refined outlook. The process of spiritual development is described in four critical phases.

Beaver, D. S. (1997). *Soul healing: A spiritual orientation in counseling and therapy.* New York: Basic Books.

This groundbreaking book shows how a spiritual orientation (which can encompass the full range of belief systems) can be used to facilitate healing at the deepest level.

Doherty, W. J., & Boss, P. G. (1991). Values and ethics in family therapy. In Alan S. Gurman and David P. Kniskern (Eds.), *Handbook of family therapy* (vol. II) (pp. 606–637). New York: Brunner/Mazel.

Of special interest in this article is the discussion of personal and cultural values in family therapy, ideological issues, ethical issues, and gender and ethics in family therapy. Future directions are also discussed.

Dykstra, C., & Parks, S. (1986). *Faith development and Fowler.* Birmingham, AL: Religious Education Press.

Fowler presents an overview of his faith development theory, and then other authors evaluate the theory and discuss how it can be enhanced.

Huber, C. H. (1993). *Ethical, legal and professional issues in the practice of marriage and family therapy.* New York: Merrill.

A new edition of a very popular text used in many marriage and family therapy professional issues courses. Several chapters are devoted to ethical issues, the professional codes of ethics, and their implications for working with families.

Kilpatrick, A. C., & Holland, T. P. (1990). Spiritual dimensions of practice. *The Clinical Supervisor, 8*(2), 125–140.

This article places values and faith in a historical context within the profession of social work, presents developmental stages of faith, and gives some practical ways that students and practitioners can think about the spiritual dimensions of professional practice.

May, G. (1982). *Will and spirit: A contemplative psychology.* San Francisco: Harper.

Within Maslow's hierarchy of needs, May (1982) found that spirituality can be found at both ends of the continuum. He states:

> *It emerges at the bottom, when physiological needs for survival cannot be met and physical existence is threatened. It also arises when most other needs have been taken care of and one has the luxury to ask, "What's it all for?" or "Is this all there is?" Thus, it is in relative affluence or in utter desolation that human spiritual longing most obviously becomes prominent. (p. 91)*

References

AAMFT Code of Ethics. (1991). Washington, DC: American Association for Marriage and Family Therapy.

Anderson, D. A., & Worthen, D. (1997). Exploring a fourth dimension: Spirituality as a resource for the couple therapist. *Journal of Marital and Family Therapy, 23*(1), 3–12.

Aponte, H. (1995). *Bread and spirit: Therapy with the new poor.* New York: W. W. Norton.

Assagioli, T. (1990). *Psychosynthesis: A manual of principles and techniques.* Wellingborough, UK: Crucible Press.

Bardill, D. R. (1997). *The relational model for family therapy: Living in the four realities.* New York: Haworth Press.

Becvar, D. S. (1997). *Soul healing: A spiritual orientation in counseling and therapy.* New York: Basic Books.

Becvar, D. S., & Becvar, R. J. (1993). *Family therapy: A systemic integration.* Boston: Allyn & Bacon.

Bray, J. H., Shepherd, J. N., & Hays, J. R. (1985). Legal and ethical issues in informed consent to psychotherapy. *American Journal of Family Therapy, 13,* 50–60.

Campbell, J., & Moyers, B. (1988). *The power of myth.* New York: Doubleday.

Canda, E. (1988). Spirituality, religious diversity, and social work practice. *Social Casework, 69*(4), 238–247.

Cornett, C. (1992). Toward a more comprehensive personology: Integrating a spiritual perspective into social work practice. *Social Work, 37*(2), 101–102.

Doherty, W. J., & Boss, P. G. (1991). Values and ethics in family therapy. In A. S. Gurman & D. P. Kniskern (Eds.), *Handbook of family therapy* (Vol. II) (pp. 606–637). New York: Brunner/Mazel.

Efran, J. A., Lukens, R., & Lukens, M. D. (1988). Constructivism: What's in it for you? *The Family Therapy Networker, 12*(5), 27–35.

Fox, M. (1983). *Original blessing.* Santa Fe, NM: Bear & Co.

Freyman, J. C. (1974). *The American health care system: Its genesis and trajectory.* New York: Medcom.

Green, S. L., & Hansen, J. C. (1989), Ethical dilemmas faced by family therapists. *Journal of Marital and Family Therapy, 15*(2), 149–158.

Holland, T. P., & Kilpatrick, A. C. (1991). Ethical issues in social work: Toward a grounded theory of professional ethics. *Social Work, 36*(2), 138–144.

Huber, C. H., & Baruth, L. G. (1987). *Ethical, legal and professional issues in the practice of marriage and family therapy.* Columbus, OH: Merrill.

Kilpatrick, A. C., & Holland, T. P. (1990). Spiritual dimensions of practice. *The Clinical Supervisor, 8*(2), 125–140.

Leiby, J. (1985). The moral foundations of social welfare and social work. *Social Work, 30,* 323–330.

May, G. (1982). *Will and spirit: A contemplative psychology.* San Francisco: Harper.

NASW Code of Ethics. (1996). Washington, DC: National Association of Social Workers.

Peck, M. S. (1987). *The different drum.* New York: Simon and Schuster.

Prest, L. A., & Keller, J. F. (1993). Spirituality and family therapy: Spiritual beliefs, myths, and metaphors. *Journal of Marital and Family Therapy, 19*(2), 137–148.

Reed, H. (1997). Finding the sacred in the profane. *Venture Inward* (magazine of the Association for Research and Enlightenment, Inc./The Edgar Cayce Foundation/Atlantic University), January-February.

Schwartz, M., & McGehee, E. (1996). Bio-psycho-social-spiritual-cosmic paradigm in social work education. In *Proceedings,* Joint World Congress of the International Federation of Social Workers and the International Association of Schools of Social Work, July, Hong Kong.

Siporin, M. (1986). Contribution of religious values to social work and the law. *Social Thought, 13,* 35–50.

Smith, A. R. (1996). A rising tide lifts all boats. *Venture Inward,* November-December.

Van Ness, P. (1996). *Spirituality and the secular quest.* World Spirituality, vol. 22. New York: Crossroad.

Woody, J. D. (1990). Resolving ethical concerns in clinical practice: Toward a pragmatic model. *Journal of Marital and Family Therapy, 16*(2), 133–150.

$Part$ II

First Level of Family Need: Basic Survival Issues

Level I families are dealing with basic survival needs such as food, clothing, shelter, protection, medical care, and minimal nurturance. A primary issue is whether there is good enough parenting capacity to support and protect the family's members. Families on this level may have presenting problems of pervasive life stresses, illness of a primary caretaker, economic deprivation, alcoholism, mental illness, or homelessness. We present two approaches that may be helpful to families who have Level I needs.

The first approach is designed to meet basic needs in high-risk families with children; Grigsby discusses family preservation theory and techniques in Chapter 5. The second approach focuses on ways to assist families and enable them to cope with illnesses (both physical and mental), disabilities, or other primary stressors. In Chapter 6, Greene and Kropf discuss the issues of family case management. They present a coordinated, congruent, and collaborative approach that can be used with both chronic and short-term problem situations. Cases presented are applicable across diverse racial and ethnic groups.

Chapter 5

Interventions to Meet Basic Needs in High-Risk Families with Children

R. KEVIN GRIGSBY, D.S.W.

Continuity of relationships, surroundings, and environmental influence are essential for a child's healthy development (Goldstein, Freud, & Solnit, 1973, p. 31). As children develop in the context of the relationship with their primary caretakers, supporting this relationship is of primary importance, as disruptions or termination of the caretaker/child relationship may lead to additional problems for the child. In some families, caretakers have been unable to meet the needs of children, or have failed in their attempts to do so. Although there are many families who experience problems, most families have either innate resources or access to support resources that enable them to provide adequate care for their children.

A small portion of families appear to be less able to provide for even the basic needs of nurturing and protection. Weltner (1982) describes these families as having an "ineffective executive system" and designates them as "Level I" families (p. 43). Level I families appear to have difficulty with issues related to food, shelter, protection, medical care, and basic nurturing. Other authors have referred to these families as being "multiproblem families" (Kaplan, 1986; Geismar & Lasorte, 1964; Spencer, 1963) whose children are at "high risk" (Adnopoz, Grigsby, & Nagler, 1996). In the parlance of the social workers who are assigned to work with these families, "perpetual crisis" is often used to describe their level of functioning.

Typical Problems of Level I Families

"Impoverished" is a good, generally descriptive term, as these families are almost always lacking in financial resources. In these families, poverty is not limited to the lack of financial resources alone. Rather, the lack of resources may provide impetus for other negative aspects of these families' lives. "Disease, poverty, alcoholism, chemical dependency, mental deficiency, constitutional inadequacy, parental discord, social isolation, and lack of familial and community support" are common features (Adnopoz et al., 1996, p. 1074) as well as parental defects such as chronic mental illness (Rutter & Quinton, 1984) or periodic incarceration. Parents' "executive capacity" (Weltner, 1985, p. 43) is often compromised by the multitude and magnitude of problems facing the family, and by a "multiproblem delivery system" (Selig, 1976, p. 526) that may blame families for their inability to make use of traditional supports, such as local social and community services. Therefore, it is important to understand that the designation, "Level I" (Weltner, 1985) is merely a tool that can be useful to helpers outside of the family, allowing them to decide "what to do, when, and with whom" (Weltner, 1986, p. 51). If the designation of Level I is seen as a diagnosis, it may lead to a deterministic view, that families on this level are doomed to perpetual crisis. Level I should be seen as a description of families' "level of functioning within an overall intervention strategy" (Weltner, 1986, p. 52), as is used in this book, and not as a "level of pathology" (Weltner, 1985, p. 39). Level of need is more accurately descriptive of these families and is used throughout this book rather than "level of pathology." Conceptual clarity is needed here in order to make the distinction between these two concepts, as they are quite different in practice and in theory building. Families may operate at a relatively high level of need and may simultaneously exhibit a high degree of pathology. On the other hand, loving, nonpathological families may find themselves in dire straits if they experience a loss of resources such as income, housing, and physical health. Nonetheless, the framework for categorizing families proposed by Weltner can be very useful, especially to novice helpers (Paquin & Bushorn, 1991).

Assessing the Level I Family: The Case of Ms. G.

All Level I families present with an abundance of problems. Novice helpers are sometimes overwhelmed as they list problem after problem, with seemingly few solutions in sight. On the other hand, experience generally leads helpers to the recognition that nearly all families have some strengths. For this reason, the approach to assessment should focus on family strengths rather than on weaknesses, psychopathology, and/or the lack of resources. Weltner (1985) suggests that the assessment of the family begin with a "survey of potential resources and strengths" (p. 43). A program that has successfully worked with these types of families operates under the assumption that "there are existing strengths in families that, once identified, can be utilized effectively" (Adnopoz et al., 1996, p. 1077). By focusing on the family strengths and resources, a starting place is established.

By focusing upon the day-to-day realities of the family situation, rather than dwelling upon the negative experiences of the past that may not be relevant to the present situation, the helper can assist the family in utilizing their own resources and strengths to "move ahead." Some families may not be aware of their own strengths, as they feel overwhelmed by the plethora of problems facing them.

The case of Ms. G. is illustrative of the history and dynamics of a typical Level I family. Ms. G. was referred to the Family Support Service, which is a program that has been developed specifically to intervene with multiproblem families with children at high risk for being removed from their homes. The source of the referral was the hospital social worker at the Women's Clinic. Ms. G. was a 21-year-old, single female who was pregnant with her second child. She had a four-year-old child, Eddie, with whom she lived in a substandard apartment near the waterfront of a medium-sized New England city. Eddie was walking; however, he did not speak, was not toilet trained, and engaged in a number of other concerning behaviors such as head-banging and spinning around and around until he was too dizzy to stand. At the eighth month of pregnancy, Ms. G. informed the social worker at the Women's Clinic that she was about to be evicted and expected to become homeless in the next day or two. At this point, she was referred to the Family Support Service. The client and the social worker feared that Eddie would have to enter foster care placement, as Ms. G. was at imminent risk of becoming homeless and had no other resources available to her that could provide adequate care for Eddie.

The worker from the Family Support Service met with Ms. G. at her apartment, which was dirty, rat-infested, and without electricity because the utility bills had not been paid. Ms. G. explained that she had been living in the apartment with her adult brothers, who had been physically abusive to her. She explained that each month when she received her AFDC support check, her brothers would take her to cash the check and then take all the money. They would routinely take her monthly disbursement of food stamps and purchase a large amount of food. The influx of money and food would in turn result in an influx of "friends," who would consume all of the food (and all of the cash through the purchase of alcohol and drugs). By the time the fifth or sixth day of the month arrived, Ms. G. had no money, no food, and no child-care supplies and had not paid the rent or utility bills, even though she actually had enough income to cover all of these expenses. She explained that she was sometimes able to hide some money, but that the father of her children would usually arrive in time to beat her until she relinquished those funds to him, leaving her to depend upon the good will of friends and soup kitchens for the rest of the month.

As might be expected, Ms. G. was depressed and felt hopeless about her situation. However, there were strengths in the family, if one looked for them. First of all, Ms. G. had a strong relationship with her child, Eddie. There had never been a report of abuse or neglect, and he had a record of consistent health care. Second, she had been consistent in obtaining prenatal care throughout both pregnancies. She also had established a trusting relationship with the Women's Clinic social worker. The fact that she had waited nearly three years between pregnancies was also seen as a strength; it represented her attempt to have some stability in her life and to provide quality care for her child. She had also been successful in maintaining her entitlements (AFDC, WIC, food stamps) and, until the present time, had not experienced any periods of homelessness in an area with a chronic shortage of affordable housing. Finally, strength was found in Ms. G.'s ability to ask for and accept help.

Treatment Goals

The immediate goals in this family were to protect the child; to prevent the unnecessary out-of-home placement of Eddie; and to promote, preserve, and support the family as the foundation for the children's healthy growth and development. The overarching goal was for Ms. G. to have happy, healthy children who had "continuity of relationships, surroundings, and environmental influence" (Goldstein et al., 1973, p. 31), thus promoting continued healthy development. Several time-limited objectives were developed, with the help and input of the family, that would lead to reaching these treatment goals. These objectives included

- locating and securing permanent housing
- obtaining utilities at new residence
- continued prenatal care at the Women's Clinic
- obtaining an evaluation of Eddie to investigate suspected developmental delay
- investigating resources available to Ms. G. through her extended family and through traditional community social services
- developing and implementing a plan to protect Ms. G. from her brothers' abuse and thievery
- preparation for the arrival of the new baby
- supporting a continuing relationship with the Women's Clinic social worker in order to facilitate a postnatal contraception plan
- arranging for an aftercare plan so that services, supports, and relationships would continue after the Family Support Service social worker was no longer involved in the case
- teaching the client assertiveness skills in order to prevent continued exploitation
- linking with a domestic violence program in order to facilitate shelter care and/or support if battering recurred
- initiating a caring, positive, and nonexploitive relationship with the client in order to help the client to recognize her own strengths, abilities, and resources
- if necessary, arrange for shelter care of all family members if eviction process resulted in acute homelessness
- advocating for keeping parent and child together rather than placing the child in temporary foster care
- in conjunction with the objective above, providing the client with emergency cash, food, clothing, or other necessities in order to prevent the out-of-home placement of Eddie

- if out-of-home placement of Eddie is unavoidable, supporting the parent-child attachment relationship by advocating for a local placement and by facilitating parent-child visitation
- advocating for the client with the placing agency in order to keep the placement to the most limited duration possible

The final objective, in any case of this type, is to renegotiate the goals and objectives according to the client's (family's) expressed desires as new issues and opportunities arise.

Treatment Approach

Many services offered to families may be home based or may espouse a "family-centered" philosophy. Level I families may need much more than most families in terms of the intensity and scope of intervention necessary to prevent unnecessary out-of-home placement of children. Over the past several years, home-based, intensive family preservation services (IFPS) have been developed in many areas of the United States. The growth of these programs has been rapid. Several program models have been described and evaluated with mixed findings about their efficacy (Nelson, K. E., Whittaker, Kinney, Tracy, & Booth, 1990; Yuan & Rivest, 1990; Wells & Biegel, 1991; Grigsby, 1993; Schuerman, Rzipnicki, & Littell, 1994). The 1993 Family Preservation and Support Services Act provides federal funding of "almost $1 billion over five years for states to improve the well-being of vulnerable children and their families" (Nelson, H, 1996, p. 18). This level of federal support has led to continued growth of these programs.

Theoretical Base and Basic Tenets

Richard Barth (1990) posits that there are four major theories upon which intensive family preservation services draw in order to articulate "ideal service delivery systems and treatments" (p. 89). Crisis intervention theory, family systems theory, social learning theory, and ecological theory appear to be integral to intensive family preservation service delivery. However, they do not appear to completely describe the theoretical framework upon which intensive family preservation services are constructed (p. 106). Grigsby (1993) argues that social attachment theory (Bowlby, 1969; Ainsworth, 1985) and functional theory (Smalley, 1967; Dore, 1990) also contribute to the common theory base of intensive family preservation services. All of these theories offer information that is useful in guiding the approach to treating Level I families. No single theory appears to offer a complete explanation of the families' problems, nor can any single theory provide a "blueprint" for intervention. Just as there is usually no single cause or condition that leads to the problems experienced by the Level I family, no single theory offers a complete guide to intervention. Therefore, it is important that the helper assigned to work with the Level I family have an excellent understanding of a range of theories. Strict adherence or commitment to a single theoretical perspective may lead to a struggle to "fit" the family to a theory, rather than making use of theory as a guide to intervention.

Application to Level I Families

A common element of the theories described here is that all of them allow for a "strength" rather than a "deficit" perspective. Dennis Saleeby (1996, p. 297) argues "the strengths perspective demands a different way of looking at individuals, families, and communities." That is, the focus of intervention is on the strengths that are inherent in families rather than on the problems that exist within the families. Generally, the strategy for intervention is to identify strengths in the family and then to build upon those strengths. In order to do so, the helper(s) assigned to the case must play a number of roles, including those of teacher, role model, advocate, and friend. Helpers working with the Level I family need to be flexible and willing to give up the notion of "therapeutic distance" and objectivity. Rather, the subjective involvement of the helper and the family is often the key to success. In many ways, the relationship between the helper and the family appears to be the "vehicle" of intervention.

Family preservation service models have several common characteristics, including

- immediate response to families in crisis
- service to children at imminent risk of out-of-home placement
- assessment and treatment focus on the family as a unit in relation to the community
- limited goals and objectives of treatment
- service provision in the home or community
- offer of concrete and psychological services
- making therapists available outside of traditional hours
- offer of intensive (5–20 hours per week) services, usually short-term (6–12 weeks) in duration
- limiting helpers to small caseloads to facilitate intensity of services necessary to prevent out-of-home placement (Cole & Duva, 1990; Kinney, Haapala, Booth, & Leavitt, 1990)

Intensive family preservation services also share several core values and beliefs, including the following:

- Children should remain with their families whenever possible.
- Families are active agents in the change process.
- Families are doing the best that they can given their circumstances, but they may need help in order to provide better care for their children (Kinney et al., 1990).
- Intervention should be based upon family strengths rather than diagnosis.

- Therapists should be nonjudgmental and should accept families "as they are," rather than emphasizing deficits.
- Intervention takes place through engagement with a "helper," who assists the family in identifying and building upon inherent strengths (Center for the Study of Social Policy, 1988).

Interventions and Techniques

In addition to common characteristics, common core values and beliefs, and a common theoretical foundation, intensive family preservation programs appear to utilize several common interventions and techniques. These interventions and techniques are not limited to IFPS programs alone. Rather, these interventions and techniques appear fundamental to any program that seeks to intervene successfully with the Level I family.

Engagement.   Families are usually first encountered in a state of crisis. The out-of-home placement of one or more of the children is usually under consideration. There is reason to speculate that the "executive capacity" (Weltner, 1985) of the family is inadequate or diminished for one or more reasons. The lack of family organization and neglect of the children may invite the novice helper to place blame on the parent(s), but there are usually many issues at hand that must be considered. Often, these families are suspicious of anyone who is offering help. However, they are often in such a state of crisis that they will respond favorably to the person who is able to approach them on terms that are comfortable to the family. In general, engaging the family in a helping relationship is sometimes the most difficult part of the intervention process. Several techniques appear to be helpful.

First of all, the social work tenet of "starting where the client is" offers the helper and the family the opportunity to begin. The intervention may begin by asking the family what is most important to them. Many of these families expect that someone is going to tell them, or even demand, that they "do something," as this is the typical intervention to which they are accustomed. In order to successfully intervene with Level I families, the families are seen as equals in a partnership that is aimed at building upon the families' strengths in order to improve overall functioning.

Some service delivery models team professionally trained (usually M.S.W. level) clinicians with indigenous community workers. These community workers are often integral in engaging families, since the families view them as peers who truly understand the situation. Sometimes, the indigenous community worker may need to make the initial contact with the family, so that the professional helper can then be introduced as the expert on "the system." At all times, it is important, and potentially empowering, to view the clients as the "experts" on their own families. Quite often, family members have been incredibly creative and adaptive in dealing with family and community issues. Much of the help they need may be in the area of intervention with the social system that exists outside of the family. For these reasons, it is vital that the family be engaged and committed to working with the helper or team of helpers from the outset. If the family is not engaged, it is often an indication that they have been approached incorrectly or inappropriately.

Support and Strengths Inventory.   In the initial phase of intervention, many families expect that the helpers will want to involve them in in-depth discussions of family problems, or in the jargon of many helpers, "family psychopathology." This approach does not appear to be useful when working with the Level I family. Rather, a listing of potential resources, such as extended family, and a listing of family strengths, may lead to a more productive intervention, as these resources and strengths are the foundation upon which improved family functioning is based. At times, families may not appear to have strengths. Further investigation may reveal that there were once many strengths, but they are no longer apparent. Sometimes, a strength may be, simply, that things are not worse than they are at present. Another "small" strength may be that the family is willing to work with the helpers. In any case, it is useful to literally sit down and discuss potential resources and strengths. The use of genograms or social network maps may be useful to professional clinicians. However, some families are intimidated by the use of a written format that they do not immediately understand. Therefore, it may be important—at least during the initial phase of intervention—that clients feel comfortable with the methods of assessment. The use of "ethnographic interviewing" in the natural setting of the family's home or community allows the family members to use their own words to inform the helpers, rather than trying to fit into a prescribed format that may be culturally or ethnically biased, or that may be intimidating to clients who are uncomfortable with certain aspects of self-disclosure. For example, a question such as, "How long have you been married?" may seem innocuous to many. To an unmarried mother of four, it may be perceived as somewhat threatening and judgmental. By allowing the client to describe the nature of the family relationships, the helper can quickly get insight into the "life" of the individual family. It is important that the helper or team join with the clients in valuing the family, rather than imposing a set of "family values" upon the clients that may be foreign to them and at times, even offensive.

Helpers may envision valuing the family as an integral part of the intervention process. This may not be as easy as it sounds. Some families may place great value on the role of the godparent and expect that the godparent will care for the children if the birth parent is unable to do so. State child welfare agencies may not recognize the godparent as having any ties to the child, because there is no biological relationship. This disparity may place the family and child welfare agency at odds. Often, the helper is expected to resolve this issue within the context of child welfare policy. To truly value the family may require adopting a position that runs contrary to state child welfare policy. Helpers must be prepared to be active participants in the day-to-day world of the clients, or clients will see them as insincere bureaucrats who are not really interested in helping them.

Nurturing the Family.   The use of the client-helper relationship is perceived as the vehicle of change, but it is only one of many behaviorally oriented interventions that are utilized in helping families. Experienced clinicians are quick to point out that all of behavioral interventions appear to be more successful if they are implemented in the context of a solid, positive relationship between the family members and clinician or team. In effect, many parents in Level I families need a supportive, caring relationship with a person who is genuinely interested in listening to them (Pharis & Levin, 1991). With the parent, indigenous community workers and professionally trained clinicians may take on the helping role of "nurturer." This often takes the form of support provided by actively participating in the day-to-day activities of the parent, like meal preparation, and cleanup or housekeeping. At the same time, these helpers may be the only other adults with whom the parent has frequent contact. The nurturing is often "passed on" to the children in the family as the adults begin to feel more confident in their own capabilities. This is a frequent "by-product" of the nurturing relationship between the helpers and the parent.

Role Modeling.   The relationship between the helper and clients often allows for a great deal of role modeling. If a trusting relationship has been established, many clients will actually ask for help with parenting skills. Very often, the executive capacity of the family may be improved as the parents watch and learn as the helpers demonstrate *in vivo* new ways of dealing with old problems. Although this information is available in books about child rearing, these families are unlikely to have access to these materials, or may not be able to make use of them without the help of someone who can answer questions or help with reading skills. In many cases, parents have been referred to parenting classes, but have not attended because they are unable to arrange for child care or because they are embarrassed that they have been singled out and "sent" to these classes. *In vivo* intervention takes away the stigma of the "parenting class" and allows for child care to continue while the learning takes place. It is ironic that clients are often seen as "resistant" when they do not attend parenting classes, when the reason for not attending is related to the need for child care.

Conflict Resolution.   Many Level I families are unable to resolve minor conflict easily within their families or communities only because they have never learned methods or techniques of conflict resolution. At times, the simple idea of convening a family meeting where individual members are able to present their own feelings and solutions is a novelty to these families. Through role playing and teaching, families can see firsthand that there are alternatives available to them.

Advocacy.   Many Level I families have been repeatedly victimized by unscrupulous landlords, salespersons, and even human services providers. Many families are shocked and surprised that others are willing to help them, and that others have enough knowledge of the "system" that they can get help for families. For example, it has become common for persons who are receiving Medicaid to be denied that benefit unless they appear at a hearing to demonstrate that they still need those benefits. While many families have no problem appearing for these hearings, a single mother of four preschool children may have a difficult time getting there because of child care issues, etc. As a result, benefits may be terminated. As helpers advocate for the needs of the family, benefits are often reinstated in a timely fashion. In turn, the families are able to learn how to advocate for themselves. In many ways, families begin to see that they have an active role in their own lives, rather than life "happening to them."

In summary, the interventions and techniques that are used with Level I families vary widely, and are used according to the wishes of the families and the issues at hand. Because all families have their own unique strengths and supports, there is no "cookbook" approach. Rather, the helping process is developed in the context of a caring relationship with trained helpers that builds upon the particular strengths of the family in question.

Evaluation of Effectiveness

Several questions must be answered when evaluating the effectiveness of an intervention with the Level I family, especially when questions related to the well-being of children in the family have been raised. Most importantly, the issue of child safety must be addressed. Are the children at continued risk for maltreatment? Are the children at risk for out-of-home placement, or has unnecessary out-of-home placement of children been prevented? Careful and thorough risk assessment should be used to determine whether the family can adequately protect the children. Most state protective services agencies have adopted risk assessment procedures that allow workers to make determinations of child safety. Theodore Stein and Tina Rzepnicki (1983) also offer a helpful guide to practitioners in *Decision Making at Child Welfare Intake. The Family Risk Scales* (Magura, Moses, & Jones, 1987) and the *Child Well Being Scales* (Magura & Moses, 1986) have also been developed and utilized as outcome measures for working with families, although one author has been outspoken in his criticism of the validity of the *Child Well Being Scales* (Seaberg, 1988, 1990). Nonetheless, examining child risk and child well-being are two areas that appear to be useful when examining intervention on a programmatic basis.

On the other hand, the idiographic or single-case design has been underutilized in work with Level I families. By examining outcome on a case-by-case basis, rather than on a program basis alone, the particular issues within each family can be dealt with in a manner that is useful to the family. Helping each family to examine their own progress toward the goals that they have set can be very useful, because it provides many families with a "success experience." By joining with the helper in the attempt to complete an objective, the family members are able to experience the sense of accomplishment (and success) that many of them have not recently—or, in some cases, ever—experienced. Client outcome should correspond to the agenda set by the family, as well as to the agenda that may have been set for them by "outsiders." Bruce Thyer (1993) argues that evaluators should avoid theory-based research studies and should concentrate on systematic efforts to evaluate their own efforts by asking whether the intervention actually helped the family to improve. The use of single-systems designs, rather than large, theory-based social science research studies, appears to be more fruitful when helpers ask themselves the question, "Did I help this family?" Therefore, the evaluation of effectiveness should be considered on a family-by-family basis where the family is involved, from the outset, in determining whether they have met their own goals and objectives in ways that are acceptable to them and to the helpers. To assist with evaluating the intervention, Craig–Van Grack (1997) describes an instrument for process measurement of family preservation service designed to enhance the evaluation of intervention with individual families.

Application to Families on Levels II, III, and IV

There are several aspects of intervention with the Level I family that are particularly applicable to families on Levels II, III, and IV (Weltner, 1985). In general, Level II families may be approached in a manner that is similar to the approach used with the Level I family. The issues of authority and limits that are omnipresent in the Level I family are the prominent issues in the Level II family as well. There is a lack of control in the family system that is due to a dysfunctional executive system. The use of a "strengths perspective" that begins with a support and strengths inventory is often a first step in engaging the family. Flexibility in the provision of home- and community-based services allows the helper to intervene, usually within the context of a family crisis, and to build upon the strengths inherent in the family to promote, preserve, and sustain the family while its executive capacity is strengthened. While a good deal of nurturing and advocacy may be necessary in the Level I family, concentration on role modeling and the development of conflict resolution skills may be more appropriate and fruitful when working with the Level II family.

The salient difference between the Level I and Level II family may be described as follows: The Level I family is often referred because there have been allegations of abuse and/or neglect and the child or children are at imminent risk of out-of-home placement. On the other hand, the Level II family is often referred because a parent has *requested* that the child or children go into out-of-home placement, because the child is "out of control." Clinicians also comment that the Level I family is often a family with young children, whereas the Level II family is a family with older, adolescent children. In either case, the approach to the family should be tailored to their needs, and should include their active participation in the planning, intervention, and evaluation.

Where the Level I and II families appear to have many similarities, families on Levels III and IV appear to be quite different from their lower-level counterparts. In general, the Level I and II families are cognizant that things are not working well. In the parlance of family therapists, issues appear to be largely of a "structural" nature.

Harry Aponte (1976) has described families like this as "underorganized." Level III and IV families are markedly different in that they have developed patterns of behavior to deal with problems that arise within the family. While some of these behaviors are adaptive and quite functional, others are maladaptive and resistant to change. In the Level IV family, the task of the helper may be focused on the development of an "inner 'richness'—insight, more sensitive awareness of the relational world, and understanding of the legacies and heritage" (Weltner, 1986, p. 54) rather than on the more basic functions of food, shelter, safety, and authority. The application of the principles and techniques described earlier for working with the Level I family have limited utility and relevance to working with the families on Levels III and IV.

Summary

Level I families present a tremendous challenge to society, because they are the families that are often described as being the most "in need." These families usually come to the attention of the social service system when family members, especially children, in the families are experiencing crisis of some sort. Because children represent our future, it is important that we invest in meeting their needs if we expect them to become productive citizens. While there are larger issues of social policy that must be addressed if we are truly interested in valuing families, we must also be prepared to intervene at the level of the individual family. The recognition that in most cases, the family is the solution rather than the problem, will lead us to provide services to families that will support, preserve, and sustain healthy families. There is no unitary cause of the problems experienced by the Level I family. Likewise, there is no unitary solution. At this point in our history, it will require significant social investment to solve the problems experienced by Level I families. It may require even greater social investment if we do not act quickly to assist these families and to help them to escape the downward spiral of poverty, neglect, and misfortune.

Discussion Questions

1. How does the delivery of family preservation services differ from other models of helping?
2. Name five strengths that are present in a family with whom you are now working. How can a practitioner use the family strengths perspective to work with Level I families?
3. Why is it especially important to use a "strengths" approach when working with Level I families? What might be the result if a problem-focused approach were used?
4. Reexamine the interventions sections. Give your own example for each of the techniques listed.
5. In the family preservation service model, a lack of family engagement is often seen as an indicator that the family has not been approached appropriately or correctly. Are there other reasons that could explain lack of engagement?

Suggested Readings

Adnopoz, D. J., Grigsby, R. K., & Nagler, S. F. (1996). Multiproblem families and high-risk children and adolescents: Causes and management. In M. Lewis (Ed.), *Child and adolescent psychiatry: A comprehensive textbook* (2nd ed.) (pp. 1074–1080). Baltimore: Williams & Wilkins.

This brief chapter presents one model of family preservation that utilizes a trained clinician teamed with an indigenous community worker as opposed to service delivery models that utilize a single clinician. It is argued that the use of the indigenous worker provides a culturally responsive intervention that maximizes the therapeutic relationship between the caregiver and family preservation team.

Cole, E., & Duva, J. (1990). *Family preservation: An orientation for administrators and practitioners.* Washington, DC: Child Welfare League of America.

Elizabeth Cole and Joy Duva offer a concise orientation to the concept and operationalization of family presevation that does not appear to favor any particular model of service delivery. The authors offer a clear description of the common elements of family preservation practice.

Geismar, L. L., & Lasorte, M. A. (1964). *Understanding the multiproblem family.* New York: Association Press.

This book was written nearly three decades ago, but the content is relevant to contemporary social work practice with families that appear to be overwhelmed with the day-to-day difficulty of their lives. It is also interesting from a historical perspective.

Kaplan, L. (1986). *Working with the multiproblem family.* Lexington, MA: Lexington Books.

A solid, practical approach to intervention with multiproblem families. Any person who is working with Level I families would benefit from the material presented in this thoughtful book.

National Commission on Child Welfare and Family Preservation. (1991). *A commitment to change.* Washington, DC: American Public Welfare Foundation.

A recently proposed new framework for child and family services that includes a commitment to family support and community investment based upon a family strengths service perspective.

Nelson, H. (1996). *What is appropriate care for the children of troubled families?* New York: Milbank Memorial Fund.

A comprehensive report describing the current crisis in child welfare and suggestions for moving toward an improved system.

Nelson, K. E., Landsman, M. J., & Deutelbaum, W. (1990). Three models of family-centered placement prevention services. *Child Welfare, 69*(1), 3–20.

An excellent, concise description of three of the more common placement prevention program models.

Schorr, L. B. (1994). Making the most of what we already know. *Public Welfare, 52*(2), 22–26.

A succinct description of the common elements in successful programs for children and families.

Selig, A. L. (1976). The myth of the multiproblem family. *American Journal of Orthopsychiatry, 46,* 526–532.

An excellent discussion of the problems faced by families who encounter the "multiproblem service delivery system" as they try to overcome problems in their own lives.

Wells, K., & Biegel, D. E. (Eds.). (1991). *Family preservation services: Research and evaluation.* Newbury Park, CA: Sage.

A collection of chapters related to documenting the effectiveness of family preservation programs.

References

Adnopoz, D. J., Grigsby, R. K., & Nagler, S. F. (1996). Multiproblem families and high-risk children and adolescents: Causes and management. In M. Lewis (Ed.), *Child and adolescent psychiatry: A comprehensive textbook,* 2nd ed. (pp. 1074–1080). Baltimore: Williams & Wilkins.

Ainsworth, M. D. S. (1985). Attachments across the lifespan. *Bulletin of the New York Academy of Medicine, 61,* 792–812.

Aponte, H. (1976). Underorganization in the poor family. In P. Guerin (Ed.), *Family therapy: Theory and practice.* New York: Gardner Press.

Barth, R. P. (1990). Theories guiding home-based, intensive family preservation services. In J. K. Whittaker, J. Kinney, E. M. Tracy, & C. Booth (Eds.), *Reaching high-risk families: Intensive family preservation in human services.* New York: Aldine de Gruyter.

Bowlby, J. (1969). *Attachment* (2nd ed.). New York: Basic Books.

Center for the Study of Social Policy. (1988). State family preservation programs: A description of six states' progress in developing services to keep families together. Washington, DC: Author.

Cole, E., & Duva, J. (1990). *Family preservation: An orientation for administrators and practitioners.* Washington, DC: Child Welfare League of America.

Craig–Van Grack, (1997). A taxonomy and recording instrument for process measurement of family preservation services. *Child Welfare, 76*(2), 349–371.

Dore, M. M. (1990). Functional theory: Its history and influence on contemporary social work practice. *Social Service Review, 64*(3), 358–374.

Geismar, L. L., & Lasorte, M. A. (1964). *Understanding the multiproblem family.* New York: Association Press.

Goldstein, J., Freud, A., & Solnit, A. J. (1973). *Beyond the best interest of the child.* New York: Free Press.

Grigsby, R. K. (1993). Theories that guide intensive family preservation services: A second look. In E. S. Morton and R. K. Grigsby (Eds.), *Advancing family preservation practice.* Newbury Park, CA: Sage.

Kaplan, L. (1986). *Working with the multiproblem family.* Lexington, MA: Lexington Books.

Kinney, J., Haapala, D., Booth, C., & Leavitt, S. (1990). The HOMEBUILDERS model. In J. K. Whittaker, J. Kinney, E. M. Tracy, and C. Booth (Eds.), *Reaching high-risk families: Intensive family preservation in human services.* New York: Aldine de Gruyter.

Magura, S., & Moses, B. S. (1986). *Outcome measures for child welfare services.* Washington, DC: Child Welfare League of America.

Magura, S., Moses, B. S., & Jones, M. A. (1987). *Assessing risk and measuring change in families.* Washington, DC: Child Welfare League of America.

Nelson, H. (1996). *What is appropriate care for the children of troubled families?* New York: Milbank Memorial Fund.

Nelson, K. E., Landsman, M. J., & Deutelbaum, W. (1990). Three models of family-centered placement prevention services. *Child Welfare, 69*(1), 3–20.

Paquin, G. W., & Bushorn, R. J. (1991). Family treatment assessment for novices. *Families in Society, 72*(6), 353–359.

Pharis, M. E., & Levin, V. S. (1991). "A person to talk to who really cared": High-risk mothers' evaluations of services in an intensive intervention research program. *Child Welfare, 70*(3), 307–320.

Rutter, M., & Quinton, D. (1984). Parental psychiatric disorder: Effects on children. *Psychological Medicine, 14,* 853–880.

Saleeby, D. (1996). The strengths perspective in social work practice: Extensions and cautions. *Social Work, 41*(3), 296–305.

Schuerman, J. R., Rzepnicki, T. L. & Littell, J. H. (1994). *Putting families first: An experiment in family preservation.* New York: Aldine de Gruyter.

Seaberg, J. R. (1988). Child well-being scales: A critique. *Social Work Research and Abstracts, 24*(3), 9–15.

Seaberg, J. R. (1990). Child well-being: A feasible concept? *Social Work, 35*(3), 267–272.

Selig, A. L. (1976). The myth of the multiproblem family. *American Journal of Orthopsychiatry, 46,* 526–532.

Smalley, R. E. (1967). *Theory for social work practice.* New York: Columbia University Press.

Spencer, J. (1963). The multiproblem family. In B. Schlesinger (Ed.), *The multiproblem family: A review and annotated bibliography* (3rd ed.) (pp. 1–12). Toronto: University of Toronto Press.

Stein, T. J., & Rzepnicki, T. L. (1983). *Decision making at child welfare intake.* New York: Child Welfare League of America.

Thyer, B. A. (1993). Promoting evaluation research in the field of family preservation. In E. S. Morton & R. K. Grigsby (Eds.), *Advancing family preservation practice.* Newbury Park, CA: Sage.

Wells, K., & Biegel, D. E. (Eds.). (1991). *Family preservation services: Research and evaluation.* Newbury Park, CA: Sage.

Weltner, J. S. (1982). A structural approach to the single parent family. *Family Process, 21,* 203–210.

Weltner, J. S. (1985). Matchmaking: Choosing the appropriate therapy for families at various levels of pathology. In M. P. Mirken & S. L. Koman (Eds.), *Handbook of adolescents and family therapy* (pp. 39–50). New York: Gardner Press.

Weltner, J. S. (1986). A matchmaker's guide to family therapy. *Family Therapy Networker, 10*(2), 51–55.

Whittaker, J. K., Kinney, J., Tracy, E. M., & Booth, C. (Eds.). (1990). *Reaching high-risk families: Intensive family preservation in human services.* New York: Aldine de Gruyter.

Yuan, Y. T., & Rivest, M. (Eds.). (1990). *Preserving families: Evaluation resources for practitioners and policymakers.* Newbury Park, CA: Sage.

Chapter 6

A Family Case Management Approach for Level I Needs

ROBERTA R. GREENE, Ph.D., and NANCY P. KROPF, Ph.D.

Case management is a process for assisting families who have multiple service needs. In reality, it may be appropriate for families who have Level I through IV needs whenever they experience multiple complex difficulties that require a range of services from numerous providers. The goals of family case management are to mobilize a family's strengths, to marshal resources, and to maximize family functional capacity. This chapter discusses family-centered case management and focuses on the Level I family.

Family Problems

Throughout the life of the family, members must negotiate changes, shifts, and alterations in their relationships with each other. This movement through the life cycle, known as "family development," requires that families establish, maintain, and adapt to new roles. In making these life transitions, the family builds on strengths and must meet stressful challenges.

Case management can help families cope with and adjust to the stress related to unexpected, or nonnormative, situations. An example of a Level I situation that requires reorganization in the family system is a severe illness of a member. For example, Kaplan (1992) has suggested that case management for families with children with HIV infection demands attention to the special developmental needs of the child over a period of years. Other Level 1 needs experienced by families include homelessness, chronic mental illness, or a developmental disability of a family member.

Case management services can also help families with adapting to normative transition phases across the life span. Structural changes that occur at family transition points, such as births, reaching adulthood, or retirement, also can disturb the family's balance. For example, a case manager can play an important role in helping a young single mother with family and household responsibilities. A case manager can be instrumental in identifying and linking a new mother with emotional, financial, and medical support for her new role as a caregiver to a young infant.

Case managers need to understand that the family is a social unit that faces a series of developmental tasks. These tasks vary along the parameters of cultural differences, but at the same time have universal roots (Minuchin, 1974). The stages of the life cycle have been defined for "intact nuclear families in contemporary Western societies" (Tseng & Hsu, 1991, p. 8) as the unattached young adult, the formation of the dyadic relationship, the family with young children, the family with adolescents, the family launching children, the family with older members, and the family in later years (Goldenberg & Goldenberg, 1980; Rhodes, 1980).

However, the structure and development of the family may vary with diverse needs and interests. Groze and Rosenthal (1991) have described the adaptability of families who have adopted special-needs children; Weston (1991), the relationship of gay men and lesbian women in their chosen families; and Kuhn (1990), the normative family crises of confronting dementia in an older family member. McGoldrick (1989) has pointed out that although women play a central role in families, only recently has there been the idea that they may have a "life cycle apart from their roles as wife and mothers" (p. 200).

Family developmental patterns may be affected by the geographical origin and birthplace of the members, and where they are in the cycle of acculturation to mainstream U.S. society. Ho (1987) has proposed that practitioners should be aware that behaviors differ, depending on whether a family and its members are foreign or native born and the degree to which they are bicultural. Falicov and Karrer (1980) have concluded that studies of the family life cycle should take into consideration the effects of cultural variables such as social class, ethnicity, and religion. When applying this perspective to family assessment, it would, therefore, be more appropriate for the case manager to think of several "typical" family life cycles.

Family Case Assessment

An important principle in family case management is that a biopsychosocial change in any one member affects the balance of the whole family group. Greene (1986) has pointed out that most elderly clients come to the attention of an agency at a time of crisis. At that time, the question "Who is the client?" must be asked. The answer is that the crisis involves the entire family. Consequently, the case manager's assessment and treatment interventions must consider both the elderly person's biopsychosocial needs and the family's role allocations, adapting, and coping capacity.

The following case example involves a family with a member who has a chronic mental illness (Kelly & Kropf, 1995). The son, who is now in middle adulthood, is being cared for by his aging parents. This case clearly illustrates the need to address the issues and needs from an entire family perspective.

Philip Jordan is a 40-year-old, single male with a diagnosis of schizophrenia. He lives at home with his 75-year-old parents in a small southern town where his father is a retired pastor from the local Baptist church. Philip, who has a 22-year history of mental illness, has experienced many psychiatric hospitalizations, but has remained out of the hospital for the past two years. Currently he has a flat affect, depressed mood, and mild paranoid ideation concerning his parents. He reports bizarre hallucinations involving religious themes and sexual thoughts.

At the time of his first psychotic break, Philip's parents were in their late fifties. His parents blamed themselves for Philip's illness and prayed for him to be "cured and return to being normal." Instead of regaining his emotional health, Philip's condition has worsened over time. His father retired prematurely, believing that if he devoted all his time to caring for his son, Philip would improve. However, the retirement has caused the parents to be estranged from their supports and has placed a financial burden on the family.

The family came to the local mental health center to discuss their situation. Their family physician had suggested that they contact the mental health program, since Philip's mother's health had been deteriorating. The parents had begun to realize that their advancing age was creating difficulties in providing care for their son. They were also concerned about Philip's lack of social contacts and the family's worsening financial circumstances due to additional medical expenses.

The mental health center intake worker gathered extensive information about family functioning. Philip's physical, emotional and social functioning, and medication management were discussed. Beyond Philip's functioning, information was acquired about the other family members. This included the parents' own health status, their knowledge of mental illness, their social support system, and their feelings of competence in managing Philip's caregiving needs in this life stage.

As a part of this family-focused assessment, the parents discussed the stress of this caregiving role and effects on their physical and emotional health. His father spoke about his disappointment over his early retirement, subsequent financial worries, and loss of status in the community. Mrs. Jordan discussed her worries about Philip's future care, and her worsening hypertension and digestive problems. Through her discussion with Philip, the case manager also became aware of his anxiety over the health of his parents and fears about his own future. The interviews with the total family unit allowed the case manager to form a holistic impression about past functioning of the family, their present situation, and future needs.

Treatment Goals

Building upon the assessment data, the case manager and family discussed service goals that were formalized into a service contract. The plan included goals that addressed the individual members, the parents as a couple, and the family as a household unit. Additionally, the plan overtly specified the relationship between the mental health service personnel and the family.

The contract addressed the issues of independence and family functioning, which had been discussed by the family during the assessment. For Philip, goals were constructed to assist with vocational training and placement. This plan was intended to decrease Philip's isolation, provide him with structured time during the day, and allow him to contribute to the household finances. To provide the parents with a temporary break, the family decided to have Philip begin taking respite care weekends at a group home. This plan also allowed Philip to experience a residential situation before a family crisis could force him to do so.

Other goals were constructed that related to the parents' issues. They were interested in becoming involved in a psychoeducational group sponsored by the mental health center to learn more about schizophrenia and behavior management. They were also interested in attending an upcoming session on estate planning being led by a local attorney.

The role of the case manager with the parents was to provide information about resources that they may use to assist in their relationship to Philip. They were also assured that their service plan would be periodically reviewed and that the family would have a voice in formulating future goals.

The case manager and family discussed future plans for Philip. The short-term goals were to have the family begin the process of exploring and considering options for Philip's future care. As an initial step in this process, they prepared a plan that helped the family specify and clarify values and preferences as a part of the process of determining what type of future care arrangements were best suited for a person with a disability (Mount & Zwernik, 1988). Intermediate goals for the family were to visit the group homes in their county, discuss Philip's care with other relevant family members (one other son who lived out of state), begin to use respite care to familiarize Philip with residential living experiences, and work with an attorney to explicate financial issues in case of parental death. These steps were all part of a long-range goal of helping the family make arrangements for the time when the parents could no longer continue as care providers.

Treatment Approach: A Generalist Model of Case Management

A variety of case management models exist, and the choice of using a particular approach depends upon numerous factors including the target client group, staff capabilities, financial resource of the agency, and organizational structure. Rothman (1992) describes four models, each having a different structure or focus. In the *generalist model,* one case manager performs a variety of roles to facilitate a client's movement through the service delivery system (Dattalo, 1992). The generalist case management model most closely resembles traditional social casework (Levine & Fleming, 1984).

A second approach is the *case management team*, where a multidisciplinary group function as the case management system for a client. Each team member is responsible for performing a specialized function (i.e., social work, physical therapy, speech therapy, psychology).

A third model, the *therapist case manager*, is used extensively in the mental health system. This approach infuses a therapeutic relationship into the case manager role.

The final model, one of *supportive care*, is based upon the natural environment of the client (neighborhood, cultural group). In this model, case management is provided to the client through the natural helping network.

In order to be effective practitioners, generalist case managers must have a broad perspective on human services, one that moves beyond the boundaries of the social welfare agencies in which they work. The use of a social system model can assist the case manager in practice with actual clients. Kuhn (1974) identified three elements of a social system. Dattalo (1992) has taken each and operationalized them in the case management process (see Figure 6.1). The first is the *detector function*, which is an information gathering phase. The case manager gathers information about both the client problem and resources and service options. The second element is the *selector function*, where information is screened for use in the treatment process. The case manager uses theoretical frameworks and practice principles to organize information in understanding client preferences, values and behaviors. The final function, the *effector element*, is the "doing function." After gathering information about the problem and possible solutions, the case manager constructs a plan of action about treatment goals.

Key Features of Case Management

Another way of examining the process is to outline the key features of case management. This practice approach is aimed at ensuring that clients with complex, multiple problems and service needs receive all services in a timely and appropriate way. This process has traditionally required that the case manager conduct a skillful assessment of the client's functional capacity and support network; and plan, advocate for, and obtain a range of suitable community-based services encompassing economic, health and medical, social, and personal-care needs (see Table 6.1).

Community-based case-managed services have been used in all fields of practice, including child welfare, aging, and mental health. Although the presenting problem of the person at risk may vary, the purpose of a case management system is to provide the client with service options along a continuum of care. The concept of a continuum of care suggests that clients may need any one of a comprehensive range of services, depending on each person's ability to function relatively independently. Clients who have greater impairments and lower levels of functioning require more structured environments and higher levels of care.

Case managers increasingly use a strengths perspective practice model (Kisthardt, 1992; Kisthardt & Rapp, 1992; Saleebey, 1992). The strengths perspective documents a client family's present daily living situation and determines what they want to change, achieve, or maintain. The strengths perspective also rests on

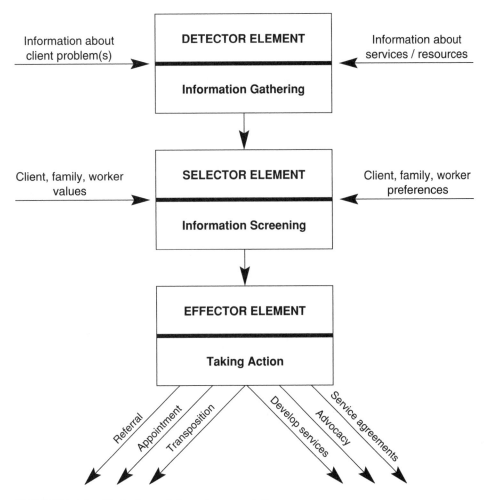

FIGURE 6.1 Kuhn's social system model.

[From R. L. Schneider and Nancy P. Kropf, eds., *Gerontological Social Work* (Chicago: Nelson-Hall, 1992), p. 141.]

an empowerment theme that seeks ways for clients to set their own agendas and further engage with others in their environment (Rose, 1992). For example, Kisthardt (1992) has suggested that people who have persistent mental illness not be labeled as being "resistant to treatment" or "lacking in social skills." Rather, clients should be understood as unique, complex individuals, coping with social pressures as well as their "talents, desires, and hopes" (p. 61).

Case management reflects the historic struggle to effect change in the person, the environment, or both (Greene, 1992). In this approach, the case manager assesses the client within the context of his or her environment, and provides both direct and

TABLE 6.1   Key Features of Social Work Case Management Practice

Social work case management practice

- is a process based on a trusting and enabling client–social worker relationship,
- utilizes the social work dual focus of understanding the person in environment working with populations at risk,
- aims to ensure a continuum of care to clients with complex, multiple problems and disabilities,
- attempts to intervene clinically to ameliorate the emotional problems accompanying illness or loss of function,
- utilizes the social work skills of brokering and advocacy as a boundary-spanning approach to service delivery,
- targets clients who require a range of community-based or long-term care services, encompassing economic, health/medical, social, and personal care needs,
- aims to provide services in the least restrictive environment,
- requires the use of assessment of the client's functional capacity and support network in determining the level of care,
- affirms the traditional social work values of self-determination and the worth and dignity of the individual and the concept of mutual responsibility in decision making.

Reprinted with permission from B. S. Vourlekis & R. R. Greene, (Eds.), *Social work case management* (New York: Aldine de Gruyter 1992). Copyright © 1992 Walter de Gruyter, Inc., New York.

indirect service. Direct service is based on a mutually trusting, therapeutic client-social worker relationship in which the case manager evaluates the client's circumstances and intervenes to ameliorate emotional problems accompanying illness or loss of functioning. The emotional problems and the stress associated with loss of functional capacity require that the case manager combine intrapsychic and interpersonal strategies with environmental interventions. Such indirect service involves community-based strategies for resource allocation and advocacy on behalf of the client at risk.

Far too often, clients with many service needs can become "disconnected" from narrowly defined programs, such as those that provide only housing, cash, or nutritional supports (Rubin, 1987). Key features of the case manager's role are responsibility for the development of a mutually agreeable care plan that offers continuity in services and assistance to the client in mediating systems problems that create disruption in service delivery (Roberts-DeGennaro, 1987). Because the case manager needs to understand how systems work and how to access them and often must coordinate the work of multiple service providers by intervening across service systems' boundaries, case management has been called a *boundary-spanning approach* (Hearn, 1969; Rubin, 1987). Key aspects of a boundary-spanning approach are developing resource systems, linking clients to resource systems, and making systems more accessible and responsible. Central to carrying out this social work approach are advocacy, or negotiating for the equitable distribution of resources, and brokerage, locating and obtaining needed resources.

Family Case Management

Family services and case management have long been important components of social work practice. Family-focused social work, with its mission to resolve family social and emotional difficulties, can be traced to the Charity Organization Societies of the 1880s. During those early years, pioneer social workers were noted for meeting with families in their homes to discuss their difficulties and to assess the need for financial relief and other tangible assistance (Hartman & Laird, 1987; Richmond, 1917). Because the Charity Organization Society social workers also were concerned with the lack of coordination among services and fund-raising activities, case management shares similar roots as one of the profession's earliest means of linking clients to service delivery systems (Rubin, 1987; Weil et al., 1985). These common beginnings reflect a strong interest in the family as the focus of intervention and an emphasis on a systematic approach to information collection and assessment, in the value of equity in resource allocation, and in case coordination. Although case management and family-centered practice share a surprising amount of common ground, little has been written about the relationship of these core practice functions.

Although most people in need of case management assistance are receiving the bulk of their care from families and other primary groups, the role of the family in the case management process is ill defined. Although practitioners increasingly have come to appreciate the value of natural helpers, or what Pincus and Minahan (1973) termed "informal resource systems" (p. 15), case management systems are largely designed for the individual client (Caragonne, 1980; Moore, 1990).

Nonetheless, when discussing case management services, some theorists have considered the individual client's resources and natural supports. For example, the National Association of Social Workers (NASW) (1984) *Standards and Guidelines for the Functionally Impaired* has defined the family as critical to the assessment process. Bertsche and Horejsi (1980) have suggested that the family be involved in the initial interview, the formulation of the psychosocial assessment, the decision-making process related to the care plan, follow-up of service delivery problems, and counseling and emotional support. They go on to describe the case manager's role vis-à-vis the family as a "liaison . . . to help the client make his or her preferences known and secure the services needed" (p. 97).

In addition, Moore (1990) has suggested that a key case manager role is to integrate formal and informal services provided by the family and other primary groups. He noted that health and social services, families, and formal organizations have complementary goals, and that the coordination of shared resources is necessary. According to Nelson (1982), the goal of coordination is to achieve a fit between formal services and primary-group caregiving, not to substitute for family care. Moore (1990) has maintained that it is often the practitioner who acts as a facilitator among the client, the family, and formal caregivers. In addition, Cantor, Rehr, and Trotz (1981) have suggested that wherever possible, members of the family should be the case managers, and that professionals should offer training to support this family responsibility. In this way, the service package is designed to support the family and to maximize its caregiving potential.

TABLE 6.2   Key Features of Family-Focused Social Work Case Management

---

Family-focused social work requires that the case manager
- identify the family as the unit of attention,
- assess the frail or impaired person's biopsychosocial functioning and needs within a culturally sound family context,
- write a mutually agreed upon family care plan,
- refer client systems to services and entitlements not available within the natural support system,
- implement and coordinate the work that is done with the family,
- determine what services need to be coordinated on behalf of the family,
- intervene clinically to ameliorate family emotional problems and stress accompanying illness or loss of functioning,
- determine how the impaired person and family will interact with formal care providers,
- integrate formal and informal services provided by the family and other primary groups,
- offer or advocate for particular services that the informal support network is not able to offer,
- contact client networks and service providers to determine the quality of service provision,
- mediate conflicts between the family and service providers to empower the family when they are not successful,
- collect information and data to augment the advocacy and evaluation efforts to ensure quality of care.

Principles for Family-Focused Case Management

Although the family case management literature is limited, the literature on family-centered practice is rich and often consistent with a systems perspective. This perspective generally views the family as promoting positive interdependence and problem resolution, and uses intervention strategies aimed at developing the family as a system of mutual aid. By moving the family to "center stage," the family social work literature recognizes the family as the "primary social service institution" and network for planning and problem solving (Hartman, 1981, p. 7). From a family systems perspective, interventions and case management care plans are designed to preserve and enhance functioning, and to modify dysfunctional family patterns (Greene & Ephross, 1991) (see Table 6.2).

As no two families are alike, once the case manager has reached out to the family as a unit it is necessary to assess the family as a group that comprises a causal network. Systems theory suggests that to understand a family, each member should not be viewed in isolation. Rather, it is necessary to examine the relationships among family members, and any one individual's behavior is considered as the consequences of the total situation (Shafer, 1969).

In case management with families, for the social worker to be able to achieve the most effective and culturally sound plan of care, it is important to recognize differences in family forms. For example, persons with AIDS (PWAs) who also are gay or lesbian may want to receive care in conjunction with their family of origin and/or their family of choice. Therefore, it is critical for the case manager to establish a helping relationship unique to that particular family.

Application to Families on This Level

Families in need of case management services have a range of needs for flexibility, adaptability, and goal achievement. Some families experience high levels of tension, use outside resources poorly, and tend to have insufficient organization to meet their goals. These are examples of Level I and II needs where attention to basic resources is indicated (financial, medical), and structural and organizational changes are required within the family. These families may appear disordered, and often require many services and clinical interventions.

Because most programs have limited resources, case finding is critical in providing case management services. This process involves delineating a target population and determining who is especially suited to receive a service because their informal support network is not able to provide a particular resource. Some families may require case management briefly during a transition in development, such as discharge from a hospital after an acute illness. Other families may need ongoing services, with the goal of maintaining functioning or preventing regression to the greatest possible extent.

Interventions

The purpose of case management is to provide the client system—in this case, the family—with service options that promote group and individual functioning. To accomplish this task, Dattalo (1992) has identified three sets of roles that a case manager performs:

1. Counselor roles that are client focused, such as being an educator and enabler.
2. Coordinator roles, matching clients with services. As such, serving as a service broker and developing information about the resource network.
3. Advocacy roles that focus on the service system, such as being a mediator and community organizer.

Using these role clusters, the case manager can establish interventions with the family to help them engage in the service system, provide support once services have been initiated, and address shortcomings in the way services are organized. Specific interventions used by case managers in working with families include building positive relationships with the family system, completing a comprehensive assessment, structuring a case plan, linking the family to needed services, monitoring service delivery, and serving as an advocate.

Building Relationships

In all practice situations, building positive relationships with clients is an important initial component. In family case management, the practitioner has the task of promoting alliances to engage all members of the family system in the service contract. Relationship building with a family may include a number of tasks for the case manager, including education about the expectations and responsibilities of both the client role and practitioner roles, assurance about the nature and use of information shared between the family and practitioner, and listening and discussing the perceptions of the family toward using services.

Due to the stigma that is a result of a psychiatric diagnosis, building a positive relationship with families who care for a member with chronic mental illness, such as the Jordan family, is critical. Even mental health professionals may blame the family for their family member's pathology (Fadden, Bebbington, & Kuipers, 1987; Lefley, 1989). This situation has caused antagonistic relationships between families and the mental health system. Establishing rapport and trust, an important phase of any helping relationship, is especially crucial with these families.

Completing a Comprehensive Assessment

Case managers use a format for examining the person who is frail or impaired within a family context. The NASW standards (1984) suggested that assessment includes a culturally sound appraisal of the client's biopsychosocial functioning and needs as well as the resources available as a member of the family system. Because the family is a unit or interdependent group, it is necessary to assess how a change in one member's functioning affects role expectations throughout the family system (Greene, 1986).

In order to gather this tremendous amount of information, data should be collected from a variety of sources. These include records from other formal service providers in addition to information from the family members themselves. Within a family case management situation, perspectives and experiences of all members of the system must be incorporated. With the Jordan family, for example, the case manager should examine the concerns of the older parents and incorporate their needs into the family service plan. The focus of service provision is broader than just identifying Philip's needs. Frequently, different family members will claim different views about their service needs. In these situations, the case manager will spend time exploring, clarifying, and negotiating with the various family members about these issues.

Structuring a Case Plan

A thorough assessment of a family provides the foundation for a case plan. A service plan is based on a psychosocial study of the client and his or her family. It is a mutually-agreed-upon blueprint for deciding what services need to be mobilized on behalf of the impaired person and family. It also involves the way in which the family will interact with formal care providers.

In constructing a case plan, the case manager builds upon the informal support network of the family. An ecomap can be used to graphically portray the supports used by the family and the quality of the established relationships. Additional resources, such as available community resources, can be added to the ecomap to demonstrate how the case plan will increase the support of the family.

Linking Clients to Services

Linking involves referring or transferring client systems to services and entitlements that are determined to be necessary and available in the family care plan. This process includes identifying available services and gathering information about service access issues. The case manager can also be involved in helping families to learn about other resources and to transition into another type of service program. Case managers can enable clients to use potential resources by demonstrating how to take appropriate and effective action, for example, how to seek out and join a caregiver support group (Dattalo, 1992).

Monitoring Service

The relative success of case management practice is based upon seeing whether work between the various services involved in a case is performed in a harmonious fashion (Greene, 1992). The case manager is the coordinator of this effort, making certain that information is exchanged among the numerous service providers who may be involved with a family. Monitoring service delivery to determine if client systems are receiving allocated resources requires that the case manager keep in ongoing contact with the client and his or her network and service providers. Where the family is not successful, it may mean mediating conflicts between the family and service providers. This may also mean that troubleshooting can fill much of the case manager's day (Steinberg & Carter, 1983).

In working with families, monitoring service delivery is intertwined with a dynamic assessment process. Changes that affect the family system precipitate changes in service needs for the family. In the Jordan family, for example, Mrs. Jordan suffered a stroke a few months after the family came to the mental health center. Mrs. Jordan's illness had a dramatic impact upon the family's ability to carry out their service goals. The case manager maintained a key role in making certain that services were not disrupted during this family emergency. The case manager was also pivotal in helping the family receive resources, such as homemaker services and transportation, that lapsed as a result of the mother's illness.

Advocacy

Advocacy is a social work intervention strategy that is concerned with poor or inequitable distribution of resources. Data collected from the client system can be used by the family and/or case manager to augment the advocacy effort to ensure the quality of care.

The Jordan family exemplifies a situation that is becoming an increasing concern in mental health—older parents who provide care to a chronically disabled son or daughter. At this life stage, the older family is concerned with the ability to continue to provide extended care for a person with a chronic mental illness. Case managers who work with older families may need to advocate for services that are specific to issues faced by older families. Examples of advocacy efforts include establishing legal/residential workshops specifically oriented to late-life caregivers, structuring an emergency respite care program for instances of health crises of care providers, and exploring the concept of "retirement" for older people who have chronic psychiatric disabilities.

Evaluation

Evaluation of services and service delivery systems is necessary for accountability to the client system, to the funding source, and to policymakers (Greene, 1992). Measures of quality to the client system help ensure that service conforms to acceptable methods of practice. Case managers engage in effort on two levels: evaluating the progress of the family in the established treatment goals, and evaluating the comprehensive quality of available services.

The evaluation of the family's advancement involves measuring progress toward treatment goals. Case plans that are constructed using behavioral objectives and time frames lend themselves to the evaluation phase. Consider the following goal for Mr. and Mrs. Jordan:

Goal: Become involved in a support group for caregivers of people with chronic mental illness.

Objective 1: Contact the support group leader to discuss the content and structure of group. Completed in one week.

Objective 2: Contact neighbors, friends, relatives to identify a companion for Philip so parents can attend meeting. Completed in two weeks.

Objective 3: Parents attend first support group meeting. Completed in one month.

Using these types of behavioral objectives within specified time frames, the case manager can help the family partialize and evaluate progress. Points of inertia, or inactivity in the family, can suggest areas to the case manager where additional support is needed. For example, the inability of the Jordans to accomplish Objective 2 suggests that they may lack social support, or that they have difficulty asking for support from others. This discovery led to enhancing the treatment plan to address this issue with the family.

Evaluating progress with a family is an empowering experience in itself. Families that cannot partialize problems may feel immobilized and overwhelmed. The case manager can motivate families by presenting them with their own progress.

In addition to evaluation of the client systems, case managers are also involved in evaluating service networks. This level of evaluation can be structured around these basic questions (Dattalo, 1992):

1. What services are available for the families?
2. How accessible are these services?
3. Are there services that are available but not used by families?
4. What needs are unmet by available services?
5. Who are potential providers of needed but unmet services?

By answering these questions, case managers gain a comprehensive understanding about how services are able to meet the needs of the families whom they serve.

Application to Families at Other Levels of Need

Case management may be used with families operating at Levels III and IV. These families appear to have a high level of organization and are well prepared or differentiated in meeting their tasks (Goldenberg & Goldenberg, 1980). Very often, however, the resources secured by the case manager make the critical difference, restoring the functional capacity of the family group in crisis.

In working with clients, regardless of their level of need, the case manager must be acutely aware of the psychosocial effects of the problem situation. For example, families who are dealing with economic survival issues may require help understanding their feelings of fear and anger. Living from day to day can be stressful, and children, in particular, may experience great anxiety. Such families may benefit from structural family interventions that work to realign hierarchical power positions: Do the parents continue to be seen as providers? Who is (are) the breadwinner(s)? (Levels I and II of family functioning).

The case included in this chapter, which discussed a family with a member who is chronically mentally ill, provides an example of how the case manager will have to fill a number of different roles. He or she needs to build a relationship with and seek resources for the identified client—the member with the mental illness. The practitioner also may examine how other family members not only are adjusting to the member who is mentally ill, but also explore what intimacy, conflict, and self-realization issues may warrant attention (Level IV of family need). In addition, families who are highly functioning may have their equilibrium severely disrupted when important resources are not available.

The key to appropriate choices of intervention rests with assessment of family need. The eclectic choice of an intervention model is carefully selected and is often a blend of approaches depending upon a particular constellation of family issues.

Summary

Although family-focused interventions and case coordination have existed simultaneously since the beginnings of social work practice, a family-centered approach to case management has not been widely addressed. This chapter has promoted an inclusive model of working with a family whose needs are primarily on Level I. The model of practice is built upon the active premise that one person in the family does not "own a problem"—issues affect all members. The case of the Jordan family provided an example of how a case manager could take a whole family approach within a mental health context. The service goals did not reduce the family to "identified client and parents," but defined the client system as the family unit.

The role of the case manager in family-focused practice is to meet family needs and promote family harmony. The case manager has the responsibility to empower family members to activate and augment their support network. Formal services are introduced where the support system cannot accomplish tasks and meet the family's needs. The case manager helps the family identify and clarify their service needs and construct a plan of action. The case manager is also responsible for determining that the plan is being implemented and evaluating its success.

Discussion Questions

1. What are the overlapping features of individual- versus family-focused case management? How would the Jordan case study differ if the approach was individual-focused?
2. What are the advantages and disadvantages of having a single case manager, as opposed to team case management?
3. Describe the roles of a case manager using a family approach.
4. How do you maintain a trusting relationship in a case management role in difficult settings (such as public housing) when you feel you have done all you can to obtain trust?
5. What issues and techniques should be considered when applying the case management model to adults with developmental disabilities?
6. B. is a 28-year-old female with a history of substance abuse and incest as a child. She recently made a suicide attempt. Would the family case management approach be useful in working with this situation? What would be the short-term goals? Long-term goals?
7. Identify a family from your practice whose primary needs are at Level I and with whom you think the case management approach would be particularly relevant. Briefly identify the family's current supports and needs, and give at least five specific ways in which you could potentially assist this family utilizing relevant family case management methods.
8. Is case management a type of family therapy? Why or why not?
9. Why would the case management approach be utilized with Levels I and II families more often than with Levels III and IV families?

Suggested Readings

Dattalo, P. (1992) Case management for gerontological social workers. In R. L. Schneider & N. P. Kropf (Eds.), *Gerontological social work: Knowledge, service settings, and special populations* (pp. 138–170). Chicago: Nelson-Hall.

This chapter addresses the role of case management with older clients and their families. Content organizes the roles of the case manager into clusters categorized as client-focused, coordination between services and clients, and system-focused.

Hartman, A., & Laird, J. (1983). *Family-centered social work practice.* New York: Free Press.

This book offers a classic rationale for and discussion of family-focused social work practice. It offers a must-not-miss introduction to anyone interested in the field.

Hegar, R. L. (1992). Monitoring child welfare services. In B. S. Vourlekis and R. R. Greene (Eds.), *Social work case management.* New York: Aldine de Gruyter.

This chapter of an edited text on case management focuses on case management in the child welfare area. It addresses such concepts as permanency planning, protective services, and family preservation.

O'Connor, G. (1988). Case management: System and practice. *Social Casework, 69,* 97–106.

> *This journal article discusses the two levels of case management—the systems level, dealing with interagency connections and the continuum of care; and the practice level, focusing on direct service to the client.*

Steinberg, R. M., & Carter, G. W. (1983). *Case management with the elderly.* Lexington, MA: D. C. Heath.

> *This text discusses case management for the elderly from the perspective of: (1) the clinician, where interventions are at the psychosocial level; (2) the administrator, where case management focuses on the program level implementing a continuum of care; and (3) the program developer, where emphasis is on instrumenting rational community-wide long-term care systems.*

Vourlekis, B. S., & Greene, R. R. (Eds.). (1992). *Social work case management.* New York: Aldine de Gruyter.

> *This book discusses the eight basic functions of case management through an examination of different fields of practice. There are chapters on private case management with the elderly, programs in child welfare, adult protective services, school social work, and pediatric AIDS.*

Weil, M., & J. M. Karls & Associates. (1985). *Case management in human service practice.* San Francisco: Jossey-Bass.

> *The authors conceptualize eight basic case management functions. Chapters illustrate practice issues in several settings and fields of practice.*

References

Bertsche, V. A., & Horejsi, C. R. (1980). Coordination of client services. *Social Work, 25*(2), 94–98.

Cantor, M., Rehr, H., & Trotz, V. (1981). Workshop II case management and family involvement. *The Mount Sinai Journal of Medicine, 48*(6), 566–568.

Caragonne, P. (1980). *An analysis of the function of the case manager in our mental health social service settings.* Austin: University of Texas School of Social Work.

Dattalo, P. (1992). Case management for gerontological social workers. In R. L. Schneider & N. P. Kropf (Eds.), *Gerontological social work: Knowledge, service settings, and special populations* (pp. 138–170). Chicago: Nelson-Hall.

Fadden, G., Bebbington, P., & Kuipers, L. (1987). The burden of care: The impact of functional psychiatric illness on the patient's family. *British Journal of Psychiatry, 150,* 285–292.

Falicov, C. J., & Karrer, B. M. (1980). Cultural variations in the family life cycle: The Mexican American family. In E. A. Carter and M. McGoldrick (Eds.), *The family cycle* (pp. 383–426). New York: Gardner Press.

Goldenberg, I., & Goldenberg, H. (1980). *Family therapy: An overview.* Monterey, CA: Brooks/Cole Publishing.

Greene, R. R. (1986). *Social work with the aged and their families.* New York: Aldine de Gruyter.

Greene, R. R. (1992). Case management: An arena for social work practice. In B. S. Vourlekis and R. R. Greene (Eds.), *Social work case management* (pp. 11–25). New York: Aldine de Gruyter.

Greene, R. R., & Ephross, P. (1991). *Human behavior theory and social work practice.* New York: Aldine de Gruyter.

Groze, V., & Rosenthal, J. A. (1991). A structural analyses of families adopting special needs children. *Families in Society, 72*(2), 469–482.

Hartman, A. (1981). The family: A central focus for practice. *Social Work,* 7–13.

Hartman, A., & Laird, J. (1987). Family practice. In A. Minahan et al. (Eds.), *Encyclopedia of social work* (18th ed.) (pp. 575–589). Silver Spring, MD: National Association of Social Workers.

Hearn, G. (1969). Progress toward an holistic conception of social work. In G. Hearn (Ed.), *The general systems approach: Contributions toward an holistic conception of social work* (pp. 63–70). New York: Council on Social Work Education.

Ho, K. H. (1987). *Family therapy with ethnic minorities.* Newbury Park, CA: Sage.

Kaplan, M. (1992). Case planning for children with HIV/AIDS: A family perspective. In B. Vourlekis and R. Greene (Eds.), *Social work case management* (pp. 76–88). New York: Aldine de Gruyter.

Kelly, T., & Kropf, N. P. (1995). Stigmatized and perpetual parents: Older parents caring for adult children with life-long disabilities. *Journal of Gerontological Social Work, 24*(1/2), 3–16.

Kisthardt, W. E. (1992). A strengths model of case management: The principles and functions of a helping partnership with persons with persistent mental illness. In D. Saleebey (Ed.), *The strengths perspective in social work* (pp. 59–83). New York: Longman.

Kisthardt, W. E., & Rapp, C. (1992). Bridging the gap between policy and practice: Implementing a strengths perspective in case management. In S. M. Rose (Ed.), *Case management and social work practice* (pp. 112–125). New York: Longman.

Kuhn, A. (1974). *The logic of social systems: A unified deductive, system-based approach to social science.* San Francisco: Jossey-Bass.

Kuhn, D. R. (1990). The normative crises of families confronting dementia. *Families in Society, 71*(8), 451–460.

Lefley, H. P. (1989). Family burden and family stigma in major mental illness. *American Psychologist, 44,* 556–560.

Levine, I. S., & Fleming, M. (1984). *Human resource development: Issues in case management.* Baltimore: Center for Rehabilitation and Manpower Services, University of Maryland.

McGoldrick, M. J. (1989). Women through the life cycle. In M. McGoldrick and F. Walsh (Eds.), *Women in families: A framework for family therapy* (pp. 200–226). New York: Norton.

Minuchin, S. (1974). *Families and family therapy.* Cambridge, MA: Harvard University Press.

Moore, S. T. (1990). A social work practice model of case management: The case management grid. *Social Work, 35*(5), 444–448.

Mount, B., & Zwernik, K. (1988). *It's never too early, it's never too late: A booklet about personal futures planning* (Publication #421–88–109). St. Paul, MN: Metropolitan Council.

National Association of Social Workers (NASW). (1984). Standards and guidelines for social work case management for the functionally impaired. *Professional Standards,* No. 12. Silver Spring, MD: NASW.

Nelson, G. M. (1982). Support for the aged: Public and private responsibility. *Social Work, 27*(7), 137–143.

Pincus, A., & Minahan, A. (1973). *Social work practice: Model and method.* Itasca, IL: Peacock.

Rhodes, S. L. (1980). A developmental approach to the life cycle of the family. In M. Bloom (Ed.), *Life span development* (pp. 30–40). New York: Macmillan.

Richmond, M. (1917). *Social diagnoses.* New York: Russell Sage Foundation.

Roberts-DeGenarro, M. (1987). Developing case management as a practice model. *Social Casework, 68*(8), 466–470.

Rose, S. (1992). Case management: An advocacy/empowerment design. In S. M. Rose (Ed.), *Case management and social work practice* (pp. 271–298). New York: Longman.

Rothman, J. (1992). *Guidelines for case management: Putting research into professional use.* Itasca, IL: Peacock.

Rubin, A. (1987). Case management. In A. Minahan et al. (Eds.), *Encyclopedia of social work* (pp. 212–222). Silver Spring, MD: National Association of Social Workers.

Saleebey, D. (1992). *The strengths perspective in social work.* New York: Longman.

Shafer, C. M. (1969). Teaching social work practice in an integrated course: A general systems approach. In G. Hearn (Ed.), *The general systems approach: Contributions toward a holistic conception of social work* (pp. 26–36). New York: Council on Social Work Education.

Steinberg, R. M., & Carter, G. W. (1983). *Case management and the elderly.* Lexington, MA: D. C. Heath.

Tseng, W. S., & Hsu, J. (1991). *Culture and family problems and therapy.* New York: Haworth Press.

Vourlekis, B. S., & Greene, R. R. (Eds.). (1992). *Social work case management.* New York: Aldine de Gruyter.

Weil, M., & J. M. Karls & Associates. (1985). *Case management in human service practice.* San Francisco: Jossey-Bass.

Weston, K. (1991). *Families we choose: Lesbians, gays, kinship.* New York: Columbia University Press.

P a r t **III**

Second Level of Family Need: Structure, Limits, and Safety Issues

Level II families have their basic survival needs met and are dealing primarily with issues of family structure, limits, and safety.

The first approach to working with families at this level is structural family interventions, discussed by Cleveland in Chapter 7. It is based on family systems theory and has been used with a wide range of families in diverse racial, ethnic, and socioeconomic groups as well as with single-parent and foster-care families. It is one of the approaches that is used more internationally.

In Chapter 8, Horne and Sayger present the social-learning family-interventions approach to families who have needs on Level II. This approach deals with both internal and external or environmental factors that impact family needs and focuses on learning more effective social skills.

Structural Family Interventions

PEGGY H. CLEVELAND, Ph.D.

"Structural family intervention" is perhaps the most widely known and used model for helping families. Although others have contributed to this model, the recognized founder is Salvador Minuchin, who has written about working with families over a span of three decades. From *Families of the Slums* (Minuchin, Montalvo, Guerney, Rosman, & Schumer, 1967) to his latest *Family Healing: Tales of Hope and Renewal from Family Therapy* (Minuchin & Nichols, 1993), he has chronicled his experiences, his evolving understanding of families, and the model of intervening with the dynamics and events that make up their lives.

This model is based on family systems theory and assumes that families are not isolated units that operate independently, but instead are units within societies and cultures that are constantly evolving. This fundamental assumption makes the structural model a very useful one within the broad context of the ecosystems perspective.

The structural family interventions model is characterized primarily by its emphasis on transactional changes in the family that are accomplished by changing the behavior of family members. The worker is the leader of the process of therapeutic change. The goal of this model is "to change dysfunctional aspects of a family system to a more adequate family organization, one that will maximize the growth potential of each family member" (Minuchin, 1981, p. 446) "while also preserving the mutual support of the family" (Nichols & Schwartz, 1991, p. 460).

In most of the literature, "family" refers to a male and female couple and their children, but the principles of this model may be applied to any type of family constellation. Its use is documented with a wide range of racial, ethnic, socioeconomic groups and with single-parent and foster-care families. In addition, Minuchin and Fishman (1981, p. 16) explain, "Our limited clinical experience with homosexual couples with children suggests that family intervention concepts are as valid with them as with heterosexual couples with children."

Typical Problems of Level II Families

Weltner's (1986) family typology has as its basic assumption that interventions with families should be selected according to particular levels of family need. While the ramifications of need can rarely be assigned clearly to one level, this designation is a very helpful tool that enables the worker to know where to begin.

On Level II, the issue is whether there is sufficient authority in the family to provide minimal structure that will provide limits for children to assure their safety and development. The following example illustrates the use of the structural model in the assessment and interventions with the Addison family, whose issues include many at this level of need.

Family Case Assessment

In the structural model, family history and personal motivation are not considered as important as the present structure of the family (Cooklin, 1986). However, some history will introduce the family and aid in the understanding of that structure. It is also very realistic to assume that the current structure is based on a family history. Minuchin and Nichols (1993, p. 43) attest that "the family organization relates to the family's view of itself, and about the fact, as time goes by, the construction of family myth reinforces the structure that guides habitual movement and vice versa. So we can listen to stories and deduce a family's systems of coalitions and balances, or we can look at behavior and infer the stories that support these behaviors."

The Addison family consisted of the birth mother, Jane; the stepfather, Mike; Tammy, the 16-year-old daughter; and Ted, the 14-year-old son. Tammy was a patient in an adolescent unit of a psychiatric hospital where she has been admitted one day before the first family session. She was given a diagnosis of "posttraumatic stress disorder and major depression, severe."

Tammy was admitted to the psychiatric facility from an acute care emergency center after she ingested a bottle of over-the-counter pain medication. The first session with the family on the second day of Tammy's hospitalization revealed a history of a system consisting of a large number of players and interesting dynamics.

The children's birth parents, Jane and Paul, were divorced when Tammy was five and Ted was three because of repeated beatings to Jane by Paul that were often witnessed by the children. Jane, Tammy, and Ted went to live with Jane's parents, both of whom worked outside their home. They had lived with the grandparents almost two years when Jane became ill with a seizure disorder and was unable to care for the children. Jane voluntarily relinquished custody to their father, Paul, and the children moved away to a distant state. During the children's absence, Jane's health improved. She lived for a brief time with a man who was abusive to her; then she met and married Mike, who had never been married before.

While visiting the children after their marriage, Jane and Mike learned that the birth father was having a homosexual affair and had sexual relations in the presence of the children. After learning about the sexual display, the Addisons petitioned the court for custody and won. At the time the children came to live with their mother and stepfather, they described the son as "almost catatonic" and explained that he seldom talked with anyone. The daughter appeared to be well adjusted and developmentally on schedule.

The father never visited the children until Tammy was 12 years old, at which time, after a visit with him, Tammy informed her mother and stepfather that her father had attempted to sexually molest her and that she had resisted. She also disclosed that for three years, when she was between ages seven and nine, he had repeatedly molested her and she was unable to resist. After an investigation confirmed the molestation, the father's visiting rights were terminated. Approximately three months before the hospitalization, the father appeared in the town where the children lived and attempted to make contact with Tammy. This event precipitated her symptoms of posttraumatic stress disorder. Her parents misunderstood the behavioral manifestations of nightmares, agitated behaviors, and decreased ability to do schoolwork. These were interpreted as acting out behaviors, which they believed showed a lack of appreciation for her "good home and all we've given you." Tammy felt accused and blamed, and reacted to it by leaving a note to them saying, "I'm sorry for putting you through so much. I do not want to hurt you anymore," and taking the medications in an attempt at suicide.

It is difficult to separate the Level II and Level III dynamics in this family because they are so interrelated. However, the assessment revealed hierarchical issues that are important to note, and also some issues of autonomy, boundary making, and patterns of behavior that were keeping the family from moving forward as the members wished to do. Minuchin and Nichols (1993, p. 43) state,

> *When families come to me for help, I assume they have problems not because there is something inherently wrong with them but because they've gotten stuck—stuck with a structure whose time has passed, and stuck with a story that doesn't work. To discover what's bogging them down, I look for patterns that connect.*

This determination was arrived at by observation of the family in the session. Although formal histories are not taken when using this model, Minuchin (1981) explains that the past history of the family was instrumental in the creation of the family's present organization and functioning. The organization and functioning, however, were manifested in the present and were available to change-producing interventions that could change both the present and the future. So the way the organization came to be is not as important as how it is presently.

A diagnosis is the working hypothesis that the worker makes from the experiences and observations in the sessions. There are six major areas for concentration (Minuchin, 1974) in making a diagnosis:

1. The family structure, the family's preferred transactional patterns, and the alternatives that are available.
2. An evaluation of the system's flexibility and its capacity to restructure (change). This can be determined by observing the members' reactions to changing alliances, coalition, and subsystems in response to changing circumstances.

3. The family resonance or its sensitivity to each other's actions. The degree of sensitivity will fall somewhere on a continuum between enmeshment or extreme sensitivity, and disengagement or inappropriately low sensitivity.
4. Family life context, which includes the sources of support and stress in the family's ecology.
5. The family's stage of development and its performance of the tasks that are appropriate to that stage.
6. The maintenance of preferred transactional patterns by the use of the presenting symptoms.

In the Addison family, the observations, their behaviors, and the family stories revealed the following information in relation to these areas of consideration:

The family structure. In the first session, mother, daughter, and stepfather sat on a sofa together in that arrangement. Brother Ted sat away from them, alone, and was quiet. The seating arrangement indicated an important dynamic. The family stories indicated that mother was burdened by enormous guilt surrounding issues of her temporary abandonment and her failure to protect her children. The stepfather was burdened with feelings of a lack of control of the people and situation, and failure to provide a perfect environment for the family. He truly believed that "father knows best," but was unable to convince mother and daughter of that. Mother and daughter colluded to make decisions about growing-up issues, such as wearing makeup, dating, spending nights with friends, and going shopping for new clothes. When stepfather was consulted, he vetoed all of these behaviors. Mother and daughter simply decided to try for forgiveness instead of permission.

Ted was withdrawn and relatively unresponsive in the session after the first moments when he saw his sister, who joined them in the hospital activity room. Probing by the worker confirmed that interactions closely paralleled the seating arrangement. The daughter's reaction to her birth father's return and attempt at molesting her exacerbated an already unsteady alliance between her mother and stepfather. Tammy wanted to spend the night with friends, stepfather became controlling, mother became protective, daughter became frustrated, and son became more frightened and lonely.

The system's flexibility and its capacity for change. The Addison family requested help because one of the children became a symptom-bearer. In these "child-centered" families, the symptom is seen as an expression of system-wide dysfunction through its most vulnerable member (Guerin & Gordon, 1986). The task for the worker is to experiment with change options and see how the family responds to them. This family seemed to have no difficulty with cognitive understanding of their situation, but had more difficulty in actually changing the interactions after their awareness of them. For example, it was very easy for Mr. Addison to understand that an adolescent needs to be involved in decisions about her clothes and activities, but it was very difficult for him to stop lecturing her when they discussed her plans to go to a school prom. It was also difficult for Tammy to stop asking her mother to rescue her, and for mother to stop colluding with her daughter against the stepfather.

Sensitivity to each other's actions. Mother, stepfather, and Tammy were all highly sensitive to each other's actions and feelings. The son was less so, and so were mother and stepfather when they were dealing with the son. The siblings were usually appropriately involved with each other—able to carry on meaningful conversations and to play games without reacting to each other.

Family life context. The major stresses of this family's life were from the developmental transitions its members were experiencing. Both parents worked away from their home and had incomes that were sufficient for the financial care of the family; however, their support systems outside of the family were quite sparse. The children were in new schools, and the parents relied solely upon each other for friendship and nurturing. Both parents enjoyed their jobs and seemed to be good at them.

Ted was described by his stepfather as doing fairly well in school, but mostly quiet at home. Tammy was described as hardworking, overachieving at school, and active in extracurricular activities. However, she was teased because of her diminutive stature. An object of pride for her was a T-shirt given to her by her stepfather with the caption "It's a Short Thing—You Wouldn't Understand!"

The family's stage of development. This family was in a precarious place in its development. There was a relatively new marriage and children who were teenagers. The issue of the parents at the time of marriage was to learn to accommodate to each other's ideas and ways of doing things. When children are born, new functions must appear. The functioning of the subsystem of spouses must be changed somewhat to meet the demands of parenting (Minuchin, 1974; Minuchin & Fishman (1981); Carter & McGoldrick, 1989).

Families with teenagers require a great deal of flexibility and adaptivity. Mr. and Mrs. Addison had not achieved their accommodation to each other before they became parents, not of infants, but of teenagers. Given that tasks of a family include support of its members and "to develop a sense of belonging and a sense of being separate" (Minuchin, 1974, p. 47), herein lie the difficulties of the Addisons. Coming together and remaining separate at the same time is a difficult task.

The maintenance of preferred transactional patterns by the use of the presenting problem. Members expressed varied meanings for the attempted suicide. For the identified patient, suicide would have been the end of her frustration and disappointment in being unable to be the perfect daughter that she believed her mother and stepfather expected her to be. For both parents, the attempted suicide was a "slap in our faces" after they had tried so hard to have a good marriage and to make a good home for the children. For the brother, the attempted suicide was an abandonment by the one person in his life that he had always depended on. All of these perceptions constituted different aspects of a multifaceted reality in a system that was stuck.

The basic, or **generic,** structure of any family involves the power hierarchy in which parents and children have different levels of authority and parents operate as a team. The second structure, or **idiosyncratic,** involves the mutual expectations of the family members (Minuchin, 1974). It is in these idiosyncratic interactions that family members begin to blame and to induce guilt, usually because someone believes that one or another is not fulfilling obligations or is not being loyal to the family.

Both the generic and idiosyncratic interactions were operating with the Addisons. Mother and stepfather were not operating as a team to parent the children, and the daughter was being blamed for being ungrateful and uncooperative.

Probing by the worker about several relationships in the family revealed examples and the nature of these interactions:

Because the mother and stepfather were not operating as a team to parent the children, the daughter became the diffusion of this fact by being blamed. One of the greatest difficulties was the parents' expectation that the children have no problems in being properly appreciative of the parents' efforts. The other was that they were not acknowledging their interdependence in parenting and trusting each other for feedback and help.

Mother considered the stepfather to be too controlling in his relationship with her and the daughter, while stepfather considered both the mother and daughter to be in need of his protection and guidance. They argued about each other's stubbornness. Since this was a pattern in the marital pair, it was also the pattern in the parental pair (one of the patterns that connect).

The stepfather expected that the mother and the children be subject to him for approval of all activities. This was especially problematic with mother and Tammy, who experienced him as too restrictive. Mr. Addison's expectation of and the reaction to it resulted in a relationship between mother and Tammy that excluded stepfather.

The relationship between mother, stepfather, and Ted was not essentially conflictual. Mother was not bothered by the stepfather's involvement with the son, and believed that it was appropriate for the two to do "boy-man" stuff together. Consequently, the mother and stepfather were able to work together with this child.

The sibling dyad was an important one in this family. This was a close relationship, but it had been burdened in the past by the necessity for the sister to protect and care for her brother even though there was little difference in their ages. Ted tended to seek guidance from Tammy instead of from his mother. When Tammy was "claimed" by the parents as the focus of the marital and parental difficulties, Ted became frightened and withdrawn. This was already an established pattern for him from the time that he lived with his birth father and Tammy protected him.

Treatment Goals and Interventions

Goals in working with this family became twofold: to acknowledge and reinforce the strengths of the family as a whole and those of individual members, and to intervene in order to change structure and interactions that were interfering with the optimal development of the family as a whole and of the individual members. Strengths that were quickly obvious were that the parents wanted a good marriage and were committed to achieving that; they worked hard at parenting and wanted to be good at it; mother and Tammy had a close relationship; stepfather and Ted had a close relationship; Tammy and Ted had a close relationship; and all of the individual members did well in their separate endeavors, that is, school and work.

Objectives for intervention (change) were to (1) facilitate a decision that suicide was not a viable option for Tammy; (2) strengthen the relationship between Mr. and Mrs. Addison as a married couple, and improve their ability to work as a team in parenting the children; (3) strengthen the relationship between Mr. Addison and Tammy, which would include realigning the triangle between mother, Tammy, and stepfather, and coaching Mr. Addison in relating to Tammy around age-appropriate developmental tasks for an adolescent girl; and (4) strengthen the relationship between mother and Ted, which would require a realignment of the triangle that included mother, daughter, and son/brother.

Theory Base and Application

In keeping with the systems perspective, the family is seen as an open system that influences and is subjected to the surrounding environment. This view recognizes that the family unit itself is not the only determinant of the structure or rules by which it operates. The broader culture of the ethnic group the family belongs to, its socioeconomic level, the community and social values and resources, and the patterns of interactions of the related families all contribute to its being "the way it is."

Families are seen as living systems; this view implies that they are in a constant state of transformation, always evolving and forming their unique patterns of interacting. This evolving nature of families is brought about by a movement through time that we call family development, and also by those stressors that are imposed on the family, such as situational crises or catastrophic events (Carter & McGoldrick, 1989).

When two people marry or come together in any relationship, they must begin a process of **accommodating** and **boundary making.** Each must adjust (accommodate) to the other's expectations and everyday living rituals. They must also begin to identify themselves as a couple while remaining separate people, and to protect that entity from the destructive intrusion of others (boundary making). It is in this part of the relationship that, without even being aware of it, couples start making the rules by which their relationship operates.

Two conversations serve as examples of how these rules are made. The first one occurred while the writer was in line at an airport bookstore behind a young couple. The conversation went something like this:

Woman: Can I get some chewing gum?

Man: Get Juicy Fruit.

Woman: I don't really like Juicy Fruit. Can I get one Juicy Fruit and one Spearmint?

Man: I said, Get Juicy Fruit!

She looked perturbed, but did as she was told. The second similar interaction was in the grocery store where a man and woman were discussing orange juice.

Man: Let's get the large size.

Woman: Get the small one.

Man: If we are going to get some, let's at least get enough to drink!

Woman: Get the small one!

It is in such ways that a couple begins to work out how they will be together, how decisions will be made, whether negotiations are options. Seemingly small transactions begin to create the big picture of the structure of the partner family.

If a child is added to this couple, then another function is acquired, that of parents. This role is very different and requires new accommodation and boundary making. When other children join the family, a sibling group is formed that must have accommodation and boundary making for itself. As time goes by, the functions of the family members change; for instance, infants require a lot of care and parents often find themselves fatigued and without much time to spend together. Teenagers, however, are away from home a lot of the time. They require some pulling away on the part of the parents while the parents stay engaged enough for guidance. Families adjust to these developmental changes and to those from the external environment, yet remain somewhat stable. Changes bring about anxiety and uncertainty, and many families seek help at times of transition; however, we must not assume that transitional stress is necessarily equated with pathology (Minuchin, 1974). Less functional families are unable to adapt to changes and, therefore, increase their rigidity and become pathological.

Interventions

Although there is room within the structural model for differences in style, there are some specific functions and tasks enjoyed by family practitioners who use this model. One is the basic assumption that the worker becomes a part of the therapeutic system, and is in that system for the express purpose of changing it. The worker must be an expert listener and observer, and must build a relationship with the family that engenders trust.

Change is perceived as occurring through the process of the workers' affiliation with the family and his/her restructuring of the family patterns in a planned way. There is a focus on the "use of self," but that focus is different from that of a worker who proceeds from other frameworks. In the structured model, the worker is not encouraged to guard against spontaneous responses, but is free to react and to become an active player in the family drama. Family pathology can be understood as the development of dysfunctional sets or patterns of interactions that develop and are used in a family without modification even when there is conflict. Those things that could restore a functional balance to the family's structure become blocked, so the family cannot proceed in a healthy way (Minuchin, 1981).

It is the goal of the worker to understand the family so fully that directing its change becomes possible. Minuchin (1984, p. 7) describes this process of understanding a family:

> *Looking into the interior of a family, one can suddenly be caught by scenarios. These may be whimsical, challenging, absurd, or dramatic, but they are all disturbing because they carry the tantalizing feeling that they are complete. It is as if one glanced into a store window and flashed the universe. But the truth is that the family therapist is always in the presence of shifting images. Often he focuses on one well-defined piece—the family's presentation of their identified patient. But there are hundreds of other pieces with clear or uneven edges that have to be fitted together in order to see the pattern, and perhaps change the position of the pieces.*

Role of the Worker

As part of this process, the family practitioner works through four phases:

1. Determination of family structure, areas of strength, dysfunctional sets; assignment of priorities of intervention (diagnosis).
2. Determination of objectives or goals for change as they continue to evolve.
3. Assessment of therapeutic options and selection of strategies.
4. Evaluation.

These phases do not occur in sequential order, but instead occur continuously.

The first task of the worker is very important in the model—that is, joining and accommodating. These are basically relationship-building techniques and serve as the basic component of the change process. Without these, change does not occur. *Joining* is used when emphasizing actions of the therapist aimed directly at relating to family members or the family system. *Accommodation* is used when the emphasis is on the therapist's adjustments of himself in order to achieve joining" (Minuchin, 1974).

These techniques can be discussed in terms of things that the worker can do, such as listen carefully, be empathetic, support each member, be caring and friendly, and speak a colloquial language that the family can understand. Such techniques are not all that there is to joining and accommodating, but it is in these two interventions particularly where a worker's individual style and sense of the art of the work is very apparent.

When a worker has joined with the family, the worker is truly *with* the family, and accommodation follows easily. A recently overheard scene involving someone trying to teach another person to fish sounded like joining and accommodating. Both the person fishing and the fish were in the water. The line by which the one fishing was hooked to the fish was the only connection between the two. Through that very tenuous connection of the line, the person had to sense where the fish was going, whether to give it slack or pull it closer, and how to guide it in the direction of the boat.

When working with people the "line" is more complex, because it's more like having two at once—a verbal and a nonverbal component. What the worker does—the body language and facial expressions—is as important as what the worker says. These two components of the worker's communication get the family to move without their having the sense of being "jerked" harder than they are willing to be. If the sense of balance isn't achieved, the line breaks and you lose the fish! Of course, this metaphor, like any other, is imperfect. If you cannot imagine ever going fishing, you might imagine something in your own experience, such as directing a choir or coaching Little League—anything that is related to the understanding of both oneself and the others who are involved in a situation. Joining and accommodating are not fully accomplished in the first few sessions, but special attention must be paid to these two interventions before the change interventions are begun. Joining and accommodating are done with the family as a whole, with each individual, and with each subsystem.

Maintenance is an accommodation technique of supporting a part of the family's structure as it is. This might be as simple as acknowledging the nature of an interaction between two members, or "going along with" a pattern that is already apparent to the worker but not yet to the family.

Mimesis is another accommodating technique. Mimetic operations are usually implicit and spontaneous, and relate to being like something else or someone else. Minuchin (1974) gives several examples—people who feed babies are likely to open their mouths as the babies do; those talking to a person who stutters may slow their own speech. The result of mimesis is for workers to adopt the family style—slowing their style if that's the way the family is; being jovial and expansive in that kind of family, and so on. This technique may also include some form of self-disclosure, such as "I have teenagers at my house, too." This approach does not include pretending or any behaviors that are patronizing. Minuchin and Nichols explain (1993, p. 42) "joining has nothing to do with pretending to be what you are not. It means tuning in to people and responding to the way they move you."

An exploration of each of these areas and an observation of how the family responds to the probing of the worker result in the diagnosis. Minuchin (1974) describes the family map as a drawing that illustrates the patterns of interactions. Please see his reference for instructions on that very helpful tool. The diagnosis of the Addison family includes several observations concerning family interactions: The conflictual marriage relationship of Jane and Mike has been detoured onto Tammy. Mother and Tammy have formed a coalition that interferes with the resolution of the conflict between wife and husband and between the stepfather and Tammy. However, the parents' interactions with Ted indicate a well-functioning relationship.

Diagnosis is very much a part of prognosis. It reveals the alternative transactional patterns that can be identified as significant for therapeutic growth. The diagnosis leads the worker and the family into the therapeutic contract.

The **therapeutic contract** is the agreement that the family and the worker have about what the problem is and how they will work on it. Often, the family comes to the worker with a definition of a problem that the worker will need to enlarge.

For example, the Addison family came to the hospital worker with a definition of the problem as the daughter's overdose, which was explained as a "slap in the face" and a lack of appreciation for her good parents and good home. It was enlarged to include the parents' expectations that the children have no problems and the family's difficulty in meeting its developmental tasks.

For the contract to be made, all must understand and agree. Statements such as "It sounds as if it's very difficult for you to agree on what's appropriate behavior for a teenager. We can work on that..." help formulate the contract and enlarge the focus of the problem. Much of this verbal problem-definition part of the contract evolves in the process of the work, but some degree of understanding must be reached at the beginning.

The contract must also include the frequency of sessions, the length of sessions, cost, and other details of implementation. This portion can be written, and it may also be verbal. There is no specified time limit for this kind of intervention; it depends on the work there is to do. The Addison family was seen for five sessions— one for one and a half hours, and the remaining four for one hour each.

Restructuring the family is the goal in structured family interventions, drawing upon a variety of interventive techniques that confront and challenge the family to change. Lists of these techniques vary across publications but usually include the following:

Actualizing family transactional patterns. This technique involves how the family and worker relate to each other and how the worker interprets the family's interactions and descriptions about themselves. The worker is assumed to be an expert and must maintain the position of the leader; however, this position must be flexible enough to allow the worker to observe the family. So, the leader must direct the family members to talk to each other instead of to the worker. This is done with simple directions, such as "Have you talked to him about that?" or "Please talk with her about that now instead of to me."

Another aspect of this technique is to ascertain whether the family's description of itself is congruent with what the worker sees and hears in the interactions. When an incongruity is seen, the worker points out this inconsistency to the family. For example, "It seems that every time she brings up something that she is angry about, you begin to talk about something that has hurt you in the past so she must take care of you. This leaves her frustrated and more angry, and you feel abandoned."

Enacting transactional patterns. "Enactment is the technique by which the therapist asks the family to dance in her/his presence. The therapist constructs an interpersonal scenario in the session in which the dysfunctional transactions among family members are played out" (Minuchin & Fishman, 1981, p. 79). In using this technique, the practitioner invites and motivates the family to search for some alternative mode of transaction (Simon, 1995, p. 19). The Addison family was asked to discuss the meaning of attempting suicide and at another point were asked to discuss preparing to go to the prom. These discussions helped this family to identify behaviors that were not working and to search for other ways to "know" about themselves or to interact.

Manipulating space. The location of the family members in a session can be a metaphor for actual closeness and distance in the family as a permanent arrangement, or in response to a particular interaction. The Addisons' seating their daughter between them was a perfect illustration of the focus of the family problem at that time. The son's distance was an accurate depiction of his role in the family during this crisis. Several times, the worker asked the family members to shift positions in order to illustrate alternative interactional patterns. The daughter was asked to sit next to the brother, the parents were asked to face each other, Mr. Addison and Tammy were asked to face each other, the worker sat next to each family member at some time in order to give support (join) and to give direction. This positioning can serve to break up coalitions and to encourage alliances and direct communication.

Marking boundaries. Healthy functioning requires that there be flexible interchanges between the autonomy of individuals and subsystems and their interdependency, both of which are needed for the growth of the family and its individual members. Marking these individual, subsystem, and family boundaries makes use of interventions that are designed to strengthen some boundaries and loosen others when such changes are necessary. In the Addison family, the parents were instructed to go out for breakfast without the children, thus reminding them of their husband-wife roles. Tammy and Ted were allowed to play a game with each other without the parents being present. One should also consider the boundaries around the family itself that determine how the family uses feedback from outside, and allows it to reach outside itself for help. These are often simple interventions that have a powerful effect on the family's understanding of how close and how separate (boundaries) people need to be in a family.

Delineating individual boundaries. A family is a distinct unit of people. In our zeal to make this system work well, we might forget that this group is made up of individuals as well as small groups. The task of delineating individual boundaries recognizes the importance and autonomy of each individual. Enacting this task requires making some rules that are imposed in the sessions. Examples of these may be that family members should talk to each other directly and not about each other. One family member should not answer a question that was directed to someone else. One member should not have to carry the responsibility for remembering all of the history of the family; everyone must have the right to a separate opinion about what is happening. The assumption that family members also have a right to develop their own autonomy and interests outside of the family should also be considered. When such rules are broken, the worker needs to redirect the family in keeping them by saying something like "I believe that Ted can speak for himself about this" or "Tammy seems to have some ideas about that" or "We have heard Dad's idea about this. What do you think?" or "It seems that you and your mother have very different ideas about this; will you talk about it now?"

Subsystem boundaries. Any family might be made up of many subsystems, though the actual number will depend on how many members a family has. A couple with no children is still a subsystem within their own families of origin. In a family with children, there are three distinct subsystems—the marital, the parental, and the sibling, and all of the others that might be formed because of shared interests or needs. The reference to boundaries around these subsystems means that the rules allow for the differentiation and development of that particular structure. For example, the marital subsystem must be able to grow and develop within a family with children, and without undue interferences from extended families.

To some extent, the sibling subsystem needs to be able to operate without interference from parents so that the children can learn such essential skills as negotiation and sharing. Many strategies were tried with the Addison family to strengthen these boundaries. For example, Jane and Mike were asked to go out for a late breakfast one morning together and not talk about the children. Tammy and Ted were given time to play games together at the hospital without their parents. A session was held with the two children alone and one with the parents alone.

Redirecting stress. The technique of redirecting stress involves changing dysfunctional ways in which the family might divert stress, such as changing the subject when something stressful is brought up or displacing anger to one member who is safer than the one who is generating the anger. The worker simply points out what is happening, and redirects the interaction in such a way that the family members learn to endure the stress and resolve the issue. Sometimes the worker produces stress in one of the subsystems in order to help the family to restructure itself and thus adapt to changed circumstances.

In the Addison family, this particular strategy was very important because of the parents' difficulty in accepting the fact of their daughter's suicide attempt. Their understanding that the daughter truly attempted to kill herself was necessary to change a dysfunctional pattern. The intensity was emphasized when the mother or stepfather refused to listen to Tammy as she explained her perception, and began to label her as ungrateful. The worker said repeatedly, "Your daughter wanted to die. Listen, your daughter wanted to die!" until the family was able to stop reframing the event and talk about the incident honestly.

An incident from another family clarifies this very important tool. A wife in a session with her husband was relating that she had learned that her husband was taking money from their joint checking account and putting it in a savings account in his name only. Upon hearing his wife report this, he yelled, "I'm the head of this family; the Bible says I'm supposed to be and you can't do anything about it." She became quiet immediately and seemed defeated. Probing brought clarity to the process: The husband maintained his power over his wife by threatening her with God's wrath, after which she was defeated because God was too big for her to fight. Her submission to this reinforced his belief in the effectiveness of the tactic. The worker's insistence that they talk about the cycle of power interactions, rather than religion, developed implicit conflict and started the process of restructuring.

Joining an alliance or coalition. The technique in which the practitioner joins an alliance or coalition is powerful and should be used with great care. It consists of sometimes joining one family member or subsystem in opposition to another. It might simply be supporting one person or subsystem in facilitating communication. This is usually not uncomfortable for family members when joining is successfully accomplished. They view it as facilitation. At other times, the worker may need to join a family member for a longer period of time in families "that rigidly deny or defuse conflict and with families that persistently refuse to accept the idea that the family as a whole is the problem" (Minuchin, 1974). It has a jarring effect, and therefore needs to be used only by those who have a good understanding of the interactions that are occurring and very sound judgment about whether this effect is actually necessary.

This technique was used with the Addison family when the worker said to Mrs. Addison, "Your husband seems to see you as incompetent. I don't see you that way at all and think that he is wrong about this. Convince him that you are competent to raise a teenaged daughter." To Mr. Addison, the worker said, "She describes you as controlling. I really think that you care a lot about her and this family. Help her to understand that." For a better understanding of this intervention, readers are referred to *Family Healing: Tales of Hope and Renewal from Family Therapy* (Minuchin & Nichols, 1993).

Assigning tasks. Tasks help the worker and family to identify and change those things that are problematic for the family. Tasks are assigned both to do in the sessions and as homework. Those assigned in the session are the ones described earlier on manipulation of space and making rules about communication. Tasks also emphasize the worker's role as the rule setter. Homework assignments are a way of taking the work of the session home with the family. Assignments may take many forms, but should always be related to the goals of the work with the family.

The Addison couple were told to go to breakfast together and to talk only about their own interests, because the boundary around this part of the family was getting very weak and they were forgetting the affection and enjoyment of each other that brought them together and made them want to stay married. Likewise, homework can be used to break up a coalition that is not healthy and to create stronger relationships.

Relabeling the symptom. Relabeling the symptom involves giving another name to a problem so that it can be perceived differently: Depression is redefined as irresponsibility, anger as anxiety. One of the ways that this technique was used with the Addison family was to reframe the father's controlling behaviors, labeling them as anxiety about the safety of the mother and daughter and his real fear that something might happen to them. This pattern was relabeled consistently in the sessions until he began to be able to talk about these things without resorting to control tactics.

Shaping competence. The final technique consists of an acknowledgment and hence reinforcement of competence in family members. This was used with the Addison family by asking mother to talk with Tammy about appropriate dress for the prom. The worker responded, "You and Tammy worked that out very well together."

The work with this family consisted of five sessions held in the hospital while Tammy was a patient. They were referred for outpatient work. By the time of discharge, the family had accepted the reality of the suicide attempt. Mother and stepfather were working well as a team in sessions, both Tammy and Ted were able to express their concerns and feelings, and stepfather was able to express his concern and anxieties without resorting to control.

Evaluation

The structural family interventions model has been used successfully with a wide range of problem areas, socioeconomic groups, races, and ethnic groups. In his first book, *Families of the Slums* (1967), Minuchin and his colleagues at the Wiltwyck School for Boys in New York City described the structure and process of disorganized, low-socioeconomic families that had produced delinquent children. Documentation of the effectiveness of this model was shown in the increased functioning of the parents as well as in more effective communication between parents and children and modification of sibling subsystem function. The model was found to be more effective with enmeshed families in this population than with disengaged ones. Similar successes were also reported by Garfield and Bergin (1986), who cite this model as successful for lower-class black clients.

Minuchin, Rosman, and Baker (1978) reported one study that compared three groups of families—psychosomatic, behavior disorder, and normal—in terms of their responses to situations in which their parents argue. The study provided documentation that psychosomatic children are used to regulate stress between their parents, and that this model of practice can effectively change that dynamic. The authors also summarized the results of the treatment of 53 cases of anorexia nervosa with a 90% improvement rate.

Structural family interventions have also been shown to be extremely effective in treating families that have children with psychosomatic asthma and cases of diabetes (Minuchin et al., 1975). Stanton and Todd (1974) showed that symptom reduction in drug addicts and their families was significant, that the level of positive outcome was more than double that of other interventions, and that the positive effects were still evident in follow-up studies at six and twelve months.

Colapinto (1982) reported that this model had been used at the Philadelphia Child Guidance Center for 15 years. This center offered training programs that included an eight-month extern program, where about 40 family therapists were trained each year. The abiding popularity of the model over a long period of time attested to its effectiveness.

In a critique of this model, Leupnitz (1988) cites and applauds Minuchin's attention to social networks of families, his interest in the politics of extrafamilial systems, and his commitment to social issues. Not all of her critique is so flattering, however. She maintains that the tendency of Minuchin and his followers to unbalance the system through the mother and thus to elevate the position of the father serves to recapitulate the mother-blaming tendency of the larger social order. She criticizes systems thinking as a whole because of its functionalist bias of "valuing the continued functioning of the whole as opposed to emphasizing the conflicting interests of the constituent parts" (p. 67).

The tenets of the structural theory do not include such biases, but the operationalizing of these tenets may often do so. Colapinto (1988) states that "unbalancing is unfair," but he believes that this unfair maneuver is necessary. Minuchin and associates (1967, p. 107) made the statement that "issues of ethics and morality are important, but they must not undercut the healing process." He, too, believes that the "unfair" unbalancing is necessary to change the family structure, even though he also says that all members of a family must feel "respected, responded to, and affirmed" (p. 107). This is an important quandary for students of this model. Is something that is deemed unfair actually necessary in a model that also espouses respect and affirmation for all members of a family?

Szapocnik, Hervis, Kurtines, and Faraci (1991) describe a structural family assessment procedure to be used in evaluating therapy outcome. This procedure includes assigning family tasks and conducting the Structural Family Systems Ratings (SFSR). Studies cited in the article indicate that the SFSR "provides a psychometrically sound measure of family functioning that contributes to further integrating structural family theory, therapy, and assessment" (p. 308). This measure further documents the effectiveness of the model and can be used for a diagnostic as well as an assessment tool.

Application to Families on Levels I, III, and IV

The issues of authority, limits, and executive abilities are often issues in Level I, II, and III families. However, the issue of parental authority and structure are usually related to those problems that we identify on Levels I and III. There are many reasons why the parental system may be unable to provide the needed structure, and it is important to understand these reasons. For example, parental structure may break down under extreme stress, such as loss of job or home, or when a parent is critically or chronically ill. In these cases, Level I interventions may be the most effective approach to working with this problem. Other examples may include situations where spousal, parental, and sibling subsystems are all so distant that the children fight for attention and are never able to work together for any common purpose. There may be almost no identifiable hierarchy of parents and children in the family, as in situations where younger children are asked to take care of the emotional needs of parents or there are no rules that govern behavior. Often, these problems can be changed by working solely with the issue of parenting. When parenting practices are related to inappropriate boundaries, patterns of interactions, and coping mechanisms, then we must address these issues as well. These problems are identified as Level III.

One may work with all of these difficulties and dynamics by using the structural model. They may be manifested in families with delinquent children, in abusive families, in psychosomatic families—any kind where hierarchy, personal autonomy, boundaries, and patterns of behavior are problems.

This model has limited relevance to families on Level IV, where the focus may be on the development of an "inner richness, insight, more sensitive awareness of the relational world, and understanding the legacies and heritage" (Weltner, 1986, p. 54).

Summary

The "structural family intervention" model is perhaps the most widely known and used by family practitioners. The model itself and the writings of the recognized founder, Salvador Minuchin, provide the practitioner with a clear organizing framework, and articulate definitions of concepts and interventions in a manner that is easy to understand. The model has been widely used with many populations of people and so has shown broad utility with many family forms as well as diverse racial and ethnic groups.

This model is especially useful with Level II and Level III families, because their issues of sufficient authority, limits, executive abilities, inappropriate boundaries, patterns of interactions, and coping mechanisms are all addressed by this model.

Structural interventions are based on family systems theory. They are characterized primarily by emphasis on transactional changes in the family that are accomplished by changing the behavior of family members. A practitioner using this model has the goal of changing the dysfunctional aspects of a family system to a more adequate one, while maximizing the growth and preserving the support of each family member. This is no small task. While concepts and interventions are usually very clear, much practice is needed to be a good practitioner of this model.

Discussion Questions

1. What are the general goals of structural family interventions?
2. What are the different ways that the concept of joining is used?
3. How do accommodating and boundary making relate to the various stages in the family life cycle?
4. Why do you think this model proves more effective with enmeshed families than with disengaged ones?
5. What makes this model effective in working with lower socioeconomic groups of people and with varying ethnic groups?
6. From your practice, choose a family that you are working with and briefly detail how you could apply the structural family interventions in addressing their particular needs.
7. Discuss the issue of "fairness" of joining an alliance. If it is unfair, are there ways to make it more fair?
8. Critique this model for its utility with issues of social justice, that is, oppression of populations, differential access to services, and so on.

Suggested Readings

Carter, B., & McGoldrick, M. (Eds.). (1989). *The changing family life cycle: A framework for family therapy* (2nd ed.). Boston: Allyn & Bacon.

This book is a prerequisite for all models of family interventions that recognize the family as an entity that changes over time and is influenced by the sociopolitical and cultural aspects of its context.

Minuchin, S. (1974). *Families and family therapy.* Cambridge, MA: Harvard University Press.

This book is the first attempt by Minuchin to identify the model of structural family interventions with the strategies that he used. Understanding the model as it was helps the reader to appreciate the evolving nature of this model through the years.

Minuchin, S., & Fishman, H. C. (1981). *Family therapy techniques.* Cambridge, MA: Harvard University Press.

> *In this book, the authors name and explain the intervention strategies that are part of the structural model. Although all authors do not always refer to all of these, this listing gives a basis for understanding the concepts of the model.*

Minuchin, S., & Nichols, M. (1993). *Family healing: Tales of hope and renewal from family therapy.* New York: Free Press.

> *This newest gift is a must for those who know or who are just learning this model. This work shows the growing wisdom of its authors.*

Szapocznik, J., Hervis, O., Kurtines, W., & Faraci, A. (1991). Assessing change in family functioning as a result of treatment: The Structural Family Systems Rating scale (SFSR). *Journal of Marital and Family Therapy, 17*(3), 295–310.

> *This article explains the structural family assessment procedure, reliability, and validity. It also summarizes clinical outcome research studies that were conducted with the measure and includes the scale, which can be used for research.*

References

Carter, B., & McGoldrick, M. (Eds.). (1989). *The changing family life cycle: A framework for family therapy* (2nd ed.). Boston: Allyn & Bacon.

Colapinto, J. (1982). Structural family therapy. In A. M. Horne & M. M. Ohlsen (Eds.), *Family counseling and therapy.* Itasca, IL: Peacock & Bacon.

Colapinto, J. (1988). Teaching the structural way. In H. Liddle, D. Breunlin, & R. C. Schwartz (Eds.), *Handbook of family therapy training and supervision.* New York: Guilford Press.

Cooklin, A. (1986). The family day unit: Regenerating the elements of family life. In C. Fishman & B. L. Rosman (Eds.), *Evolving models for family change.* New York: Guilford Press.

Garfield, S. L., & Bergin, A. E. (Eds.). (1986). *Handbook of psychotherapy and behavior change.* New York: Wiley.

Guerin, P. J., & Gordon, E. M. (1986). Trees, triangles, & temperament in the child-centered family. In C. Fishman & B. L. Rosman (Eds.), *Evolving models for family change.* New York: Guilford Press.

Leupnitz, D. A. (1988). *The family interpreted: Feminist theory in clinical practice.* New York: Basic Books.

Minuchin, S. (1974). *Families and family therapy.* Cambridge, MA: Harvard University Press.

Minuchin, S. (1981). Structural family therapy. In R. L. Green & J. L. Framo (Eds.), *Family therapy: Major contributions.* Madison, CT: International Universities Press.

Minuchin, S. (1984). *Family kaleidoscope.* Washington, DC: Howard University Press.

Minuchin, S., Baker, L., Rosman, B., Liebman, R., Milman, L., & Todd, T. C. (1975). A conceptual model of psychosomatic illness in children. *Archives of General Psychiatry, 32,* 1031–1038.

Minuchin, S., & Fishman, H. C. (1981). *Family therapy techniques.* Cambridge, MA: Harvard University Press.

Minuchin, S., Montalvo, B., Guerney, B. G., Rosman, B. L., & Schumer, F. (1967). *Families of the slums: An exploration of their structure and treatment.* New York: Basic Books.

Minuchin, S., & Nichols, M. (1993). *Family healing: Tales of hope and renewal from family therapy.* New York: Free Press.

Minuchin, S., Rosman, B. L., & Baker, L. (1978). *Psychosomatic families, anorexia nervosa in context.* Cambridge, MA: Harvard University Press.

Nichols, M., & Schwartz, R. (1991). *Family therapy concepts and methods.* Boston: Allyn & Bacon.

Simon, G. (1995). A revisionist rendering of structural family therapy. *Journal of Marital and Family Therapy, 21*(1), 17–26.

Stanton, M. D., & Todd, T. C. (1974). Structural family therapy with drug addicts. In E. Kaufman & P. Kaufman (Eds.), *The family therapy of drug and alcohol abuse.* New York: Gardner Press.

Szapocnik, J., Hervis, O., Kurtines, W., & Faraci, A. (1991). Assessing change in family functioning as a result of treatment: The Structural Family Systems Rating scale (SFSR). *Journal of Marital and Family Therapy, 17*(3), 295–310.

Weltner, J. S. (1986). A matchmaker's guide to family therapy. *Family Therapy Networker, 10*(2), 51–55.

Chapter 8

Social Learning Family Interventions

ARTHUR M. HORNE, Ph.D., and THOMAS V. SAYGER, Ph.D.

Family life has become increasingly stressful during the past century. There has been more isolation of family members due to the urbanization of society, and a move toward small nuclear families instead of extended families. The urbanization process has led to a focus on work outside the home for most adults. Increased costs of living have resulted in more parents working longer hours out of the home, with fewer support systems available to provide parenting and child care. There has been a significant rise in violence in American society, coupled with drug and alcohol abuse; there has been a concomitant increase in sexual experimentation among young people, and more teenage parenting and single-parent households. There has been dramatic growth in the numbers of children and family members living below the poverty level and a corresponding increase in suicidal and homicidal behavior among young people. In many communities, gang membership has supplanted family membership as the primary source of identity.

Family Problems

Within American society there are substantial numbers of families that are functioning above the crisis level, the level at which families need support from the community for their very survival needs. Although the survival needs of these families have been met, they still have very real and serious problems. Examples of families with problems that fall within the second category of need include families with disruptive, acting-out children; families that are experiencing considerable disarray in the form of poor family organization and structure; families with difficulties in communicating and effective problem solving; families that have children in difficulty with school or community agencies; and families experiencing high levels of disruptive affect, as in violent anger or disabling depression.

Many of the families that have needs on Level II are there because of internal and external (environmental) factors that have impacted them. These include the following:

Parental Traits:	Psychopathology of one or both parents
	Antisocial behavior of family members
	Susceptibility to stressors
Family Stress:	Disrupted family management practices
	Unemployment
	Marital conflict
	Divorce
	Single-parent head of household
Demographics:	Family income level
	Level of family/parent education
	Neighborhood
	Ethnic group

Families that have sought help have included ones such as the following:

The McCallisters called, requesting to be seen at the center because of a referral from the school psychologist. Their son, Kevin, had experienced high rates of behavioral conduct problems in school for a number of years. Now that he had reached sixth grade, he had become a serious enough problem to be perceived as a danger to other children. The father was a carpenter who worked long hours when employed and who had little time for the family. The mother, a waitress, worked afternoons and was seldom home when the children came home after school. Kevin, the oldest, had been a behavioral problem throughout his school career and had been referred for testing several times.

Each time he was evaluated, Kevin was identified as marginal in terms of special needs; consequently, he had not received any special placement. The two younger children, also boys, had behavioral problems, but had not demonstrated the extent of physical aggression that Kevin had shown. The initial interview with the family indicated that the father was quite removed and distant from parenting, seeing the role of parenting as the mother's responsibility. He was angry that he had been called into the situation. The mother, who scored in the clinical range on a depression inventory, indicated that she loved the children, but that they had been a disappointment, causing her more pain than pleasure. Kevin was antagonistic to being involved in treatment, while the two younger boys were curious and rambunctious.

The Washington family was referred because Randolph Washington, a 15-year-old, had been caught shoplifting. He had a history of aggressive behavior, including attempting to extort money from children at school, threatening to hurt other children if they didn't pay him for "protection," and stealing items from school. Randolph had been arrested at a convenience store and held overnight at a juvenile detention center. He had attended juvenile court, and the judge had ordered that Randolph, his single-parent mother, and the siblings living at home participate in family counseling. Mrs. Washington was angry at the inconvenience, and Randolph was quite rebellious. None of the family members indicated that they saw counseling as a positive experience. They indicated that they would participate in counseling only by showing up for the minimum number of times the judge had ordered.

The Wnukowskis contacted the center and requested marriage counseling. They indicated that Mr. Wnukowski came from an Eastern European background, while Mrs. Wnukowski was of Irish heritage. They had been married for six years. While the marriage had started out amicably, the last two years had been marked by conflict, arguments, and recently by physical aggression between the two of them. They had attempted religious counseling by their priest, but he had encouraged them to follow traditional roles of husband and wife, with the wife deferring to Mr. Wnukowski as the head of the household. Mrs. Wnukowski indicated that she had been willing to accept that role when they were first married, but that it was no longer tolerable to her. They both reported significant conflict in the area of sexuality within the marriage. There were no children.

Robert Verde, a recent university graduate, came for his first session at the center and reported that his lover had just left him for another man. Robert was very distraught and reported the possibility of inflicting personal harm on himself. He stated that he had experienced a number of lovers during his university education but that his recent partner had been with him for more than a year. They were very close and trusting with each other. Robert was devastated that his lover left him after such a close and involved relationship. Robert indicated that his family had not been told about the partnership because Robert did not want his fundamentally religious farming family to know he was gay.

Assessment and Treatment Goals

Each family described presented very real pain and need for assistance in addressing the pressing problems that they were experiencing in their lives. There are general goals that are established for all families receiving treatment:

1. Develop a sense of optimism and hope about their particular situation.
2. Become aware of the alternative ways of addressing the problems they are experiencing so that they see more options available to them.
3. Learn more effective basic living skills: communication, problem solving, decision making, environmental interaction.
4. Develop independence in living skills.

The goals of treatment become focused as each family member presents his or her unique and individual issues.

The McCallisters. The McCallisters require a careful negotiation to determine the level of change and restructuring that would be acceptable and agreeable. Mr.

McCallister has reported little interest in participating in treatment, seeing the problem primarily as one for the mother. Here, the therapist must make a decision about family responsibility and power: Should the therapist support the traditional roles that have been assigned and accepted by family members, or should there be a focus on realigning the roles and responsibilities for the parents? The goals for the McCallister family might include

- empowering the mother to take greater control over how family members spend their time (father absent; chaotic family schedule)
- teaching both parents more effective parenting skills
- helping the boys learn anger self-control skills
- identifying problem-solving skills and, especially important, couples communication skills

The Washingtons. The Washington family does not want to participate in treatment. A goal for this family would be to identify ways in which their family is functioning well, and to help them see that they are not "bad" or "sick" but doing the best they can, given their economic and social circumstances. However, they need assistance in learning more effective ways of dealing with their environmental circumstances. Specific goals for the Washington family might include

- empowering the mother to be able to take greater responsibility for the behavior of the children
- teaching the family effective disciplinary techniques
- helping the boys learn self-control strategies that will help them stay out of trouble
- establishing better communication skills within the family
- addressing environmental issues (employment, leisure time, etc.)
- working with school issues such that greater success is experienced in the school environment

The Wnukowskis. The Wnukowskis have demonstrated difficulties in maintaining and enhancing intimacy. They need to learn more effective communication and basic problem-solving skills. They are experiencing an evolving and developing relationship, but have become "stuck" at a level of development that is not acceptable and is, in fact, detrimental to their growing closer together. Goals might include

- developing more effective problem-solving skills
- learning better communication skills
- addressing the beliefs or narratives they have about their relationship
- discussing the power and role relationships that have become troublesome

Mr. Verde. Robert Verde is having difficulty managing his needs for intimacy and relationships in light of his homosexuality and negative social pressures. He needs assistance in learning to manage issues of intimacy (being discarded) and sexual orientation, developing personal strength to manage his loneliness, and learning communication skills, both to facilitate meeting other persons and to learn ways of talking with his family members. Goals might be

- learning to develop the strength to manage developmental passages, such as the loss of a loved one
- developing effective coping skills to manage his loss and fear
- practicing communication skills that will allow greater means of meeting people and sharing with his current family and friends
- developing self-control skills to manage his life more effectively

Consistent with other families at Level II, the four families in the case examples are experiencing difficulties with inefficient and ineffective family structures. In turn, these structures inhibit the effective solving of current problems, confusion in family rules, roles, and responsibilities that exacerbates the current low level of functioning. As a result, these kinds of confusion limit the families' capacities to overcome their life challenges and their feelings of insecurity, dissatisfaction, and discomfort with the level of intimacy within the family.

Social Learning Family Interventions

Several principles aid in our understanding of family needs and the contingencies upon which current family interactions are based. The social learning family treatment approach, as outlined in Fleischman, Horne, and Arthur (1983) and Horne and Sayger (1990), has been successfully employed with a variety of families and with many levels of family needs. This model enables the practitioner to utilize a well-structured series of intervention strategies, yet allows for the necessary flexibility when working with diverse, chaotic, and unique family systems. Since social learning family interventions allow for unique family structures and flexibility in implementing change according to the expressed needs of each family, this approach can be effective across cultures and with varying gender roles and responsibilities. The effectiveness of social learning family interventions has been researched in a variety of clinical settings. It has been shown to be useful in the remediation of difficult child behavior problems, marital conflict, ineffective power structures and coalitions, and poor community–school–home relations (Horne, Glaser, & Calhoun, 1998; Sayger, Horne, & Glaser, 1993; Sayger, Horne, Walker, & Passmore, 1988; Szykula, Sayger, Morris, & Sudweeks, 1987).

Theoretical Base and Basic Tenets

Many theoretical approaches to family intervention have been utilized with Level II families, with varying degrees of success. All of these models attempt to approach clinical work with families from a positive viewpoint, and focus upon the families' strengths and current abilities to cope with the chaotic and challenging living environments. Clearly, no one theoretical approach provides the answer for all families experiencing difficulties; thus, family practitioners must be clear about the needs of each family they plan to assist, and how they will develop their intervention to meet those needs. An underlying knowledge of how one believes individuals and families develop and learn their behavioral patterns is the cornerstone for effectively implementing a family intervention.

For those clinicians who practice social learning family interventions, the following beliefs and assumptions about human/family development are the bases for intervention:

1. People learn within a social context through watching how other people in their environment behave, reacting to these behaviors, and interacting with those individuals in their social system (e.g., spouse, child, parent, extended family members, teachers, coworkers, etc.).
2. The problem behaviors demonstrated by the individual or family are logical from a learning perspective, given the contingencies within that family's or person's environment.
3. People behave the way they do either because they have learned that behavior, or because they have not learned alternative, and often more positive, ways to behave.
4. People attempt to maximize the rewards of their behavior while minimizing the costs. People are more likely to perform in ways that result in praise, encouragement, or expected responses than they are to perform in ways that result in punishment, pain, or unknown consequences.
5. In order to change how someone else behaves, a person has to change the way he or she typically responds to that behavior.
6. The more consistent the consequence and the more immediately it occurs after the behavior, the faster the person will learn. Inconsistent consequences make learning harder because people do not know what to expect.
7. Since people rarely learn from only one act of behaving and receiving a consequence, repeated trying or testing is a necessary part of learning.
8. The family is the expert on what is happening in its life, and each family is unique.

This framework is appropriate for families at the second level of functioning. The intervention focuses upon the development of effective communication skills, establishes appropriate limits and levels of authority, encourages strong parental alliances, and aids families in the development and use of self-control and problem-solving skills for coping with individual and family life. In essence, social learning family interventions help family members not only to learn how to survive family life, but also to make their family life healthier from a psychological perspective and more enjoyable in general.

Applications and Intervention Strategies

Social learning intervention strategies focus on families at Level II and fall into three general categories. First, cognitive restructuring addresses any disruptive or maladaptive thoughts that might result in painful or disturbing feelings and, consequently, maladaptive behaviors. Second, coping skills training, such as relaxation training, self-control strategies, behavior rehearsal, and modeling, addresses inappropriate learning experiences. Third, problem-solving skills training (e.g., behavioral contracts, negotiation, brainstorming) assists families in developing alternative strategies for resolving current and future conflicts or concerns. Perhaps the most important objective of intervention with Level II families is to focus upon creating a structured learning environment in which family members can learn and practice new behaviors that alter their currently ineffective family structure.

Therapeutic Relationship.   The development of a positive therapeutic relationship is central to effective family intervention. The relationship between professional and client develops in much the same way as all social systems are formed, that is, through modeling appropriate social behavior, coaching the family members in effective social communication, and setting up positive consequences for establishing the therapeutic alliance. To accomplish these goals, the family practitioner must first help the family establish positive expectations for change. Level II families are characterized by a negative view of their chances for remediation. They feel that they have tried everything they know how to do, and nothing has worked. Thus it is important for the practitioner to communicate to each family that she or he believes that the family can successfully deal with its current problems. The process of preparing the family for success can be initiated by

1. Defining all members in the family as victims of their circumstance. Most families attempt to find someone or something to blame for their problems. Objects of blame may be the child, parent, judge, social service system, neighborhood, teacher, school, social caseworker, extended family members, or the therapist. In defining all members in the family as victims, everyone acknowledges that each family member is affected in hurtful ways and that blaming will not solve the problem.
2. Normalizing the family problems. Families may communicate hopelessness or feelings of "Why me?" when they are first referred for treatment. It is important to inform the family in treatment that all families have problems and, although the family's current problems may seem to be overwhelming and uncontrollable, families in similar situations have been successful in overcoming their conflicts.
3. Emphasizing the family's strengths and positive motivation. Although many families may initially proclaim their reluctance to participate in treatment, the fact that they have attended a session shows that they still have some concern for their family and hold some hope for change.
4. Communicating empathy. The family must believe that the practitioner understands what it is like for the family to be experiencing these problems. Assuming the position that family members are the experts on their own family can assist the professional in communicating positively to the family that he or she is there to listen, understand, and help the family successfully overcome their concerns.

5. Using humor. Although the problems facing the family may be enormous and difficult, a positive attitude and an ability to see the irony and humor in the situation are necessary. Most families at Level II have forgotten how to laugh and enjoy themselves; thus, the practitioner must attempt to make the treatment intervention enjoyable and even fun, without diminishing the seriousness of the problems being addressed.

Other relationship-building skills that the professional would utilize include

- breaking complex problems into manageable units
- dealing with one issue or task at a time
- giving everyone a chance to participate
- teaching new skills in specific, nontechnical language
- modeling new skills
- personalizing in-session rehearsals
- predicting feelings and behavior changes
- soliciting and anticipating concerns
- encouraging client initiative and giving credit for positive changes
- determining reasons for client resistance
- checking for comprehension and understanding when teaching new skills
- sharing treatment/session agenda
- gathering information about what family members do
- gathering information about cognitive and emotional reactions
- gathering information about behavioral sequences and patterns

Structuring for Success.   Structuring for success begins with the initial contact between the family and the practitioner. Not only does the professional want to be successful in assisting the family to function in a more effective manner, but the family must also establish a belief in their own ability to succeed. To establish this positive expectation for change and success, interventions begin with clearly and objectively defining the problem, establishing specific behavioral goals, emphasizing consistency and persistence in developing family routines, interacting with respect and dignity, emphasizing family strengths, and enhancing the couple's and/or parent–child relationship. Families are encouraged to begin tracking the instances of problem behaviors in their family to determine patterns, sequences, frequency, intensity, and duration of the problems. Usually, families will discover that the incidence of problem behavior is less frequent than they had perceived; yet, the discomfort, anger, pain, and disruption created by the behavior is no less real. However, in discovering that the behavior occurs less frequently, the family becomes more hopeful that positive change can be achieved, and, thus, their motivation and commitment to treatment will increase.

Self-Control Skills Training.   Individuals who cannot gain and maintain control of their emotions and behaviors find it very difficult, if not impossible, to interact with family members in a positive and respectful manner. A study conducted by

Morris et al. (1988) found that fathers of aggressive boys reported five times more negative thoughts about their families and eight times more negative thoughts about their child than did fathers of well-behaved boys. This finding further supports the belief that the maladaptive thought processes that family members have about their relatives must be altered if they hope to develop a more functional family environment. Self-control strategies that might be utilized to assist family members in gaining and maintaining self-control are

1. *Relaxation Training.* Family members may receive training in deep-breathing exercises, progressive muscle relaxation, counting to ten, or other relaxation strategies to aid the family member in becoming physically relaxed.

2. *Positive Imagery.* Most individuals have some idea of an idyllic place where they might retreat in times of difficulty. Through guided fantasies or imagery, family members are taught to visualize their place of retreat to escape the emotionally charged atmosphere they experience in the family environment.

3. *Positive Reframing.* Individuals will typically react to behaviors based upon some perception they have regarding the intent of that behavior. For instance, a parent who is constantly being interrupted by a child may assume that the child is being an ill-mannered pest. This belief might lead the parent to respond in a negative manner. However, if the child's reaction was reframed as an attempt to gain the parent's highly valued attention, the parent might respond more positively. Functioning under a more positive frame of reference, the parent can then teach the child more appropriate ways of gaining parental attention. This reframing can also be identified as an attempt to replace upsetting, and possibly irrational, thoughts with calming thoughts that allow the family members to interact in healthier ways.

4. *Child Self-Control Strategies.* The most effective way to implement and train children to use self-control strategies is by aiding the parent in instructing the child. The turtle technique (Schneider & Robin, 1976) assists younger children in gaining control over impulsive, aggressive, and disruptive behaviors, and teaches children to slow down, "pull into their shell," calm down, and think of their behavioral goal. This strategy encourages the child to think before he or she acts.

5. *Disciplinary Strategies.* For families in which parental authority has been undermined, it becomes important to assist them in gaining control through consistent and effective disciplinary methods. Many Level II parents have relied on spanking, lecturing, or grounding to punish children for their misbehavior. These punishments are typically ineffective, particularly if the parents' authority is not secure or respected. Emphasizing modeling, direct instruction, and rehearsal to develop effective discipline, parents can be instructed in the development of strategies that allow the child to fully experience the consequences of his or her misbehavior. The following disciplinary strategies are often recommended:

> *Time-out.* Time-out is useful for general child noncompliance or defiance or when immediate cessation of the behavior is important. Short-term time-out is most effective with children before the age of 10, and requires the parent to

send the child to a nonreinforcing environment for a specified length of time to "cool off" and gain self-control.

Premack principle. Often referred to as "Grandma's law," the Premack principle requires the child to complete a desired or expected activity before doing something the child prefers to do. A form of contract, this strategy is often misused and reversed, and therefore rendered ineffective. For example, the child must eat his or her vegetables before he or she has dessert; this is an appropriate contract. However, because the child is whining or yelling, most parents will allow the child to eat the dessert to make them quiet. Typically, the child will continue to refuse to eat his or her vegetables. In essence, the child has won the battle.

Natural and logical consequences. Particularly useful with irresponsible children, natural and logical consequences allow children to experience the consequences of their behavior; thus, a child learns which behaviors have negative costs and which provide positive rewards.

Assigning extra chores. Effectively used with older children and adolescents, extra chores are assigned for children who lie, damage property, or steal. The child should be assigned to do one hour of work for each transgression. It is important that the chore be something that would not disrupt other family functions if not completed (e.g., cooking dinner). Additionally, the child is restricted from the telephone, friends, food, and fun until the work is completed. In instances of property damage or stealing, the child should also be expected to pay restitution.

Loss of privileges. To be effective, the loss of a privilege must entail something the child values. For instance, telling the child that he or she cannot use the car on the weekend when he or she does not have a driver's license would not be effective. Also, parents must not go overboard. If the child loses a privilege for too long, he or she will soon find a replacement of equal or greater value, and the suspended privilege will lose its effectiveness. Loss of privileges is often effective when other disciplinary strategies have been unsuccessful.

Communication Skills Training.   Healthy and functional family communication begins with ensuring that the message being sent is the message that is being received. Family members must be specific and brief, and utilize I-messages instead of you-messages if they hope to increase the effectiveness of their communication. Effective communication involves the following:

1. Speaking your piece. Individuals in the family must express their desires and opinions instead of relying on others to "read their mind."
2. Finding out what others are thinking. Many individuals make the mistake of believing they know what other family members are thinking. To be sure, family members must ask others what they are thinking.
3. Showing others that you are listening. Maintaining good eye contact and otherwise indicating that you are interested and trying to understand what others

are saying will communicate that you are concerned and committed to open communication.
4. Asking questions when confused. If family members do not understand what other members are trying to communicate, ask them for clarification.
5. Stopping and letting others know when communication is breaking down. During arguments, many things that are said in haste and anger may cause others to feel hurt or angry in return. It is best to stop the interaction before it progresses to this stage and to wait until a more calm and rational discussion can occur.

Other behaviors can derail communication and should be avoided. Such behaviors as put-downs, blaming, denial, defensiveness, mind reading, sidetracking, or giving up only lead to the demise of effective communication.

Problem-Solving Skills Training.   Most families at Level II are relatively unskilled problem solvers in many aspects of their lives. To overcome these deficiencies, interventions will assist family members in problem-solving exercises specifically designed to address the unique problems of each family. Basic to problem-solving skills training is the act of brainstorming alternative solutions for specific problems. An approach that seems particularly useful with such families is to ask these questions:

1. What is your goal? What would you like to see happen?
2. What are you doing to achieve this goal?
3. Is what you are doing helping you to achieve this goal?
4. If not, what are you going to do differently?

At first, most families will require a great deal of assistance to generate positive alternatives to their current behavior. However, through modeling this four-step process, the family will soon be able to generate many alternative solutions. The task for the practitioner then becomes helping the family evaluate the potential consequences for each solution and selecting and implementing the alternative that is deemed to be the most satisfactory in resolving the problem.

Evaluation of Effectiveness

Sayger, Horne, and Glaser (1993); Sayger, Horne, Walker, and Passmore (1988); and Szykula, Sayger, Morris, and Sudweeks (1987) have measured the effectiveness of social learning family interventions in a variety of settings with children with behavior disorders and their families. The results have been impressive, noting significant decreases in negative child behaviors and corresponding increases in positive child behaviors both at home and in school. Sayger et al. (1988) also reported that these behavioral changes were maintained after a nine-to-twelve-month follow-up. In a comparison of strategic and behavioral family therapies in an outpatient child psychiatric facility, Szykula et al. (1987) reported that 100% of the families participating in social learning family intervention demonstrated gains toward their treatment attainment goals, while 67% of those in the strategic family therapy group made gains toward treatment goals.

In a study of the impact of social learning family treatment for child conduct problems on the level of marital satisfaction of parents, Sayger et al. (1993) noted that those parents reporting low marital satisfaction prior to treatment reported scores in the maritally satisfied range after treatment.

Sayger, Szykula, and Sudweeks (1992) noted that parents participating in social learning family interventions reported significantly more positive than negative side effects of their participation in treatment. These studies suggest that consumer satisfaction ratings show that family treatments are both efficacious and effective in the positive treatment of many aspects of poorly functioning families with problems ranging from marital conflict to child behavior problems.

Application to Families Functioning at Levels I, III, and IV

Social learning family treatment offers a structured approach to dealing with a variety of family concerns. As such, it can be effectively employed with families at all levels of functioning. Families functioning at Level I can benefit from the positive focus on structure, organization, and problem solving. Even with families at levels higher than Level I, instances may occur in which their safety and security are challenged through unemployment, death, divorce, or other life events. The need to define and develop a new family structure and organization can become a focus in treatment. Families at Level III can benefit from the focus upon establishing clear boundaries and emphases on communication skills building. Level IV families can benefit as they develop self-knowledge and awareness regarding their behavior patterns, goals for the future, and general understanding of family systems and structures.

Summary

Social learning family interventions with Level II families focus on learning more effective social skills. People learn in social settings, with the family being the primary such setting. Through live and vicarious modeling, each member of the family learns to interact consistently with how other family members act ("nastiness begets nastiness"). People seek the maximum pleasure and least pain that they can experience in life, and as a result, often use aversive methods of interacting to obtain the greatest payoffs. Frequently, this tendency results in an environment focusing on aversive interactions, the abuse of members of the family, and a lack of family (community) happiness because individual desires at times take precedence over the best interests of the group.

Social learning family interventions present a relearning opportunity, helping family members learn to interact with one another in more pleasant, affirming, and respectful ways. Two primary contributions are the teaching of family members on how to interact in positive rather than aversive ways, showing respect and dignity for the members of the family; and a provision of structure and organization that brings order to chaos, predictability to uncertainty, trust rather than fear.

While this approach is not proposed as the only intervention for all families, it has been demonstrated to be highly effective for assisting families experiencing considerable chaos, with clinicians using aversion to control family members. When families are functioning with inadequate or inappropriate social skills, social learning family interventions facilitate the learning of more adaptive and fulfilling ways of living together.

Discussion Questions

1. Identify the particular population that the social learning family intervention model has been used with the most. Why has this population been targeted? What is there about the social learning family intervention model that particularly lends itself to working with this population?

2. The authors provide extensive evidence substantiating the efficacy of social learning family intervention. Describe why behavioral research methods have been especially applicable to this model of intervention, and discuss whether the information is useful for the clinical practitioner.

3. It often appears that clinicians are guided more by intuition and feel than by research supporting particular models. Family treatment adheres to a research model for evaluating the development and application of principles. Discuss why family treatment makes use of this research model, whereas many other models do not.

4. The authors noted that the social learning family treatment model is not necessarily the only or the best intervention to use. Describe guidelines that could assist you in deciding whether the social learning family treatment model is applicable to a given case.

5. The authors address the "softer" clinical skills necessary to be effective with families. Discuss the importance of relationship skills to a program that is predominantly technique- and intervention-oriented.

6. Explain from an ethical/professional position how you can justify using or not using a model that is less appealing but more efficacious.

7. Identify the aspects of treatment that seems to be key for impacting families at Level II.

Suggested Readings

Goldstein, A., & Huff, C. (1993). *The gang intervention handbook.* Champaign, IL: Research Press.

> *This handbook describes interventions useful for addressing gang problems, including two chapters describing family interventions.*

Horne, A. (1998). Social learning family therapy. In A. Horne (Ed.), *Family counseling and therapy* (3rd ed.). Itasca, IL: Peacock.

> *This text presents an overview of models and theories of family therapy intervention. The chapter on social learning family therapy includes a historical foundation for the model and reviews the research supporting the model. The chapter also describes applications to marriage work.*

Sayger, T. V., & Heid, K. O. (1991). Counseling the impoverished rural client: Issues for family therapists. *The Psychotherapy Patient, 7,* 161–168.

Discusses the problems facing family therapists when working with the rural poor and possible strategies for family intervention.

Sayger, T. V., Szykula, S. A., & Laylander, J. A. (1991). Adolescent-focused family counseling: A comparison of behavioral and strategic approaches. *Journal of Family Psychotherapy, 2,* 57–79.

This article presents a hypothetical case and discusses the application of social learning and strategic family therapy in addressing the family issues.

References

Fleischman, M., Horne, A., & Arthur, J. (1983). *Troubled families: A treatment program.* Champaign, IL: Research Press.

Horne, A., Glaser, B., and Calhoun, G. (1998). Conduct disorders. In R. Ammerman, C. G. Last, & M. Hersen (Eds.), *Handbook of prescriptive treatments for children and adolescents* (2nd ed.). New York: Pergamon Press.

Horne, A. M., & Sayger, T. V. (1990). *Treating conduct and oppositional defiant disorders in children.* Elmsford, NY: Pergamon Press.

Morris, P. W., Horne, A. M., Jessell, J. C., Passmore, J. L., Walker, J. M., & Sayger, T. V. (1988). Behavioral and cognitive characteristics of fathers of aggressive and well-behaved boys. *Journal of Cognitive Psychotherapy: An International Quarterly, 2,* 251–265.

Sayger, T. V., Horne, A. M., & Glaser, B. A. (1993). Marital satisfaction and social learning family therapy for child conduct problems: Generalization of treatment effects. *Journal of Marital and Family Therapy, 19,* 393–402.

Sayger, T. V., Horne, A. M., Walker, J. M., & Passmore, J. L. (1988). Social learning family therapy with aggressive children: Treatment outcome and maintenance. *Journal of Family Psychology, 1,* 261–285.

Sayger, T. V., Szykula, S. A., & Sudweeks, C. (1992). Treatment side effects: Positive and negative attributes of child-focused family therapy. *Child and Family Behavior Therapy, 14,* 1–9.

Schneider, M., & Robin, A. (1976). The turtle technique: A method for the self control of impulsive behavior. In J. Krumboltz & C. Thoreson (Eds.), *Counseling methods.* New York: Holt, Rinehart & Winston.

Szykula, S. A., Sayger, T. V., Morris, S. B., & Sudweeks, C. (1987). Child-focused behavior and strategic therapies: Outcome comparisons. *Psychotherapy: Theory, Research, Practice and Training, 24*(3S), 546–551.

Part IV

Third Level of Family Need: Problem-Focused Issues

Families with needs on Level III have their basic survival needs met and have achieved some success in dealing with the issues of family structure, limits, and safety. They have a structure and style that usually works for them. As a result, they are able to focus on more specific problems, such as clear and appropriate boundaries and control. In the house analogy for Level III, the primary focus is on the inner architecture, since the presence of the outer structure and basement are assumed.

In Chapter 9, Cleveland and Lindsey discuss solution-focused interventions, one of the brief intervention approaches appropriate for families at this level of functioning. The emphasis on health and strengths in this approach make it an especially useful model for families functioning at Level III. The second interventive approach for such families is presented by Pippin and Callaway in Chapter 10. Family systems interventions draw heavily on Bowen's family theory, which is an intergenerational approach.

Chapter **9**

Solution-Focused Family Interventions

PEGGY H. CLEVELAND, Ph.D., and ELIZABETH W. LINDSEY, Ph.D.

Solution-focused interventions emphasize a focus on solutions or exceptions to problems, rather than on the problems themselves. This major difference from problem-focused treatment approaches has significant implications for intervention. Solution-focused treatment is based on a series of assumptions that guide interventions and strategies. The major assumptions are summarized in the next section (de Shazer et al., 1986; O'Hanlon & Weiner-Davis, 1989).

Assumptions

Families have resources and strengths to resolve complaints. The practitioner's role is simply that of a facilitator of change, one who helps clients access the resources and strengths they already have but are not aware of or are not utilizing.

Change is constant and the practitioner's role is to identify and amplify that change. The solution-focused approach emphasizes the dynamic rather than homeostatic nature of phenomena. Clients frequently complain that problems are unchangeable. It is the practitioner's job to help them see changes that may have already occurred and to be able to recognize changes as they occur in the future by focusing client attention in those directions.

It is not necessary to know the cause of the complaint or even very much about the complaint itself in order to resolve it. This is perhaps one of the most radical positions of the solution-focused approach. It implies no need for extensive diagnosis of the problem situation or for complete understanding of its origins. Solution-focused practitioners believe that it is more important to come up with a solution that "fits" the situation rather than one that exactly "matches" the situation (de Shazer et al.,

1986). de Shazer and colleagues use the analogy of a key and a lock to explain this assumption: The solution to a given problem functions like a skeleton key. It is not necessary to have the exact specifications for a given lock if one has a skeleton key that will open it. (The key must "fit," but does not necessarily need to "match" the lock.) Since solutions are not tailor-made for specific situations, it is not necessary to know everything about the problem, only what is required to solve it.

A small change is all that is necessary: A change in one part of the system can affect changes in other parts of the system. Problems are maintained by unworkable solutions that continue to be tried because clients do not see the potential for other solutions. Recursive cycles result when the problem and attempted solutions interact in ways that maintain each other. To break this cycle, all that is needed is some small change in the patterns of interaction.

Clients define the goal: Practitioners help families define goals that are amenable to change. Those practitioners who use the solution-focused approach focus attention only on the complaints their "customers" want to change. A "customer" is defined as a person with a complaint who is willing to make changes in order to resolve the complaint. Some problems may be defined in ways that render them unsolvable, for example, "My husband's personality is such that he just cannot accept responsibility." The practitioner might work with the client to reformulate a goal in a way that makes the problem less intractable, for example, "I would like my husband to take more responsibility for certain household chores."

Rapid change or resolution of problems is possible. Solution-focused interventions are usually brief. de Shazer and colleagues report an average of fewer than five sessions per case, but emphasize that time is not the primary factor that makes solution-focused treatment brief. Rather, it is considered "brief" because of its approach to solving problems. By focusing on solutions rather than problems, families frequently notice significant improvements in their situations almost immediately.

There is no one "right" way to view things. Those who practice the solution-focused approach draw extensively upon the theory of social constructionism, recognizing that any situation has many points of view. However, there may be some perspectives that are more helpful than others in facilitating change. The practitioner does not seek a "correct" understanding of the situation, but a point of view that will open up the potential for change. Since families frequently enter treatment with rather constricted perspectives of their situations, part of the practitioner's job is to help them get a different slant on the problem. The practitioner, therefore, focuses on exceptions to the problem rather than on the problem itself.

Typical Problems of Level III Families

Level III families tend to have "a structure and a style that is often perceived as working" (Weltner, 1985, p. 46). The analogy for this level is the inner architecture of the house. When one is working with the inner structure, the presence of the outer structure is assumed. In these families, it is assumed that "there is sufficient strength and health to allow for resolution" (p. 47). This assumption is congruent with the use of a solution-focused approach to family treatment.

Family Case Assessment

The Brown family consists of the mother, Barbara, 27; the son, Joe, who is six years old; and the sister, Sharon, who is seven years old. Joe and Sharon are in first and second grades, respectively. For her family's support, Barbara depends on child support from the children's father, Aid to Dependent Children, and food stamps. Barbara is not married to the children's father, and although he lives in a nearby town, he has virtually no contact with the children. Joe would like to see his father more often. Barbara attends a technical school part-time, but is planning to enter school full-time in the next few months.

Barbara Brown and her children came to a counseling clinic at the suggestion of a counselor at school who was concerned about Joe's behavior in the classroom and on the playground. Ms. Brown, too, was concerned about Joe's behavior at home, with sitters, and at his aunt's house when he was visiting without his mother. She reported that Joe had hit children, had hit one teacher, was kicking and throwing chairs in the classroom, hit his sister, and was generally noncompliant while visiting his aunt. Barbara's goal as she stated it was "I need help in learning how to help my child express his anger without throwing a tantrum." Barbara, Joe, and Sharon all agreed on a goal of improving Joe's behavior in school and in other places when his Mom is not with him.

It was learned that there were many exceptions to Joe's undesired behavior; for example, Joe often helped around the house by washing dishes and cleaning his room, the living room, and the bathroom. He enjoyed reading to his mother and sister. He sometimes did not hit Sharon even when he was angry with her. He was often able to control his own anger by going away from the family until he cooled off. He was generally considered to be honest and trustworthy.

At school Joe was reported to be very helpful to the teachers and other children. He usually followed directions and obeyed teachers' directives. He worked well in the learning centers, and generally got along well with the other children.

Theory Base and Basic Tenets

Solution-focused treatment is an outgrowth of problem-focused strategic treatment (particularly from the Mental Research Institute brief therapy model) and thus shares many similarities with that approach. For instance, both are time-limited approaches (six to ten sessions) that focus only on symptoms or complaints specified by the client. They share a similar notion of problems being maintained by ongoing interactions in which attempted solutions do not "fit" the complaint, and share an Ericksonian influence. Both approaches try to create the smallest possible change, with the assumption that any small change in the system will be amplified by the system itself, and both deemphasize history and underlying pathology.

The major differences from the other approaches are that in order to discover attempts at resolutions that do not work, strategic therapists talk with families about sequences of interactions around the problems that they are presenting, while solution-oriented practitioners lead clients to focus on solutions that have worked or might work and talk about the context of the problem.

Solution-oriented practitioners do not maintain that problems serve a function in the family system or that people do not want to change (de Shazer & Molnar, 1984). O'Hanlon and Weiner-Davis (1989, p. 54) emphasize that practitioners may create or maintain problems because of their own framework.

> *If the client walks into a behaviorist's office, he or she will leave with a behavioral problem. If clients choose psychoanalysts' offices, they will leave with unresolved issues from childhood as the focus of the problem. If a client seeks help from a Jungian analyst, he or she is likely to get a problem that can be treated most effectively by examining symbolism in the client's dream.*

So much of the work in the solution-focused treatment approach is in the "co-creation" of an achievable goal by the client and therapist that is not related to what might have originally caused the problem. Those who work with this approach borrow from the constructionist idea that there is no true external reality, so elaborate theories of development or notions about what is normal or expected for all people are superfluous.

Solution-focused practitioners view clients as possessing the resources and strengths that are needed to resolve their complaints, with the practitioner as a facilitator of that process. This view is different from that of strategic therapy, where the practitioner is seen more as an expert to whom the client comes for the resolution of the problem.

Those who practice this approach aim for one (or more) of three types of change: a change in behaviors, a change in perceptions, or a recognition and tapping of client resources and strengths that can be brought to bear on the problematic situation (O'Hanlon & Weiner-Davis, 1989). Thus, successful work with a father who comes to treatment complaining of a rebellious adolescent son may focus on solutions that will result in behavior change in the son (or the father), on a change in the father's perceptions of the son's behaviors (which may not change at all), or on helping the father to realize that he has the capacity to deal effectively with his son, perhaps by considering how he has handled similar situations in the past with the same son, with other children, or even with other people in similar, but not necessarily identical, situations.

The primary process of change involves selective attention,whereby the practitioner focuses family attention on exceptions to the problem, what life was like before the problem, or what life would be like without the problem. Rather than examining the problem and its concomitants in great detail, the practitioner gets a brief description of the problem and then directs the family's attention to its exceptions.

This selective attention can impact family perceptions in several ways. First, by recognizing exceptions, families may realize the problem is not as serious or as ubiquitous as they originally thought (a change in perception). Second, by focusing on exceptions or what life without the problem would be like, the family becomes more likely to recognize times in the future when the problem is *not* happening, instead of selectively attending to problem occurrence and only seeing the behaviors that are objectionable. As a result, the family's behaviors are likely to change. Instead of being constantly critical of the son, the father might actually begin talking about the son in more positive ways. If the father is less critical, it is likely that the son will become less rebellious. A self-fulfilling prophecy seems to operate here: If one talks about problems, one sees them; but if one talks about solutions or exceptions to problems, that is what one begins to see.

Solution-focused interventions are literally a "talking cure." Anderson and Goolishian (1988) describe the role of the practitioner as "that of master conversational artist—an architect of dialogue—whose expertise is in *creating a space for* and *facilitating* a dialogical conversation" (p. 372). The focus of the talk is on exceptions, solutions, strengths, resources, and the inevitability of change. When sessions are filled with solution-focused talk, families leave prepared to see exceptions and solutions, whereas if the session is filled with problem-focused talk, they are likely to leave with their attention focused even more extensively upon the problem. Similarly, if the talk of the session emphasizes strengths and resources, families are likely to leave with a sense of competency and resourcefulness, while if the talk of the session focuses on problems, they are likely to leave with a sense of inadequacy and a perceived need for someone else to take a major role in problem solving for them (e.g., the practitioner).

Treatment Goals and Interventions

O'Hanlon and Weiner-Davis (1989) outline a typical structure for a solution-focused first session. Steps include joining, getting a brief description of the problem, exploring exceptions to the problem, normalizing, and goal setting. In addition, they recommend that the practitioner take a "think break" (either with or without a reflecting team), followed by the delivery of compliments to the family and an intervention, including a formula first-session task, which is given to all families. This task involves family reflection on aspects of their relationship that they value and want to sustain.

Language is very important to this therapeutic approach. The practitioner who uses the solution-focused approach assumes that change is inevitable and that families themselves have the potential to create the type of change they desire. All communication by practitioners implies—or at the very least does not contradict—these assumptions. Thus, solution-focused practitioners use the strategy of "presuppositional questioning," which serves not only as an assessment tool but also as an intervention, since such types of questions plant the seeds in families' minds that desired change will occur. Gale (1991) explains how presuppositional questioning works: "Either by selecting a specific verb tense, or implying the occurrence of a particular event, the family is led to believe that a solution will be achieved" (p. 43). For instance, "What good things happened since last session?" rather than "Did anything good happen since last session?" or "How will you know *when* your son has become more responsible?" rather than, "How will you know *if* your son becomes more responsible?"

Application

Specific interventions and how they apply to the Brown case provide further elucidation.

Joining

Joining is the process of building rapport. There are several activities identified by O'Hanlon and Weiner-Davis (1989) that facilitate this harmony. They may be as simple as chatting and asking a few questions at the beginning about their family's life in a way that shows a nonjudgmental interest in them. Matching the family's language or initially using the same words that they use in describing their subjective experience helps the family members to feel that they are understood and appreciated. They are much more likely to cooperate and relate easily with someone they feel can identify with them. Another approach for joining entails translating negative, fixed labels that the family uses to describe themselves or others into descriptions of actions. This change has the effect of depathologizing or normalizing situations. For example, when a family member says, "I'm codependent," we might say "You care a lot." Avoiding confrontation and topics that might cause disagreements in the beginning allows time for the family and practitioner to become more acquainted and to be more comfortable. In discussing the idea of resistance, de Shazer and colleagues (1986) explained that when people are labeled "resistant," they are showing us ways that we can help them. The key to cooperation is described as follows:

> First we connect the present to the future (ignoring the past, except for past successes), then we point out to the families what we think they are already doing that is useful and/or good for them, and then—once they know we are on their side—we can make a suggestion for something new that they might do which is, or at least might be, good for them. (p. 209)

Nyland and Corsiglia (1994) warn against a "solution-*forced* phenomenon" in using this method. "Solution-*forced*" interventions instead of "solution-*focused*" interventions occur when the practitioner does not attend sufficiently to the relational and emotional aspects of the client's presentation. Instead the practitioner forces the client to move into future talk too early, and the client feels invalidated.

In the first session with the Brown family, the practitioner began by chatting informally with each of the children, Joe and Sharon. She decided to talk with Sharon first to avoid focusing on Joe as the problem. They talked about favorite subjects in school and fun times. Both of the children responded eagerly to the practitioner's show of interest, although Joe seemed somewhat more shy and less outgoing than Sharon.

Barbara, the mother, seemed to become more comfortable as the practitioner talked with Joe and Sharon. After establishing a beginning level of rapport with the children, the practitioner "began a conversation with Barbara about herself, her extended family, and her work. It was then that the practitioner learned that Barbara was taking advantage of an employment program open to AFDC recipients and also planned to go to the local technical school in the near future.

Talking with families about their perceptions of the problem is actually a component of the joining process. Families come in expecting to talk about their problem, and a failure to attend sufficiently to their concerns about it can seem disrespectful and hinder the joining process.

The practitioner began to explore the Brown family's conceptualization of the situation by asking a general question, "So what brings you here today?" This question was followed by a few moments of silence. Barbara finally said that the counselor at school had suggested they come because of Joe's recent disruptive behavior in class. The practitioner asked her to elaborate on the disruptive behavior, but she was unable to give much detail. She could say only that Joe had hit teachers and other children and had tried to throw chairs in the classroom. She said Joe kept being sent to the office. The practitioner asked Joe if he knew why he was sent to the office, but he only shrugged and looked away.

In a conversation about Joe's behavior at home, the practitioner was surprised when Barbara began talking about how cooperative Joe usually was around the house, as long as she was there. Although she did mention that Joe was not cooperative when he stayed at her sister's house or at home with sitters, and that he sometimes hit Sharon, most of her description of Joe's behavior outside school indicated that there were many situations in which Joe's behavior was not a problem, especially if his mother was present. This surprising finding enabled the practitioner to move directly into one of the central components of solution-focused treatment—exploring exceptions.

Exploring Exceptions. The primary reason for exploring exceptions is to identify and amplify any changes or differences in the problem situation in the desired direction. O'Hanlon and Weiner-Davis (1989) suggest that the practitioner begin by finding out if the clients have noticed any changes in the problem since they called to make an appointment. If so, the practitioner explores those exceptions. If not, the next question is, "What is life like when this problem does *not* occur?" Again, the practitioner explores these times in detail, highlighting what the family member did to make these exceptions occur, for example, "How did you manage to have that happen?"

Most clients are able to remember exceptions. If they are not, O'Hanlon and Weiner-Davis (1989) offer alternate approaches, for instance, the miracle question: "What if you were to wake up tomorrow and a miracle had occurred and this problem no longer existed. What would life be like?" From this imaginary situation, the practitioner can lead the family to talk about problem exceptions. If family members continue to be unable to imagine any exceptions, switching to a problem-focused approach until an exception arises that the family is willing to pursue is appropriate.

In the first session with the Brown family, Barbara facilitated the exploration of exceptions when she began to talk about situations in which Joe's behavior was not a problem. The practitioner expressed great interest in these situations, and began to write down all of the exceptions the mother mentioned. Joe seemed fascinated and began to pay particular attention as the practitioner began writing. The practitioner began to include Joe in the process by asking him to contribute to the list of situations in which he was cooperative around the house. Joe became much more animated and involved in the discussion. Clearly, he preferred to talk about his good behaviors rather than his troublesome behaviors. As a result of this conversation, the practitioner ascertained that Joe generally followed his mother's directions even when he did not want to, that he helped around the house by washing dishes and cleaning bathrooms, his own room, and the living room, that he read to his mother, and sometimes did not hit Sharon even when he was angry with her. In addition, exceptions to problem behavior at school emerged. Joe stated that he had taught another child at school how to tie her shoes, that he followed directions, obeyed, and worked. Joe also indicated that his good behavior at school included not kicking, hitting, and punching others. Barbara indicated that Joe was doing well in school, and generally behaved well for at least half the day. In addition, Joe always told his mother when he got in trouble at school. Thus, his mother considered him to be honest and trustworthy.

Continuing the focus on exceptions to problem behavior rather than on the problem itself, the practitioner asked Barbara, what of the things that Joe is doing well at home, would she like to see Joe do more of. She said that she would like Joe to do what she asked even if he did not want to, to do what the sitter asked even if Mom was not there, and not to hit Sharon even if he was angry with her. These were all behaviors that Joe had shown in the past. By talking about increasing these behaviors rather than decreasing problem behaviors, the practitioner tried to focus Joe's and his family's attention on what he should be doing rather than on what he should not be doing.

Telephone conversations with both of Joe's teachers between the first and second meetings with the family enabled the practitioner to add to the lists of exceptions she had started during the initial family session. With information gained from the family and teachers, she created two lists that she then used during the second session to further highlight exceptions and emphasize positive behavior. Joe became so interested in these lists that he asked for copies to give each of his teachers and the aunt who sometimes cared for him. He also took a copy to post on the refrigerator at home.

Normalizing. Normalizing or depathologizing problems relieves family members' minds and can make them less focused on the problem. Normalizing can be done by such simple comments as "Of course it's understandable you would feel that way" and "Most people in your situation would react just as you have." Anecdotes and stories about other families with similar problems, or even self-disclosure by the practitioner who has experienced a similar problem, can be reassuring. Normalization begins to change everyone's perceptions of the situation. A father may be helped to see that his "rebellious" son's behavior is, in fact, typical of young men his age; the father may stop seeing his son as being "disturbed" or "troubled" and begin seeing him as being only normally obnoxious. One of the most powerful normalizing techniques is the question, "How can you tell the difference between (the stated problem) and (a normalized explanation of it)?" For instance, "How can you tell the difference between your daughter's depression (which the parent fears) and normal teenage moodiness?" (O'Hanlon & Weiner-Davis, 1989, p. 97).

With the Brown family, the practitioner had an opportunity to begin normalizing Joe's behavior in the second session, which occurred three weeks after the initial meeting. All three family members reported that Joe's behavior had improved both at home and at school. The practitioner asked Joe how he accounted for these changes, and he replied that he had decided that he wanted to behave better. The practitioner normalized Joe's need to learn self-control by reframing what he was doing as learning to grow up. Conversation with Joe and his family elicited more examples of "growing-up" behaviors.

Joe's behavior continued to improve, and the practitioner met with the family only two more times. The last time she met with them was after school was out and Joe and Sharon were in full-time day care for the summer because Barbara was now in school during the week. Barbara reported that Joe's school behavior had continued to be fine, but after entering day care full-time the past week, he had been in time-out three times. However, during the current week, he had not been in time-out at all. The practitioner normalized Joe's regression to previous poor behavior by framing it as not unusual behavior for a child trying to adjust to a new situation. The practitioner emphasized how much his behavior had improved in the current week, and suggested that Barbara monitor the situation to see how the improvement continued.

Another instance in which the practitioner used normalization with this family was in a conversation with Barbara alone during this last meeting. Barbara complained that Joe still did not obey her sister when she cared for him. However, exploring how the sister interacted with Joe, it became apparent that at the sister's house, there were no consequences for poor behavior. The practitioner suggested that perhaps it was normal for children to try to get away with doing things they knew they shouldn't do if they realized there would be no consequences. The practitioner suggested that perhaps it was a lot to expect a 6-year-old to behave perfectly all the time. She suggested that Barbara talk with her sister about providing consequences for Joe's misbehavior, but she said she had tried and that her sister would not do so. The sister did not even have consequences for her own children. Barbara seemed to realize that her sister might have a part in why Joe did not behave well at her home, and seemingly resigned herself to the situation. Her primary concerns were Joe's behavior at school and day care, and she was able to credit the improvements he had made in those areas.

Compliments.   The use of compliments serves two functions: they reinforce family strengths, and they set in motion a positive response set that the practitioner can capitalize on when delivering interventions. Compliments are normally delivered immediately after the "think break" and before the intervention. Compliments focus on what the family is already doing that is positive in spite of the situation that is causing distress. Throughout the session, the practitioner will be looking for things that can be used as compliments, such as ideas the family has already had about how to solve the problem or solutions already attempted. The practitioner may use positive connotation by "ascribing positive intent and motivation to behaviors which have previously been considered problematic" (O'Hanlon & Weiner-Davis, 1989, p. 105). With the Brown family, the practitioner used compliments in several ways. At the end of the first session, the practitioner took a brief break in order to review the notes she had taken about Joe's positive behaviors and to construct the message she wanted to give to the family. The message she delivered focused on the positive behaviors Joe was already demonstrating at home and at school. The practitioner also complimented Joe on being such a good student that even though he got into trouble from time to time, he could still make good grades. She also complimented Barbara on doing such a good job of raising Joe and Sharon, and for caring enough about her family to bring them in to try to improve the situation.

At the end of the second session, when the family reported improvements in Joe's behavior at school, again the practitioner complimented Joe, emphasizing his decision to grow up and learn to behave more maturely.

In the third session, the practitioner spent some time talking alone with Barbara, who expressed concerns about raising her children in the low-income housing area where they lived because of the presence of drugs and illegal behavior. She was very concerned that Joe not grow up to "hang out on street corners" and "get in trouble." She expressed concerns about her ability to parent him effectively. At the end of the conversation, the practitioner suggested that perhaps Barbara was not taking enough credit for how good a parent she really was, pointing out some of the effective parenting she was already doing. The practitioner continued to try to reinforce Barbara's perception of herself as a good mother by complimenting her again in the fourth session on how hard she was working by going to school and by insisting on good behavior from both of her children.

Interventions

Solution-focused practitioners are known for their use of formula interventions, that is, using certain interventions for all families, regardless of the presenting problem. de Shazer and Molnar (1984) describe four interventions often used in brief family treatment. The first is called the "formula first session task" (de Shazer et al., 1986; O'Hanlon & Weiner-Davis, 1989). At the end of the first session, all families are asked, "Between now and next time we meet, we (I) want you to observe, so that you can tell us (me) next time, what happens in your (life, marriage, family, or relationship) that you want to continue to have happen" (de Shazer & Molnar, 1984, p. 298).

The second intervention de Shazer and Molnar (1984) describe is "Do something different" (p. 300). Rather than giving specific instructions about what the family is to do differently, this intervention is deliberately vague, leaving it up to the family to decide what to do. This intervention is based on the assumption that families will know (although they may not realize it) what to do differently. Any small change in the usual recursive cycle of attempted solutions to their problem will be amplified and create additional changes in the system.

The third intervention is "Pay attention to what you do when you overcome the temptation or urge to...(perform the symptom or some behavior associated with the complaint)" (de Shazer & Molnar, 1984, p. 302). This intervention implies that families can exert some influence over the symptom or complaint even though they may perceive themselves as helpless in the face of the problem. This instruction also presupposes that the family *will* do something different, implying that change is inevitable.

The final intervention mentioned by de Shazer and Molnar (1984) is "A lot of people in your situation would have..." (p. 302), which is used to suggest alternative solutions in a way that implies families have perhaps chosen more difficult alternatives in the past. Stability is framed as "the most difficult course of action, one that really demands the most changes. This redefinition of stability as change then permits the practitioner to suggest change as being the way to promote the desired stability" (de Shazer & Molnar, 1984, p. 302).

O'Hanlon and Weiner-Davis (1989) describe other solution-focused interventions, several of which are elaborations on the "do something different" theme. Complaint pattern intervention involves having the family alter the pattern of the complaint in some small or seemingly insignificant manner. For instance, if a couple complains of frequent arguments, the practitioner may instruct them to go into the bathroom every time they begin to argue. The conscious effort required to stop the argument long enough to go into the bathroom is an example of introducing a small change that can interrupt the recursive cycle. O'Hanlon and Weiner-Davis describe various ways in which complaint patterns can be altered, including changing the frequency or rate, the timing, the duration, the location, or the sequence of elements or events in the performance of the complaint.

Context pattern intervention involves altering patterns that do not directly involve the performance of the complaint; for instance, asking a person who avoids socializing with friends on days when she binges on food, to make a point of going out with friends when she feels the urge to binge. Again, this intervention creates likelihood of a change in the complaint pattern, although that pattern was not directly addressed by the intervention.

A third intervention O'Hanlon and Weiner-Davis suggest is called the "surprise task." "Do at least one or two things that will surprise your parents (spouse, if doing marital treatment). Don't tell them what it is. Parents, your job is to see if you can tell what it is that she is doing. Don't compare notes; we will do that at the next session" (p. 137). This is another version of "do something different" that introduces randomness into the system. As people begin behaving in unpredictable ways, families cannot continue to maintain the illusion that they are "stuck." This intervention also introduces a fun, gamelike quality to the process of change.

A final class of interventions described by O'Hanlon and Weiner-Davis (1989) involve "solution-focused hypnosis," based on the work of Milton Erickson. Although it is beyond the scope of this chapter to explore this complex therapeutic approach, this strategy uses such Ericksonian techniques as naturalistic trance induction, utilization, the "illusion of alternatives" (p. 142), and the creation of the expectancy of change.

With the Brown family, the practitioner used the "formula first session task" at the end of the first meeting. She asked all three family members, "Between now and the next time we meet, notice things that happen in your family that you want to have continue." This request did not specifically mention Joe's behavior because the practitioner wanted to open up the family's thinking about interactions that occurred in the family. However, the fact that the practitioner and family had spent so much time talking about Joe's behavior during the session placed the request in a certain context. That is, the family would be especially likely to notice aspects of Joe's behavior, and Barbara and Sharon would probably be most likely to note aspects of their interactions with Joe.

During the second session, the practitioner asked what they had observed regarding this task. This question, asked early in the session, set the stage for a conversation that focused almost entirely on improvements in Joe's behavior and things the family members liked about being together.

Evaluation

Evaluation of interventions with the Brown family indicated that the solution-focused approach had been an effective approach to use with them. Barbara asked that her case be kept open over the summer, even though she did not feel a need to meet with the practitioner because Joe's behavior in school continued to improve. In a follow-up phone call shortly after school started the next fall, Barbara indicated that Joe was having no problems in school. At that point, her case was closed, and she was sent posttreatment assessment materials to complete. Barbara provided feedback about her perception of the treatment process on a standardized form used in the clinic. She indicated that the problem was better, although it was not completely resolved. She believed that treatment had met her goals to a large extent and reported that Joe's behavior was "a lot better." She expressed confidence that the changes would last for at least three to six months and indicated she was completely satisfied with the treatment received.

Comparison of Barbara's scores on the McMaster Family Assessment Device (Epstein, Baldwin, & Bishop, 1983) before and after treatment indicated improvement in all areas of family functioning measured by the FAD. Specifically, Barbara reported improvements in family problem solving, communication, roles, affective responsiveness and involvement, behavior control, and general functioning.

This intervention approach makes an easy task of evaluating the effectiveness of the work on a session-by-session basis because of the standard question "What is better?" Others have studied its effectiveness on a more formal basis. Adams, Piercy, and Jurich (1991) reported their examination of the differential effects of the "formula first session task" (FFST) formulated by de Shazer compared with a standard problem focused (PFT) structural-strategic intervention. The FFST was as follows:

> *Between now and the next time we meet, we would like you to observe, so that you can describe to us next time, what happens in your (pick one: family, life, marriage, relationship) you want to continue to have happen. (Adams et al., 1991, p. 278)*

Another group was given the following problem-focused task at the end of the first session:

> *Between now and the next time we meet, we would like you to observe, so that you can describe to us next time, the problem(s) occurring in your (pick one: family, life, marriage, relationship). (Adams et al., 1991, p. 280)*

Forty-five couples and families were seen at two clinical sites and were in one of three treatment conditions: a formula first session task (FFST) followed by problem-focused treatment; the FFST followed by solution-focused treatment; or a problem-focused intervention followed by problem-focused treatment.

According to the practitioners' judgments, families who had received the FFST were more compliant with the task itself than those who were given the PFT. They also judged that those who completed the FFST showed improvement in the presenting problem and had a clearer sense of the goals of treatment. And they determined that neither group was more optimistic about the family's ability to change or about a positive treatment outcome.

In a study of treatment with Asian American families, Berg and Miller (1992) assert that the solution-focused approach provides a balance between both the macro- and microviews of families, and is sensitive to ethnic and cultural factors. They cite its successful use at the Brief Family Treatment Center in Milwaukee, Wisconsin, where families from diverse ethnic and cultural backgrounds were seen.

Webster (1990) compared solution-focused treatment with traditional nursing and feminist values, and declared that all three are congruent.

Selekman (1991) reported on his use of "a strength-based, family wellness–oriented, 'Solution-Oriented Parenting' group approach" (p. 36) in which was integrated ideas from "Solution-Focused Brief Treatment," the Mental Research Institute approach, Michael White and his colleagues, and the constructivist ideas of von Foerster, Von Glaserfeld, and Maturana. This approach was found to be effective in empowering parents and in helping parents set realistic goals. It was not effective with highly disengaged families or with families where there were multiple substance abusers.

Application to Families on Levels I, II, and IV

Weltner's (1985) analogy for the issues of those families who might be considered at Level I is the basement of a house. These issues refer to life and death issues, such as housing and health care needs, and sufficient parenting to nurture and protect the family. The goal for intervention is to add resources. The Level II analogy is the foundation, and refers to authority and limits within the family unit. At Level IV, the goal is "the development of an inner 'richness'—insight, more sensitive awareness of the relational world, an understanding of legacies and heritage" (p. 47). The utility of this approach in dealing with these issues has not been established. It is probable that this approach is more effectively used with issues at Level III than with those in Levels II and IV.

Summary

Solution-focused interventions emphasize the exceptions to problems rather than the problems themselves. Solution-oriented practitioners believe that it is important to look for solutions that fit the situation. These solutions are not based on the complete understanding of a problem situation or upon a standard diagnosis of a disorder. When clients present problems that are unsolvable, the practitioner must help the client to reformulate a goal in a way that makes the problem less intractable. Then the practitioner makes interventions that help clients make changes in their perceptions and behaviors.

Many of the interventions in this framework are standard and are used by all practitioners. Others are made by a particular practitioner in response to what the client is presenting.

This framework presents an easy-to-understand and easy-to-follow paradigm. Literature is beginning to be available that shows its effectiveness especially with those families who might be identified as Level III families.

Discussion Questions

1. Someone once said, "If all you have is a hammer, everything looks like a nail." Discuss the meaning of this as it relates to the approaches of practice with families (all of them, including solution-focused).
2. Discuss the possibilities of using this approach for issues at Levels II and IV.
3. How is the future-oriented perspective of this theory different from other theories?
4. How would history taking differ in solution-oriented interventions as opposed to other approaches to family treatment?

5. Social constructionism emphasizes the use of language. Discuss the nature and implications of the language that is used by practitioners who use this framework. Discuss the possibility and advantages or disadvantages of using the language of social constructionism with the other models that are presented in this book.

6. Critique this model for its utility with issues of social justice, for example, oppression of populations, differential access to services, and so on.

Suggested Readings

Furman, B., & Ahola, T. (1992). *Solution talk: Hosting therapeutic conversations*. New York: Norton.

These authors show the reader how to engage in "solution talk" rather than "problem talk" through vignettes, including work with individuals, families, and organizations.

O'Hanlon, W. H., & Weiner-Davis, M. (1989). *In search of solutions: A new direction in psychotherapy*. New York: Norton.

This book presents a very clear description of this approach and where it came from. It is a very good place to start to get enough information to practice.

Walter, J. L., & Peller, J. E. (1992). *Becoming solution-focused in brief treatment*. New York: Brunner/Mazel.

This book is a good resource book for "how to do it." It contains definitions and examples for skill building in this approach.

References

Adams, J. F., Piercy, F. P., & Jurich, J. A. (1991). Effects of solution focused treatment's "formula first session task" on compliance and outcome in family treatment. *Journal of Marital and Family Therapy, 17*(3), 277–290.

Anderson, H., & Goolishian, H. A. (1988). Human systems as linguistic systems: Preliminary and evolving ideas about the implications for clinical theory. *Family Process, 27*(4), 371–394.

Berg, I. K., & Miller, S. D. (1992). Working with Asian American clients: One person at a time. *Families in Society: The Journal of Contemporary Human Services, 73*(6), 356–363.

de Shazer, S., Berg, I. K., Lipchik, E., Nunnally, E., Molnar, A., Gingerich, W., & Weiner-Davis, M. (1986). Brief treatment: Focused solution development. *Family Process, 25*(June), 207–222.

de Shazer, S., & Molnar, A. (1984). Four useful interventions in brief family treatment. *Journal of Marital and Family Treatment, 10*(3), 297–304.

Epstein, N. B., Baldwin, L. M., & Bishop, D. S. (1983). The McMaster Family Assessment Device. *Journal of Marital and Family Treatment, 9*(2), 171–180.

Gale, J. E. (1991). *Conversion analysis of therapeutic discourse: The pursuit of a therapeutic agenda*. Norwood, NJ: Ablex.

Nylund, D., & Corsiglia, V. (1994). Becoming solution ~~focused~~ forced in brief therapy: Remembering something important we already knew. *Journal of Systemic Therapies, 13*(1), 5–11.

O'Hanlon, W. H., & Weiner-Davis, M. (1989). *In search of solutions.* New York: Norton.

Selekman, M. (1991). The solution-oriented parenting group: A treatment alternative that works. *Journal of Strategic and Systemic Therapies, 10*(1), 36–49.

Webster, D. (1990). Solution-focused approaches in psychiatric/mental health nursing. *Perspectives in Psychiatric Care, 26*(4), 17–21.

Weltner, J. (1985). Matchmaking: Choosing the appropriate treatment for families at various levels of pathology. In M. Marikin & S. Koman (Eds.), *Handbook of adolescents and family treatment.* New York: Gardner Press.

$$Chapter \quad 10$$

Family Systems Interventions

JAMES A. PIPPIN, Ed.D., and JANICE T. CALLAWAY, M.S.W.

Working with families is usually exciting, often rewarding, but sometimes problematic for the practitioner. Joel Bergman's (1985) account of his work with a certain group of families that always challenge and sometimes consume the helper is aptly titled *Fishing for Barracuda.* In his preface he recounts an experience of snorkeling in the Red Sea off Israel. He was told that it was safe to snorkel except for the poisonous coral—which one should avoid—and the barracuda. When he asked if the barracuda would attack him he was told, "Only if you scare them." "What will scare them?" Bergman asked. His friend responded with a smile, "If you show panic" (p. xiii). A word to the wise for the practitioner working with such families.

These are the same families Weltner (1985) identifies as Level III families. He suggests that these families have a "rich mixture of coping mechanisms...to which they are committed." When working with such families to bring about change, Weltner concludes with an understatement, "we can anticipate some struggle." Beavers and Hampson (1990) are more accurate with their appraisal: "Such a family can chew up naive or unwary therapists and (figuratively, most of the time) eat them for breakfast, if not brunch" (p. 155). Whereas, as we have seen, Level I and Level II families generally are receptive and appreciative of help, Level III families dare you to help them.

Typical Problems of Level III Families

Weltner (1985) identifies the central issue in Level III families as a lack of clear and appropriate boundaries. Beavers and Hampson (1990) say these families "worship control over all else—over satisfaction, over apparent success, perhaps over a place in heaven" (p. 154). Boundary and control issues manifest themselves in a wide range of individual and interpersonal problems. Where there are children in these families, one will likely find poor school performance. Their behavior at home may be sullen and negative. Among the parents as well as the adolescents, it is not unusual to find evidence of alcohol abuse and abuse of other substances. Eating disorders, such as anorexia nervosa with restricted food intake and abuse of laxatives, are also manifested in family dynamics (Minuchin, Rosman, & Baker, 1978; Beavers & Hampson, 1990).

If the family has an intact marriage, that marriage is inevitably conflictual. Bergman (1985) believes that all symptoms in such families serve as stabilizers in the unstable marriages. Marital conflict may not be overt or acknowledged by either of the couple, but the more serious the symptom of a member of the family, the more severe the marital conflict is likely to be. Minuchin and associates (1978) identify specific ways in which a symptomatic child may be triangulated in parental conflict.

Adults in Level III families may be symptomatic either through significant overfunctioning or underfunctioning in any of three major areas: productivity, relationships, and personal well-being (Guerin, Fay, Burden, & Kautto, 1987, p. 123). Productivity has to do with how persons are functioning in whatever areas they consider to be their "jobs." Assessing productivity involves consideration of the satisfaction received, energy invested, and meaning attached to the particular work. The relationship area encompasses all those connections with important others.

An assessment of relationships takes into account the amount of energy and creativity invested in maintaining and nurturing these relationships. Personal well-being refers to "the amount of attention and creativity invested in taking care of one's own physical and emotional needs." Signs of underfunctioning in this area include obesity, abuse of alcohol and other substances, and significant inattention to general health maintenance routines.

Assessing the Level III Family: The Case of the Callahan Family

Bill Sr. and Carmen have two children, Bill Jr., aged 14, and Sonia, aged 12. Bill Jr. has always been difficult to manage. Currently, his school performance is poor, he is sullen and negative at home, and he has recently shown clear signs of being involved in alcohol and marijuana abuse. On several occasions he has driven the family car without permission. Most recently, he and a friend had gone for a "joy ride," during which Bill Jr. lost control of the car and struck a tree in a neighbor's yard. The police were called and the family ended up in Juvenile Court, where the judge directed them to receive family treatment.

Sonia has been regarded as a model child. She is quiet and cooperative and has a good record of school performance. Carmen is a pretty, rather sad-looking woman who frequently attempts a smile but rarely speaks. Though not expressing it openly, she seems to be pleased with Sonia and appalled at Bill Jr. Although the connection is not overtly apparent, she appears to be bonded with Bill Jr. Bill Sr. is a hard-driving, successful surgeon. He expresses frustration and irritation over the demands of meeting a rigorous professional schedule while attempting to keep members of his family in line. These feelings are usually expressed in remarks that denigrate his wife and threaten his son. When he does express satisfaction with another family member, it is about Sonia. Much of his energy when at home is dedicated to bullying his son. At the scene of the automobile accident following the joy ride, Bill Sr. broke his hand in a tussle with Bill Jr. This injury prevented him from doing surgery for a period of time.

In assessing this family in the interview setting, there is little doubt there is a sense of absolute authoritarian control by Bill Sr. Others in the family have chosen to respond with varying degrees of compliance or rebellion. The effort to control is felt by everyone, but the effectiveness of that control is tenuous. Communication among family members is limited. Most comments, with the exception of Sonia's, go unacknowledged. Most of the conversation in the family is a series of monologues with occasional interruptions. The feeling/tone of the family is depressed, with occasional expressions of anger and frustration.

The current involvement in treatment follows two previous episodes with helping professionals, neither of whom Bill Sr. considers competent, since the family continues to have problems.

Figure 10.1 is a three-generation **genogram** of the Callahan family. This Irish-Anglo-American family has several notable patterns that have repeated through two generations. Bill Sr. had a heavily conflictual relationship with his father, whom he described as a heavy drinker and womanizer prone to abuse his wife and his children. Bill Sr. is repeating the pattern with his son, Bill Jr. Bill Sr. was described by Bill Jr. as a heavy drinker. Early in his medical practice, Bill Sr. abused alcohol but has been sober for six years. He is an active member of AA. Bill Jr. has abused alcohol and marijuana by the early age of 14. Bill Sr. describes his parents' relationship as conflictual. His wife, Carmen, describes her parents'

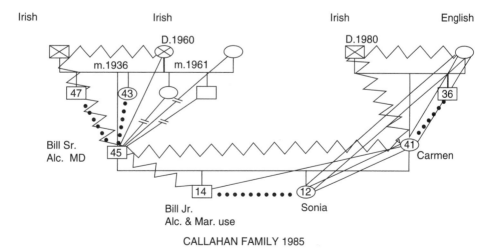

CALLAHAN FAMILY 1985

FIGURE 10.1   Callahan family genogram and relationships.

relationship as conflictual and the relationship between Bill Sr. and Carmen as conflictual.

There are three significant intergenerational triangles. The first involves Bill Jr., his mother, and his father. Bill Jr. and his mother are allied against his father, with Bill Jr. acting on behalf of his mother against his father. Carmen was caught in a similar triangle with her own mother and her father. Carmen, like her mother, was subject to abuse and ridicule throughout her early life. In turn, she and her mother had an overinvolved relationship where she was her mother's confidant and supporter. That pattern is repeated in the overinvolved relationship she has with her daughter Sonia. The third significant triangle is that of Bill Sr., Carmen, and Bill Jr. This is the identical triangle in which Bill Sr. was involved in his own family of origin, where he was caught in his parent's conflict and took his mother's part in that triangle. In this family, it is Bill Jr. who has challenged his father on behalf of his mother. As with Bill Sr. and his mother, Bill Jr.'s relationship with his mother is open but not overinvolved.

The significance of these intergenerational conflicts and overinvolved relationships lies not so much in the amount of pain the individuals experienced—and it must be said that though there appeared to be villains, even they were experiencing significant pain—rather, the most important aspect these relationships indicated is the degree of fusion. Members in this nuclear and these extended families are deeply enmeshed, and they experience a level of overinvolvement in their relationships that binds them together so tightly that the inevitable growth and change with age is viewed with terror. The family seems frozen in its anxiety over what will happen to them if a member separates or becomes emotionally independent, as demonstrated in the emotional control exerted by the father with the mother and the son. Weltner (1985) describes this fusion as a powerful commitment of family members to the very problematic behavior that hurts them.

Treatment Goals

The overarching goal of treatment with this Level III family is the realignment of the family system. Boundaries in this family are not sufficiently clear to allow and require individuals in the family to address their own needs and goals without distractions and invasions from others. A second overall goal is to identify and ameliorate the sources of chronic anxiety within the family system that undermine individual growth and autonomy. The members of this family need to develop new roles and arrangements among themselves.

Within this major framework of goals, there are several interim objectives that should be addressed by the family practitioner:

- The practitioner should connect with each member of the family in order to engage them in the change process.
- The parental subsystem must be a strengthened, supporting team in the management of the children.

- The covert marital conflict must be made overt and distinguished from parental issues.
- Bill Jr.'s vulnerability to alcohol abuse must be identified and addressed with appropriate educational and skill development interventions.
- Sonia's overinvolvement with her mother must be reduced with a concomitant increase in her involvement with peers (reducing her vulnerability to being drawn into the marital conflict, which will recycle over the coming years).
- Clear expectations for Bill Jr.'s behavior must be set forth with equally clear outcomes articulated regarding rewards and punishments to be associated with both success and failure to meet those expectations.
- The practitioner should identify and facilitate with Carmen the development of her personal goals and the actualization of these goals.
- The practitioner should identify and address with Bill Sr. his abusive behaviors toward Bill Jr. and Carmen.

Treatment Approaches

The primary intervention in this case was the intergenerational approach of Bowen. His theoretical base lends itself to addressing each of the specified objectives and is compatible with intervention techniques drawn from the strategic and structural approaches that will be suggested.

Theoretical Bases and Basic Tenets

In his work with families in which a member was identified as being schizophrenic, Bowen concluded that relationships with such families were "endowed with high emotionality" (Guerin, 1976, p. 49). Members of these families were often unable to distinguish between their own feelings and intellectual processes. In such families, the feelings and intellectual processes were fused. The actions that these families' members took were often in response to emotional processes rather than intellectual processes. Further, these family members were unable to separate what they felt from what they thought of other family members. Often they contended that their actions were well considered and thought out, but a trained observer easily sensed the high degree of emotionality in the exchanges between family members, as well as the similarity of interactional patterns involving various triads within the family.

Under stress, any problematic interaction between two family members drew in a third party, thus diminishing the tension between the original dyad and stabilizing the interactional process. Several concepts were developed by Bowen as a result of these studies.

Differentiation of self is a cornerstone concept of Bowen's family theory (Guerin, 1976, p. 65). This concept defines people according to the degree of fusion or separation between emotional and intellectual functioning.

> *At the low extreme are those whose emotions and intellect are so fused that their lives are dominated by the automatic emotional system.... At the other extreme are those who are more differentiated. It is impossible for there to be more than relative separation between emotional and intellectual functioning, but those whose intellectual functioning can retain relative autonomy in periods of stress are more flexible, more adaptable, and more independent of the emotionality about them.... In between the two extremes is an infinite number of mixes between emotional and intellectual functioning. (Guerin, 1976, p. 65)*

Bowen's (1978) concepts are built on the assumption that the family is an emotional system. Family boundaries, the rules regarding who participates in a subsystem and how they participate, are membranes of varying degrees of permeability that "give varying degrees of access to personal emotional space" (Guerin et al., 1987, p. 45). In times of high stress, the boundaries of some individuals become highly permeable, inviting others into their personal space almost at random, while spilling anxiety and emotional upset on anyone within reach. Others may demonstrate their own sensitivity to high levels of stress by closing up emotionally and withdrawing from all others.

Both of the parents in our case example are responding emotionally to the high level of anxiety within the emotional system, one by enmeshment and the other by cutoff. Both may be viewed in Bowen's terms as having the same low level of differentiation of self.

Under extreme circumstances, individuals in such families may take essentially permanent positions of enmeshment, with some clinging to others in such a fashion as to be unable to operate without a high level of interchange for any period of time, even at great geographical distances. Others may cut themselves off by divorce, separating and refusing all contact, or even suicide. Guerin et al. (1987) discuss this residue of chronic anxiety in a concept they call the "premorbid state of the family." By this they mean the stress likely to be funneled to a family from the extended family. They consider the best markers of the premorbid state of the family to be the "number and severity of the individual dysfunctions in the multigenerational family system and the number of conflicts and cutoffs in relationships in that system" (Guerin et al., 1987, p. 23).

Bowen concluded that occurrences in the history of a family such as alcoholism and other forms of substance abuse, divorce, suicides, and extramarital affairs are indicative of the degree of fusion in the family system. Such events leave a residue of chronic anxiety within the system that is passed down to each generation, adding to the acute anxiety that is normal when stressful events occur in everyday life. Of particular significance are the occurrences of events in current life that match with events from the family's past, thus contributing an already high level of anxiety (Carter & McGoldrick, 1988).

Bowen considers the triangle as "the smallest stable relationship system." A two-person system is unstable, and quickly adds a series of interlocking triangles. The triangle has definite relationship patterns that predictably repeat in periods of stress and calm (Bowen, 1978, p. 199). "Triangulation is the reactive emotional process that goes on between the three people who make up the triangle" (Guerin et al.,

1987, p. 62). As a family is observed at any moment in time, one may identify the variety of ways in which three people relate with one another. In addition, it is important to observe over time the pattern to which such patterns regularly return. These significant relationship patterns may be identifiable over several generations.

The triangulation process need not be destructive, but it becomes so when it blocks the life stage development of individuals. A child who is triangulated into a conflictual marital relationship may develop a wide range of symptoms from organic to behavioral (Bergman, 1985). Additionally, the overinvolvement of the child with the parents will hamper his or her own development of a self that feels and thinks autonomously. As the child ages, and particularly as the adolescent years approach, the importance of the child to the marital relationship will preclude the changes in participation within the family system that are necessary to allow the child ever-increasing involvement with peers and a more solid sense of self as a developing adult. Another child in the same family might not be as caught up in the emotional triangle because of the overinvolvement of the sibling. Such a child has more appropriately permeable boundaries and is more likely to develop a higher level of differentiation of self than either of the parents or the sibling.

Interventions and Techniques

In addition to techniques that have been developed within the Bowen family model, interventions based on structural and strategic approaches have been found useful with Level III families (Bergman, 1985; Beavers & Hampson, 1990). These interventions will be discussed along with those developed specifically within the Bowen approach.

Engagement.   Connecting with the Level III family is difficult. Since high emotionality within the system is a characteristic of these families, the practitioner must be extremely careful not to be drawn into the system by reacting emotionally to the "undertow" that will be felt immediately upon contact. There is a power struggle in these families, and the practitioner who is co-opted into it immediately stabilizes the system, providing it with homeostasis rather than change. This requires practitioners to control their automatic emotional participation in the emotional process.

> *This control I have called detriangling. The concept of triangles provides a way of reading the automatic emotional responsiveness so as to control one's own automatic emotional participation in the emotional process. . . . No one ever stays outside (the emotional system), but a knowledge of triangles makes it possible to get outside of one's own initiative while staying emotionally in contact with the family. (Bowen, 1976, p. 53)*

When the practitioner operationalizes the principle of detriangling, she or he remains well connected and emotionally involved with the family, but is experienced as a casual but concerned individual. Beavers and Hampson (1990) refer to this technique as the practitioner maintaining a "meta-position to the family in a manner that can induce change.... Such a system exerts maximum pressure on therapists to be somebody other than themselves" (p. 156). Another way of describing such a response to a family system is to "have a life philosophy of not taking too many things seriously" (Bergman, 1985). This approach is sometimes referred to as the practitioner remaining "one-down" to the family.

A Level III family presents as a powerful force in the interview setting. The practitioner has to be careful not to appear to disagree with—or worse, appear to ignore—the excessive statements of a member describing the sad state of affairs in the family: a rebellious and disrespectful son; a wife who is incompetent as a mother; a verbally and emotionally abusive husband and father. It is extremely important to join with each member of the family in such a way as to communicate to each a level of respect and interest. Among the implications of this approach is that it would preclude siding with any member against another.

Bergman (1985) suggests extensive use of *joining* techniques in the first interview. These procedures were developed by Minuchin in his structural approach and involve underscoring similarities between the practitioner and the family as their story unfolds. Similarities might involve common histories, such as where one is born; socioeconomic situation; and similar family structure such as birth order, or other cultural similarities.

Joining with each member of a Level III family is not easy. Beavers and Hampson (1990) remind us that it is extremely tempting to forget systemic thinking and find villains. The villains are always there, and identifying them as such always means a confrontation. Such a confrontation at this early stage of involvement nearly always results in the family not returning. The overtly powerful family member is a person who is experiencing pain and misery along with every other member of the family. Joining means going beneath the power struggle and connecting with the pain and loneliness each of these individuals feels as well. The flip side of not finding a villain is not rescuing a victim. In these families the system is a controlling one. Although one individual may appear more overtly in control, there is no greater control than that exercised by the most passive member of the family.

Passivity may be incorrectly perceived by the therapist when cross-cultural differences are not taken into consideration. Overt behaviors may at first appear passive when in actuality the family member is actively engaged in a nonverbal manner.

In families with members exerting influence through passivity, joining can be initially instituted on an emotional level through nonverbal exchanges. These characteristics fit within the Irish and Anglo cultures of the case study family (McGoldrick, Giordano, & Pearce, 1996). In the case of the Callahan family, Carmen influences the family through passivity. As a more active oral participation by Carmen in the interview is encouraged, its generation will be difficult. The practitioner must be prepared to navigate possible derisive comments from Bill Sr. countered by supportive comments from Bill Jr.

Joining can and must be accomplished within the context of conflict. However, it is important that the practitioner offer a safe environment for the joining process to occur. While being careful not to appear to be walking on eggshells, in dealing with the Level III family the practitioner will walk a tightrope.

Genogram

Bowen developed the use of a graphic representation of the multigenerational family. The genogram is both an assessment tool and an intervention tool. It can be used with the family as a way of gathering data and organizing it before their eyes. Family members begin to identify patterns in relationships; nodal events in the history of the family that occurred simultaneously, such as births, illnesses, and deaths; and other stressors in the life of the family that led to emotional cutoffs or added to the level of chronic anxiety present in the extended family system. The practitioner will find this graphic presentation particularly useful in identifying the intergenerational triangulation process that is so significant in maintaining fusion in families. The genogram is the major instrument used in assessing the premorbid state of the family.

The genogram is incorporated into the first interview with the Callahan family, and is shown in Figure 10.1. By engaging the parents in an exploration of their own families of origin, all family members may briefly detach from the current dilemma in the nuclear family. Bill Jr. and Sonia become an audience for their parents as each is led in an exploration of earlier events in their lives. Only after the past is thoroughly explored with each of the parents will the immediate nuclear family be drawn on the genogram. Even then, the practitioner must be careful not to identify too quickly the nature of the relationships between family members in the nuclear family. Such observations may be made by the family members themselves, but they are best left by the practitioner to later interviews. At this tender stage in the joining process with such an emotionally volatile family, adults easily hear any interpretation of problems in their past as accusations of responsibility in the present. This response will raise anxiety and increase the difficulty of the joining process. Culture-specific discussion may be included at this point in order to examine how tradition and historical context can influence a family's schema. The genogram should be treated as an exploration process that provides both information for personal thought during and after the interview, and information to be used in future contacts with the family, particularly in individual coaching sessions with members of the family.

Coaching

"Coaching" is the term used by Bowen (1978) and his colleagues to describe the ongoing consultative process in family of origin therapy (Carter & McGoldrick, 1988). It consists of work done with family members (usually on an individual basis) to identify multigenerational dynamics and issues that are limiting individual and family functioning. Following this initial exploration, plans are then developed to guide the individual in a deliberate and a conscious manner to make contact and interact with specific members of the nuclear and extended families. The purpose of these contacts is to bring into balance old relationship patterns and to neutralize toxic issues. The process is intended to provide an opportunity for direct renegotiations of emotional ties that have a significant bearing on the ability of individuals to remain attached to significant others while not losing their autonomy in relation to the significant others. In other words, the individual should be able to reenter the emotional field of the family without being overwhelmed by it.

Coaching is intended to reverse the processes of enmeshment, cut-off, and triangulation that occur as family systems develop tension over time. The goal of coaching is to bring about open adult relationships among family members such that the individuals involved may share themselves without emotional reactivity distorting the sharing.

It will be important for Bill Sr. and Carmen to reconnect with living members of their families of origin in a more open manner. Bill Sr. has only occasional and mostly superficial contacts with his brother and sister. He is totally cut off from his stepmother and half-brother and half-sister, as shown in Figure 10.1. Carmen continues to be overinvolved with her mother and has only occasional contact with her brother.

Steps in the coaching process include detriangling, person-to-person contact, reversals, and reconnecting.

Detriangling involves the deliberate act of shifting one's allegiance from a person with whom one is overly close to another in the same triangle from whom one is more distant. This might involve taking sides with the more distant one, or refusing to listen to a critical comment made by the closer person about the more distant one. In the case of interracial or cross-cultural families, connection to family members of the opposite couple member can be facilitated in small steps. Person-to-person contact, such as a member asking for ethnic recipes or family stories, encourages directness, limits triangulation, and supports connection (McGoldrick et al., 1996). In the case of the Callahan family, Carmen might be coached to increase contacts with her brother while at the same time refusing to join with her mother in discussions of her brother's incompetencies and failures.

Person-to-person contact involves planning a contact with a family member in order to share something meaningful with that person. Bill Sr. might visit or write to his brother or sister and tell them how important they have been in his life. Or he might share some genuine concerns with that person. The idea is to move from a distanced or overclose relationship to an experience of intimacy.

Reversals are deliberate efforts to behave in an opposite fashion from that expected of you. This aspect of coaching will be important in altering the relationship between Bill Sr. and Carmen. Bill might be coached to demonstrate confidence in Carmen by asking her if she is willing to attend a parenting group that deals with teenage use of alcohol. He must be able to convince her that he believes she can bring back information useful to him and to Bill Jr., and that he is not trying to set her up for later criticism. Any new behavior that more accurately communicates who the person is is appropriate, as is surprising others by responding to a situation differently from one's typical way. An example is not taking so many things seriously, or finding humor in the criticisms of others.

Reconnecting involves expanding one's contacts within the nuclear family in order to broaden the network of persons with whom one is involved. Opening new lines of communication will reduce cutoffs and diffuse overinvolved nuclear-family relationships. Although it will be difficult to accomplish, the practitioner working with Bill Sr. may coach him to connect with his stepmother and step-siblings. Such actions would not be early goals in the treatment process.

Paradoxes and Other Side-Door, Back-Door Methods

Beavers and Hampson (1990) recalled the injunction of noted family therapist, Carl Whitaker, that practitioners should always leave the initiative and control of the family in the hands of the family and the control of the sessions in the hands of the practitioner. In order to maintain control of the session, many practitioners believe they must use indirect methods, which are a way of avoiding head-to-head power struggles. Prescribing symptoms, prescribing setbacks, and blessing the status quo are suggested by Beavers and Hampson (1990) as ways of avoiding linear power struggles. They caution, however, that such procedures must not be gimmicks, but must represent the genuine assessment of the practitioner that such an action is the appropriate one for the family to take. "Paradoxical interventions are only effective when they are not paradoxical, we say paradoxically" (Beavers & Hampson, 1990, p. 159).

Other practitioners have developed techniques to incorporate storytelling into their family sessions, drawing from social constructionism. Usually those stories are unplanned and spontaneous, and come out of the practitioner's own personal experience. Such stories may carry embedded meanings, suggest ideas, touch emotional states and attitudes, or provide a parallel to a family member's view of the world or to their own current situation. Stories may be useful in derailing family members' control efforts and avoiding direct conflict with these members. The Callahan family may respond positively to the use of stories, remembering the heritage of storytelling and humor as passed through many Irish-American family members (McGoldrick et al., 1996). For an extensive discussion of storytelling in family practice, see Combs and Freedman (1990).

Evaluation of Effectiveness

Extensive studies have been reported regarding the clinical relevance of the multi-generational model of family therapy (Bowen, 1957, 1966, 1976, 1978; Guerin, 1976). Most are anecdotal and rely on the practitioner's judgment regarding the accuracy of assessments and the effectiveness of interventions. Few scales exist that are of sufficient validity and reliability to serve well a practitioner committed to measuring the outcomes of family practice, particularly one who is attempting to measure aspects of family systems thinking. When considering additional characteristics of families, such as the presence of alcoholism (Rolls, 1995), refugee status (Kelly, 1994), injuries (Sachs & Ellenberg, 1994), and adolescent violence (Mucucci, 1995), the outcome evaluation may incorporate assessment of systems concepts, as well as other indicators of family and individual functioning (Harris, 1996).

As much as systems thinking has assisted practitioners in assessment and evaluation of families, there are limitations that must be remembered. A purist approach to systems thinking may disregard the social and historical contexts in which families find themselves (Berman, 1996). Additionally, the metaphors of family systems theory themselves obscure various issues pertinent to system analysis or evaluation (Rosenblatt, 1994): observer subjectivity, randomness of family events, individual functioning in isolation, embeddedness within multiple systems, fluidity of the family entity itself, and so on.

Application to Families on Levels I, II, and IV

For the most part, families at Levels I and II respond to more straightforward interventions, such as those described in Chapters 6, 7, and 8. However, the genogram is quite useful to the practitioner in working with any family to determine the extent to stress being experienced by the family through the extended family system. Whereas a practitioner may often use the genogram with the Level III family as an intervention as well as an assessment tool, it may be used more indirectly with a Level I or Level II family. The practitioner may construct the genogram outside of the clinical setting, utilizing data gleaned in family contacts, rather than directly with the family as a mutual discovery process. Level IV families often find working through the genogram experience in the interview setting to be enriching.

Summary

Level III families usually pose a significant challenge to practitioners working with them. The challenge exists not so much because they have fewer resources than other families, since often they are well defended and have coped well at various times over the years. Rather, the greatest challenge is the vulnerability of the practitioner. Many of the issues confronting the Level III families are those that the practitioner's own family has addressed and may be continuing to address. The reverberations of the presenting family may set off vibrations within the practitioner that are like an undertow pulling her or him into the presenting family's systemic process. The wise practitioner is sensitive to these forces and learns to "move with the flow," soon to resurface, all the while maintaining some distance and control in the interview process. Bowen's intergenerational approach provides excellent markers for assessment and intervention strategies.

Discussion Questions

1. What subsystem does this theory suggest as the focal point of intervention?
2. How does the strengths perspective affect the way this theory is applied?
3. Explain a point of fusion in your own immediate family of origin that would involve you and state how you would modify this triangle.
4. Why does Bowen describe the triangle as "the smallest stable relationship system"?

5. Describe the techniques used by the practitioners to maintain a metaposition with respect to the family.
6. Why are Level III families difficult to engage in the treatment process, and what techniques from Bowen's family systems model can be used to overcome this problem?
7. Discuss the interventions used in treating Level III families and the hazards or precautions that practitioners must be aware of in treating these families.
8. Discuss the purposes, goals, and steps involved in the process of "coaching." How would you apply this process in your own family?

Suggested Readings

Bowen, M. (1978). *Family therapy in clinical practice.* New York: Jason Aronson.

This is a compilation of most of Murray Bowen's significant writings. Any serious student of the intergenerational approach will more fully grasp the central concepts of this approach by reading the papers and presentations that first presented the ideas.

Gilbert, R. M. (1992). *Extraordinary relationships: A new way of thinking about human interactions.* Minneapolis: Chronimed.

This book is based on Murray Bowen's family systems theory. It gives a blueprint to better relationships and tells how the principles of Bowen's family theory can be used in all areas of life. Roberta Gilbert studied and worked with Bowen and has presented here a most helpful formulation and application of his theory. It is a refreshing alternative to common self-help approaches. Every chapter can be seen as a therapy session in itself.

Guerin, P. J., Fay, L. F., Burden, S. L., & Kautto, J. G. (1987). *The evaluation and treatment of marital conflict.* New York: Basic Books.

These writers have developed an excellent application of Bowen's intergenerational concepts. Although primarily focused on couples, the presentation easily lends itself to broader applications within the family.

McGoldrick, M., & Gerson, R. (1985). *Genograms in family assessment.* New York: Norton.

The genogram is a primary assessment tool when working with families from an intergenerational approach. These authors provide a comprehensive outline for organizing the great variety of material gleaned through a genogram. Their illustrations are interesting and clearly present their ideas.

References

Beavers, W. R., & Hampson, R. B. (1990). *Successful families: Assessment and intervention.* New York: Norton.

Bergman, J. S. (1985). *Fishing for barracuda.* New York: Norton.

Berman, M. (1996). The shadow side of systems theory. *Journal of Humanistic Psychology, 36,* 28–54.

Bowen, M. (1957). *Treatment of family groups with a schizophrenic member.* Paper presented at the annual meeting of the American Orthopsychiatric Association, Chicago. In M. Bowen (1978), *Family therapy in clinical practice.* New York: Jason Aronson.

Bowen, M. (1966). The use of family therapy in clinical practice. *Comprehensive Psychiatry, 7,* 345–374.

Bowen, M. (1976). Theory in the practice of psychotherapy. In P. J. Guerin (Ed.), *Family therapy: Theory and practice*. New York: Gardner Press.

Bowen, M. (1978). *Family therapy in clinical practice*. New York: Jason Aronson.

Carter, B., & McGoldrick, M. (1988). *The family life cycle* (2nd ed.). New York: Gardner Press.

Combs, G., & Freedman, J. (1990). *Symbol, story and ceremony*. New York: Norton.

Guerin, P. J. (Ed.). (1976). *Family therapy*. New York: Gardner Press.

Guerin, P. J., Fay, L. F., Burden, S. L., & Kautto, J. G. (1987). *The evaluation and treatment of marital conflict*. New York: Basic Books.

Harris, S. M. (1996). Bowen and symbolic experiential family theories: Strange bedfellows or isomorphs of life. *Journal of Family Psychotherapy, 7*(3), 39–60.

Kelly, P. (1994). Integrating systemic and postsystemic approaches to social work practice with refugee families. *Families in Society, 75,* 541–549.

McGoldrick, M., Giordano, J., & Pearce, J. K. (Eds.). (1996). *Ethnicity and family therapy* (2nd ed.). New York: Guilford Press.

Minuchin, S., Rosman, B. L., & Baker, L. (1978). *Psychosomatic families*. Cambridge, MA: Harvard University Press.

Mucucci, J. A. (1995). Adolescents who assault their parents: A family systems approach to treatment. Special Issue: Adolescent treatment: New frontiers and new dimensions. *Psychotherapy, 32,* 154–161.

Rolls, J. A. (1995). The recovering female alcoholic: A family affair. *Contemporary Family Therapy: An International Journal, 17,* 317–329.

Rosenblatt, P. (1994). *Metaphors of family systems theory*. New York: Guilford Press.

Sachs, P. R., & Ellenberg, D. B. (1994). The family system and adaptation to an injured worker. *American Journal of Family Therapy, 22,* 263–272.

Weltner, J. S. (1985). Matchmaking: Choosing the appropriate therapy for families at various levels of pathology. In M. P. Mirken & S. L. Koman (Eds.), *Handbook of adolescents and family therapy* (pp. 39–50). New York: Gardner Press.

Fourth Level of Family Need: Family and Personal Growth Issues

Families on Level IV of family need have their basic needs met. There is adequate parenting, and structural boundaries and limits are relatively clear. Generally there exist generational boundaries and parent–child differentiation, and personal and family growth are the primary issues. Presenting problems often focus on the wish for greater intimacy and commitment, more adult autonomy, interpersonal competence, self-actualization, more constructive resolution of conflict, or changing destructive patterns. Based on the accomplishment of lower-level needs, this higher level of need is represented by a focus on inner richness and quality of life in the house that the family is building.

The two chapters in this section offer ways to work with families who have needs at Level IV and are experiencing growth issues at that level. The first is narrative family interventions, discussed in Chapter 11 by Kurtz, Tandy, and Shields. Their emphasis is on the meanings families make of problems, instead of the cause of the problem, making use of a collaborative, co-learning therapeutic relationship.

A second approach is presented in Chapter 12 by Kilpatrick and Kilpatrick. Object relations family intervention is a bridge between working with individuals and working with families, and is essentially interactional in its treatment processes.

Chapter 11

Narrative Family Interventions

P. DAVID KURTZ, Ph.D., CYNTHIA C. TANDY, M.S.W.,
and JOHN P. SHIELDS, M.S.W.

We all have stories of our life experiences. Some of these stories we tell to others, and some we keep private. From a social constructionist point of view, these stories are much more than simply the mirroring of life. Instead, metaphorically speaking, people live their lives by stories, or the narrative. The narrative serves to interpret life experiences, to give them meaning, to make sense of them. These stories (1) determine which features of the experience persons choose for expression, (2) the interpretation or meaning that persons give to the experience, and (3) insofar as behavior is prefigured by the meaning making, stories shape actions (White, 1993). The dominant story of a troubled family is usually a disempowering and pathologizing description of each member and the relationships among the members. Using a narrative approach to treatment, the therapist facilitates the bringing forth of the problem-saturated story. And, primarily through the use of curious questions that enable family members to attend to other features of their lived experiences, they are able to bring forth alternative stories. The process of narrating and witnessing the new or alternative stories helps to inform new meaning. This restorying process creates possibilities for alternative meanings and, correspondingly, alternative ways of acting. In the narrative approach, it is imperative that the therapist see the family members as experts in their own lives, validate the meaning they give their problem stories, and assist them to bring forth their alternative stories.

Family Problems

Lisa believed in a world of spirits, thought energy, and other extrasensory powers. To her dismay, she often didn't "fit in" socially. She described feeling dejected and alone, and yearned to accomplish more in life. Her goal in therapy was to have more successful relationships while focusing on her spiritual concerns. Lisa's therapists accepted her and her assumptions, and diligently attempted to understand her unusual ideas and their effects on her life and relationships. New understandings were created by using Lisa's language and story (Joyce & Taylor, 1990).

Lyn, age 15, was described by her mother as a chronic worrier with a history of depression. Their therapist, a social worker, asked Lyn how long she and her family had been "under the influence of Worry," and how she and her family had responded to it. How had they attempted to find solutions? How often did Lyn "lead Worry around by the nose," and how often did it control her? Were she and her family satisfied with this situation, or would they "stage a comeback and rally against further domination" (Esler, 1987, pp. 16, 18)?

Pauline described herself as a "clam," concealing her thoughts and emotions, close to no one aside from her son. Lately, however, she had become quite emotional and frequently a bit confused. She was experiencing herself and her feelings differently, and was uncomfortable with the change because it contradicted her problem-saturated story of herself as having been trained to a lifetime of stoicism by cold, aloof parents. The practitioner asked her, "If I could look into your past, what might I see that would have enabled me to predict that you would be able to become emotionally aware and sensitive, and that you would encourage this in your son?" Pauline slowly began to recover memories of emotional openness that challenged her dominant story as a person without feelings (Hewson, 1991).

Each of these examples reveals individual and family self-narratives, and therapist responses of respect for individuals' experiences, beliefs, and language. In Lisa's case, the therapist listened intently to her transpersonal story, accepted her assumptions, and assisted her in developing new ways for her to make sense of her experiences. Lyn's problem was "externalized" or separated from her; this separation implied that she had some ability to control or influence the metaphor of "Worry" (Esler, 1987). Pauline's problem-saturated story of emotional detachment was challenged as memories were brought forth that she had previously ignored. These memories were given meaning and significance. Little by little, Pauline recognized them as evidence that she had always valued, if not practiced, emotional openness. Pauline's dominant story of herself as an emotionally dead "clam" had been shaped by her selected memories. She decided that a drastic change was not necessary, and that she had merely gone through a "temporary phase" of thinking of herself as emotionally closed (Hewson, 1991).

The narrative framework along with several related approaches to family therapy is based in the metatheory of social constructionism, as discussed in Chapter 2. In this postmodern model, the emphasis is on the meanings attributed to problems, rather than to their causes. Reality is assumed to be invented, rather than discovered, and derived from individuals' beliefs, values, culturally based attitudes, and feelings (Hoffman, 1985; Neimeyer, 1993b). We make the assumption that we create versions of our lives as we attempt to make sense of any particular situation. Using a text analogy, we can say that the meanings of our versions flow and evolve in the form of stories, or self-narratives. Similarly, meanings are cocreated between individuals as they communicate. Lynn Hoffman illustrated this point by quoting comedian Steven Wright: "I have a seashell collection. I keep it scattered on beaches all over the world." The collection exists in the interchange and cocreation of meaning between comedian and audience, not as "reality" in the comedian's mind or in the world-out-there (Hoffman, 1990, p. 3).

We cannot include every experience in our life stories. Our current attitudes alter what we remember, and what we remember strengthens our commitment to those attitudes. Like Pauline, we selectively include or exclude information to "fit" into the dominant yet ever-changing stories that we are creating and that we perceive others are creating about us (White & Epston, 1990; Hewson, 1991). According to Gregory Bateson (1972), if the information "fits" into the way we view ourselves (our dominant story), we keep it. If it is information that doesn't fit the story, we disregard it or throw it out. Thus, distant and recent memories inform and shape the current living as well as future retelling of our story.

Furthermore, each selected memory carries meaning or personal significance that allows one to make sense of and find continuity in one's experiences. The meanings that individuals and families attach to situations and events influence their behavior around those events. Without planning or intending to, individuals support and maintain problems. They cooperate with the problem until it seems to develop its own lifestyle or "career" (White & Epston, 1990).

It becomes the therapist's job, through a process of therapeutic conversations, to assist in drawing out and identifying experiences from the past that are exceptions to the individual's problem-saturated, old story. The exceptions or unique outcomes are evidence that, upon occasion, the person has not experienced, or has successfully challenged, the problem. As the significance and impact of the exceptions are explored and elaborated, the individual's sense of personal efficacy intensifies. Exceptions with their new, re-authored meanings contribute to the new story's past history. The therapist, and eventually the client, can then decline to accept the validity of the old story (White & Epston, 1990; Hewson, 1991).

The narrative framework is appropriate for Level IV individuals and families, and for the other levels as well. In the three vignettes at the beginning of this chapter, each individual and family could be described as having needs at Level IV. Nevertheless, probably the best-known narrative example is Michael White's (1988/1989) case study of Nick and "Sneaky Poo," which describes a family that appears to have Level III needs. The case illustrates some narrative treatment techniques often utilized for both children and adults at all four levels.

Before introducing the case, however, it is important to understand the place of assessment within the narrative model. Assessment from the narrative perspective is not concerned with diagnoses or classification into pathologizing categories, but rather is an intervention itself, concerned with the bringing forth of stories from a stance of respectful curiosity. Assessment occurs through enactment of a person's stories rather than through the uncovering of "facts." When stories and their meanings are revealed, strengths emerge. Alternative stories (Nick, who can outsmart Sneaky Poo) can "deconstruct" the dominant, problem-saturated story (Nick, who has an entrenched history of an embarrassing problem of encopresis).

Thus, assessment and treatment are not separate processes, but become blurred (Epston, 1993b). This explanation of assessment is intended to increase the reader's understanding of the language employed in the Sneaky Poo case, which follows.

Family Case Assessment

Ron and Sue arrived with their six-year-old son, Nick, who had a long history of encopresis and many past visits to other therapists. Daily "accidents" of soiling his underwear occurred. Nick had virtually turned the "poo" into his pal. He smeared it up walls, under tables, and into corners. The poo trotted along to the bathroom with Nick at bath time, where Nick would squeeze it into the tub and shower drains.

White began by assessing the effect the problem was having on the family. It was preventing Nick from maintaining friendships with other children. It was too embarrassing for Nick to invite his friends for sleepovers, and it was likewise impossible for him to visit them. The poo was particularly cruel to Sue, as she felt its presence proved her to be less than a "good mother." Sue felt overwhelmed with guilt and despaired of ever being an adequate parent. Sneaky Poo was just as humiliating a secret for Ron. The embarrassment prevented him from talking to friends about it, as he would freely do with other problems.

Further, Sneaky Poo was wreaking havoc on the relationships between the family members. It was straining the relationship between Nick and Sue. The relationship between Nick and Ron had likewise "suffered considerably under the reign of terror perpetrated by the poo." Sue and Ron were rarely able to spend time together and talk casually; their conversations seemed dominated by Nick and the poo.

After talking about how the problem had been negatively affecting the family, White inquired about how the family had been affecting or influencing the "life" of Sneaky Poo. Nick was able to remember and describe situations in which he defied Sneaky Poo and refused to fall for its attempts to trick him into "smearing" or "plastering." During these occasions, Nick had outsmarted Sneaky Poo, refusing to play its games. In addition, Nick was doubtful that Sneaky Poo had managed to destroy all the love between Nick and his parents. Sue recalled an incident during which she refused Sneaky Poo's invitation to retreat into guilt and misery. Instead, she focused her attention on music rather than on her supposed inabilities as a parent. In spite of Sneaky Poo, she still had moments of enjoyment with her son.

While Ron had not yet given up on his relationship with Nick, he insisted that there were no situations in which he had defied the embarrassment of Sneaky Poo and its effects of isolating him from friends and coworkers. He decided, however, that he was interested in protesting Sneaky Poo's demands by confiding the humiliating secret to a coworker.

Treatment Goals

Michael White deliberately externalized or separated the oppressing problem of encopresis from Nick. This removed blame from Nick as the "identified patient" with a long history of the problem and previously failed therapies. Instead, White focused on the *problem* as the problem, and encouraged the family to explore the detrimental effects the problem had on them. He encouraged the family to organize their strengths and resources in challenging their oppressive story of encopresis. He actively facilitated their finding significance and meaning in their occasionally successful encounters with Sneaky Poo. The dilemma of whether to cooperate with the problem or to protest against it was raised. The family was presented with the options of resisting or acquiescing to encopresis. Refusal to cooperate with the problem began to undermine its effects and "life-support system." The family was encouraged to build on successes so that their story might be re-authored into a new story of a family that has conquered the problem of encopresis.

At a six-month follow-up session White heard a new story in which Sneaky Poo was unable to trick Nick into playing with it again. Nick was doing much better in school and with his friends, and the family was delighted with his progress.

Intervention Approach

Theory Base and Major Tenets

The narrative model has been developed and elaborated in the past few years by Michael White and David Epston. The narrative approach is a postmodern framework in its recognition of social and political influences and constraints and in its agreement with the social constructionist contention that "reality" is a social construct. Although congruous theoretically, narrative therapy and the solution-focused therapy defined by Steve de Shazer have distinct differences (Chang & Phillips, 1993). Specifically, these authors note differences in therapeutic intent and the stance toward the problem. Despite important differences, narrative and solution-focused therapies are focused on strengths and solutions, placing these methods at the cutting edge of the constructionist perspective. Major theoretical and philosophical influences have included Michel Foucault, Gregory Bateson, and Jerome Bruner. Their contributions may be seen in three types of assumptions of the narrative model: theory of power and oppression, theory of problems, and theory of change.

Theory of Power and Oppression.   Michel Foucault, a French philosopher, had much to say about society and power. According to Foucault (1979, 1980), a dominant knowledge is imposed by society. The culture shapes behavior and trains individuals to conform, and in turn to judge those who refuse to or are unable to follow the prescribed norms. Those who conform to the dominant or expert knowledge are accepted, but nonconformists come under the "gaze" of others and are viewed as deviants. Psychotherapists are trained to identify and label individual deviants with clinical diagnoses such as obsessive, alcoholic, or codependent. Family therapists also have their own language for categorizing or storying families as enmeshed, blended, triangulated, and so on. The language of the broader society is also filled with words and phrases that convey less-than-acceptable or normal behavior such as "gay/alternative lifestyles," or even "single parents." Deviants are often isolated and persecuted, and such reactions can provoke more deviant behavior (Besa, 1994).

Drawing extensively on the ideas of Foucault, Michael White aligns with individuals and families in protesting oppressing social forces and problematic beliefs. The creative exchanges he calls "externalizing conversations" (Tomm, 1993) are not merely reflective of a technique designed to depersonalize the problem. They also enable families to objectify the problem and to protest its oppression. For example, women, who for years have come under that "gaze" of the cultural value that "thin is beautiful/perfect," come to see themselves under the influence of anorexia (rather than being anorectic) and begin to take a stand for antianorectic ways for self and others.

White and Epston (1990) and Madigan (1991) have cautioned professionals to be aware that because the therapeutic situation lies within the domains of power and knowledge, it always includes the possibility of social control and is never value-free, apolitical, or context-free. Therapists approach a therapeutic situation with their own narrative that may limit or shape what they think is relevant or important in a client's story (Hart, 1995). Therapists and family members alike are subject to restraints of race, gender, culture, and theoretical position (see Chapter 2 for a discussion of this issue) (White, Summer 1989; Fish, 1993).

The narrative tradition stands theoretically distinct from the restraints of deterministic theories and frameworks. David Epston (1984) contrasted narrative therapy with "therapies of degradation" and "missionary" therapies. These approaches, he argued, seek to rank individuals according to notions of pathology and "correct" behavior. They imply that "truth" is possessed by the therapist (messengers of society) and will somehow be forced upon the "dysfunctional" and probably "resistant" client. The narrative model, on the other hand, assumes a respectful attitude toward human variation, avoids pathologizing, and places particular value upon personal responsibility (Anoretic & Anoretic, 1991).

Theory of Problems. Gregory Bateson (1972, 1979) argued that individuals behave according to information that they have selected out according to its meaning or significance. If it has no significance and doesn't fit into the individual's perceived pattern or dominant story, then it has virtually no existence as fact (White & Epston, 1990). Problems develop as the inevitable consequences of "vicious cycles" of events that are inadvertently reinforced. Problems are maintained even though solutions may have been attempted, because nothing has happened to break the cycle and allow new information or "news of a difference" to enter the individual's world of meaning.

Not only has the cycle remained intact, but restraints have operated to prevent changes. These restraints may take the form of beliefs, presuppositions, assumptions, or attitudes that prevent individuals and families from noticing new information. "They may claim to have heard it all before, when in fact, they have never heard it" (Anoretic & Anoretic, 1991, p. 142). Thus, restraints may prevent people from noticing at-hand information about their own strengths and abilities to deal with the problem. For instance, a battered woman may escape to a shelter and then return to her abuser because she believes she cannot survive economically without him. Or, a middle-aged man may remain miserable in a boring, unfulfilling job because he fears the scorn of family and friends should he make a career change.

In each of these examples, individuals had dominant stories of themselves ("I can't survive without him"/"I'd be crazy to leave this steady job") that conflicted with alternative stories of themselves with happier lives (an independent woman/ a man with a more challenging career). This is the point at which families and individuals often seek therapy (White & Epston, 1990). The problem and its oppression of individuals can be deliberately "placed" by the therapist outside the individual or family. The cause is not sought. White argues that the search for a cause is itself a problem, leading to vicious cycles of blame and guilt.

Likewise, the concept of a symptom's function is foreign to the narrative approach (Chang & Phillips, 1993) and serves only to distract from the problem and its effects on the individual or family. In the narrative model, symptom functionality is replaced by the view that problems are inevitable, that restraints have prevented the discovery of effective solutions. As these negative explanations are employed, the pertinent question is not "Why are things this way?" but "What has stopped things from being different?" (Anoretic & Anoretic, 1991).

"News of a difference" is news that makes a difference. It provides a twist that allows the individual and family to see and experience the old story in a new way. The changed meaning provides a new story line for daily living. For example, Jeff, a 34-year-old male who was attending marital therapy with his wife, found new meaning in his rebelliousness. He realized that rather than "rebelling against" his family of origin, he had instead been "rebelling for" taking care of himself; now he was rebelling for his marriage.

Theory of Change.   According to Edward Bruner (1986) and Jerome Bruner (1990), stories provide the dominant means for individuals to structure or organize their lived experiences. As life stories are told with their inevitable gaps and inconsistencies, lives are changed through the process of interpreting situations and filling the gaps with both experiences and imagination. As narratives or stories are enacted or performed, they affect lives. In fact, White asserted, life is enactment of text, and the enactment of text is a process of re-authoring lives and relationships (White, 1988/1989). Hart (1995) challenges the apparent simplicity of this arrangement and warns therapists to be aware of their own narrative that may limit or shape what is chosen for re-authoring in a therapeutic situation.

The narrative therapist who is presented with a dominant, problem-filled story challenges it by focusing predominantly on previously disregarded exceptions (or "unique outcomes") to the dominant story. The narrative therapist attempts to cocreate with the family new ideas, new information, and new perceptions around the exceptions that will challenge former presuppositions and create a context for change (Anoretic & Anoretic, 1991). As problem-saturated beliefs are challenged, possibilities for alternative ways of behaving are enhanced. These alternative ways compose the new story, which can gradually replace the steadily less influential old story. In the case of children, it is often effective to tune into their fantasies and imaginations as well as their behaviors. These can be rich sources for identifying exceptions and authoring solution-focused stories.

Interventions and Techniques

The style of narrative therapy is caring, collaborative, curious, conversational, and cautious. All who are involved in the therapeutic endeavor are viewed as cocreators of any transformations that occur. Accordingly, the professional does not cause change, but simply provides the opportunity for change to occur (Sluzki, 1992). The style and behavior of the narrative family therapist is akin to that of a curious explorer or researcher who intends to discover and challenge restraining patterns of ideas, beliefs, and contexts (Tomm, 1988; Anoretic & Anoretic, 1991).

One of the primary techniques of this approach is the use of a variety of questions. The narrative therapist asks many gentle, curious, respectful questions in this process of interventive interviewing. It is assumed that questions will elicit experiences of exceptions, which is the stuff of restorying (Tomm, 1987; White & Epston, 1990). Curious questions, by and large, are the means by which restraining patterns are revealed and challenged. New opportunities are discovered for positive, affirmative, more flexible action around the problem. As part of this search, any information that represents positive moves toward change is noticed, seized upon, and highlighted. Language and metaphors are used creatively.

Narrative interventions include an eclectic collection of treatment methods, of which any or all may be used. Several of the more commonly used techniques are described in the following paragraphs. The order is intended to reflect a somewhat logical sequence, although some interventive methods can be repeated many times or possibly even eliminated. The process should be seen as rather more like loops and curves than steps.

1. *Externalization of the problem.* Michael Anoretic (1989) described meeting for the first time a family of five who had been referred because of the eight-year-old's tantrums. When Anoretic entered the room, the father greeted him: "Hello. I'm George Adams. This is my wife Mary, my daughter Susan, my son John, and this (gesturing towards the youngest) is the problem!" (p. 4). What is the effect of such a statement? Can the child feel that he has any ability to exercise self-control? After all, he is the problem! Such a classifying and objectifying description, Anoretic argued, damages a child's self-esteem and adds to feelings of hopelessness. It weakens the family's ability to see possibilities for change. A cycle is set in motion: the very language they use suggests that change is unlikely.

In the earlier family case, Michael White first attempted to externalize the problem of encopresis by giving it the name "Sneaky Poo." This clever and sometimes humorous technique of naming the problem enables the family to combat the problem itself rather than one another. The problem is seen as the problem, rather than the person being the problem. Next, he engaged in externalizing the problem by discussing the influence of the problem on the family. Questions such as "How long have you been under the influence of the problem?" "How has the problem affected your family life?" and "How has the problem interfered with your relationships?" can enable family members to be ready to externalize the problem. White then proceeded to further externalize the problem by asking the family about the ways in which they stand up to it. How had the family managed to be effective against the problem? Children and adolescents in particular enjoy the imagery of pushing around, challenging, or defeating a problem.

Externalization is more than a reframing and depersonalizing of the problem. It is a way for families to gain control over the problem. As each person involved "faces up" to the problem, the therapist is not seen as being in control over the parents, and the parents are not in the position of controlling the child (Anoretic, 1989). Quite to the contrary, therapist and family work together to define the problem situation or pattern as something outside of and distinct from the "identified patient." As the problem is shaped through metaphor into an "entity" that can be named, the individual or family can distance themselves from the problem, challenge it, and defeat it (Neimeyer, 1993a).

Frequently, family members have had previous experience with therapists who have labored with them to "work through" or "come to terms" with particular "pathologies" or "dysfunctions." As a result, families are often restrained by the belief that a family member has intentionally maintained a problem or that the problem reflects a character defect or personality weakness. Externalizing the problem challenges these notions. For example, it may be more productive to work with a teen who is "under the influence of some habits" than one who "has a dependent, addictive personality." In addition, externalization allows the family to visualize the solution in terms of family teamwork against the problem rather than pitting family member against family member (Anoretic & Anoretic, 1991, p. 152).

2. *Influence (effect) of the problem* upon the person. In this process and the next (effect of the person on the problem), reciprocal patterns emerge that have been supporting the problem. The problem and its impact upon the individual's and family's life and relationships are scrutinized at length. The narrative therapist asks each family member to give a detailed, no-holds-barred account of the distressing effects of the problem and the extent to which each individual has been supervised (dominated, pushed around, controlled) by it. For example, if fear of inadequate parenting has been externalized, then the question, using the family's premise, might become "How is the *fear of failure* as a parent interfering in your family relationships?"

3. *Influence (effect) of the person* upon the problem is the "flip side" of the influence of the problem. Michael White (1986b) has referred to these combined questions as mapping the relative influence of the problem in the life of the person, and the person in the life of the problem. For instance, the question in the preceding paragraph, using the therapist's premise, now becomes "How much have you been able to *stand up to* the *fear of failure* as a parent and not *allow it to dominate* your family relationships?"

TABLE 11.1   Relative Influence Scale

A. To what extent has the problem of _____ been interfering with or dominating your life and relationships?

    (1) _____ rarely interferes with or dominates my life and relationships.

    (2)

    (3)

    (4)

    (5) Moderate interference

    (6)

    (7)

    (8)

    (9) _____ to an extreme extent has been interfering with or dominating my life and relationships.

B. Would you say the problem of _____ has been interfering with or dominating (what percentage) ____% of your life and relationships?

C. To what extent have you been successful in resisting the interference or domination of _____ in your life and relationships?

    (1) To no extent of success at all

    (2)

    (3)

    (4)

    (5) Moderate extent of success

    (6)

    (7)

    (8)

    (9) Successful resistance: _____ no longer dominates my life and relationships.

D. Would you say you have been (what percentage) ____% effective in resisting the interference or domination of _____?

From C. Tandy & J. P. Gallant, *Narrative therapy: A case study* (unpublished manuscript, University of Georgia, School of Social Work, Athens, 1993).

A simple, self-anchored "Relative Influence Scale" (see Table 11.1) was developed to function as a blend of assessment tool and intervention (Tandy & Gallant, 1993). It was designed to measure the relative influence of the problem/person at the beginning and end of therapy. The scale has been used in initial sessions with individuals at a community mental health center and then again several weeks later. Reactions were interesting: People were puzzled, intrigued, and surprised by the questions. One individual in particular, who had tamed a dangerous and troublesome temper problem, was pleased with both his new story and the scale that indicated to what extent he had turned the tables on his temper's previous hold on his life and relationships. Such an informal clinical scale creates possibilities and highlights personal efficacy.

The substantial content of narrative therapy (White, 1991) is found in questions relating to the relative influence of the person upon the problem (Exceptions Questions, History of Exceptions Questions, Significance Questions, and Spectator Questions). We will describe those questions in some detail. Before those questions are begun in earnest, however, the narrative therapist can raise some dilemmas.

4. *Collapsing time and raising dilemmas* highlights the relative influence of the problem. It also allows individuals to peer into the past and future and predict how the problem (e.g., "Trouble") might have developed, how it is likely to evolve, and then to make a decision around the resulting dilemma: Is it worth the effort to challenge "Trouble?" Some questions that might be introduced include the following:

- To a teen: Is Trouble more of a problem for you now than it was say, six months ago? How is the influence of Trouble different in your life now than it was then?
- To a teen: If you were to continue to allow Trouble to get the best of you, in what other ways would you invite your parents to treat you as fragile and protect you from their opinions?
- To the parents: If Worry gets a stronger grip, how might it invite your son/daughter to place responsibility for his future in your hands?

5. *Enhancing changes* can be accomplished through the respectful challenge of a client's dominant story. This serves to motivate individuals to reexamine their narratives, leading to an amplification of changes already under way. The goal here is to demolish the problem-saturated narrative and to begin to re-author a more adaptive story. Children and adolescents seem particularly open to this method and respond with energy and devotion to proving the problem-saturated story to be wrong. Motivational questions or comments may include these:

- To a teen: But wait a minute, you told me that you were always sad, and now you're telling me that you were happy on Saturday! Are you telling me that you were able to keep sad out of your life on Saturday?
- To a parent: You said you noticed that Billy kept fear from pushing him around and you were able to go to the mall. I don't get it! I thought you said fear controlled him all the time! Something is different here. What happened?

6. *Predicting setbacks* can be done before the dilemma (item 4) is even settled. Because the problem-saturated story still dominates, setbacks are virtually inevitable. Thus, they must be anticipated and their distress expected and planned for, but in a manner that highlights and encourages self-efficacy. The following example assumes that the family argues for change:

- If you are really determined to make a radical change in your relationship with Apathy, do you think you'll be able to handle a setback? Or will you be tricked by Apathy into returning to cooperate with it (White, 1986a)?

7. *Use of questions.* At this point, the narrative therapist can begin to ask many questions involving the influence of the person upon the problem.

- *Exceptions Questions.* Sometimes called unique outcome questions, these questions focus on situations of successful exceptional outcomes that don't square with the dominant, problem-filled, story. Some examples:

  - *When* could you have given in to Fear, but stood up to it instead?
  - *What* are the times when you resist the control of Irresponsibility?

- *History of Exceptions Questions.* Sometimes called unique account questions, they discover past clues to accounts of current competence. Michael White (1991) urged therapists to treat these discoveries as significant and as intriguing mysteries "that only persons can unravel as they respond to the therapist's curiosity about them. As persons take up the task of unraveling such mysteries, they immediately engage in storytelling and meaning-making" (p. 30). Some examples:

  - *How* did you achieve this? Have you been advising yourself differently?
  - *What* led up to it?

  Patterns of connecting ideas and beliefs can often be discovered through circular questions that involve other family members (Tomm, 1988). Such History of Exceptions Questions might be

  - *What* have you seen Ann doing that could reveal how she was able to achieve this?
  - *What* have you witnessed in your life that could have provided a clue that this development was a possibility for you?

- *Significance Questions.* Sometimes called "unique redescriptions questions," they search for and reveal the meanings, significance, and importance of the exceptions. Some examples:

  - What do you think these discoveries reveal to *you/me/your family* about your motives and what is important to you and your life?
  - In more fully appreciating John's achievement, what conclusions might you reach about what he stands for?

  Questions of significance help draw attention to the importance of the exception and the possibility of new meanings.

- *Spectator Questions.* Sometimes called experience-of-experience questions, they invite individuals to imagine how other people that they have known might experience them. For example:

  - If *I* had been able to look in on your earlier life, *what* might I have seen you doing that would reveal to me how you have been able to take this step?

- Of all who have known you, *who* would be the least surprised that you have been able to challenge Trouble, and *what* would they have seen that would enable them to predict it?

Questions such as these are effective in bringing forth alternative "landscapes" of action (White, 1991). They encourage the articulation and performance of these alternative actions.

   8. *Reflecting team.* As Tom Andersen (1991) became curious about ways to introduce more available but unasked questions during family therapy conversations, he and his colleagues developed the "reflecting team." The feedback provided by the reflecting team includes new descriptions to add to those that have been brought forth by the family and the therapist. A team of observers (from one to several), functioning as an audience, silently listens to the therapist and family. At a designated time, the therapist invites the team to share its observations with one another about what they have just observed. The family and therapist silently listen to the team, which reflects upon the story of the family with positive and curious comments and questions. Questions often begin with "I seemed to notice..." or "I couldn't help but wonder what would happen if..." The team attempts to be sensitive, imaginative, and respectful, and to avoid any negative connotations, advice, or criticism. They introduce new ideas, bring out unnoticed exceptions, and expand the family's new story. This process usually lasts about five minutes, after which the family and therapist can reflect with each other upon the reflecting team's conversation (Andersen, 1991).

   9. *Letters and audiotapes* can serve as media for continuation of the dialogue between therapist and family members. Therapist-authored letters and tapes can be rich sources for summarizing sessions, highlighting emerging new stories, and rendering lived experience into a narrative or story. The therapist can ask curious questions (such as those discussed in item 8) that may give cause for individuals to further reflect on their circumstances, and that may unearth new meanings, affirming exceptions, and unique outcomes, and pose new ideas or possibilities.

   A seven-year-old boy named Bjorn was unable to see himself as having control over his urinary frequency. He felt the need to use the toilet so strongly and so often that it was interfering with activities such as school and sleep (Epston, 1992). He was quite fearful that he would wet his pants. Medical experts detected no physical reason for the problem. David Epston used child-appropriate themes (dreams, magic, stories, and fantasies) to externalize the problem and create a context within which Bjorn could discover new strengths. After the first session, Epston made a taped story to help Bjorn consolidate his new view of himself. The following are a few excerpts from the tape.

   Hello Bjorn,
   David speaking.... Your problem has weakened your bladder and I am sorry about that...but it (the problem) will learn that your name means Bear....I had a sense of that bear-like strength inside you. I wasn't surprised when you told me that on October 31st you had beaten your habit and proven how bear-like you were....You

told me you felt proud of yourself for winning ... and then when I asked you how it was that you got so strong all of a sudden, you said that your strength just came up in a hurry and lasted a fair while. Now, Bjorn, that's not the only place or time your strengths have come up. (Epston, 1992, p. 183)

Epston proceeded to note other exceptions to the problem and proposed a secret formula of magic words that Bjorn could use to fight the problem.

Letters can be long or short, and to children or adults. For example:

Dear Marion, Keith, Michelle, Steven,
After our meeting I was thinking about how I could take your side in your plans to escape from isolation ... thought I would write to ask how your plans are work-ing out. I'll be interested to find out at the next meeting. (White & Epston, 1990, p. 109)

Longer letters may substitute for case notes, and can be shared with the individual or family. Decisions made to take or not take new steps or to come or not come to appointments can be seen as matters of readiness, not failure. For example:

Dear Paul,
I'm sorry that you didn't come to your appointment. . . . I missed you. . . . I did, however, respect your decision not to come in. . . . My guess is that you were not ready ... and therefore it was probably wise of you not to come. It also gave me a good chance to talk things over with your Mum and Dad. (White & Epston, 1990, p. 149)

10. *Certificates and celebrations* can serve as tangible affirmations of a defeat of the problem or a new description of an individual. Certificates employ the written word as celebrations of victories. Literal celebrations complete with balloons, cake, and punch signify problems successfully challenged and defeated. These personal affirmations contribute to an individual's new story. To illustrate, Michael White (White & Epston, 1990) has a professionally printed certificate, complete with photo and logo, that reads, in part:

MONSTER-TAMER & FEAR-CATCHER CERTIFICATE
This is to certify that _____ has undergone a Complete Training Pro-gramme in Monster-Taming and Fear-Catching, is now a fully qualified Monster-Tamer and Fear-Catcher, and is available to offer help to other children who are bugged by fears. (p. 193)

Another certificate, suitable for an adult, reads:

ESCAPE FROM GUILT CERTIFICATE
This certificate is awarded to _____ in recognition of her victory over guilt. Now that guilt doesn't have such a priority in her life, she is able to give her-self a priority in her own life. . . . This certificate will serve to remind _____, and others, that she has resigned from the position of super-

responsibility in the lives of others, and that she is no longer vulnerable to invita-
tions from others to live their life for them and to put her life to one side. (p. 199)

Evaluation of Effectiveness

The effectiveness of narrative therapy has been reported in case studies. These studies explain the problems families and individuals present, the treatment method employed, and the short-term (and in some cases, long-term) outcomes. Listed in the "Application" section are illustrations of problems for which case studies have been published.

Despite the impressive treatment effects noted in many case studies by Michael White and others, there has been a dearth of quantitative literature examining the effectiveness of narrative methods. This is mostly likely due to the narrativist conclusion that traditional empirical investigatory methods differ with the values espoused by the narrative school. At the core of this dialogue is the issue of epistemology. With a different view on the nature of reality itself, narrative therapists have mostly used the case study method to testify to the method's effectiveness and have been slow to experiment with ways of using quantitative methods to measure success.

A few quantitative studies have appeared in the literature. For instance, an outcome study of White's family narrative therapy with a group of individuals with schizophrenia demonstrated a significant improvement over a control group (Hafner, 1987). A two-year follow-up study of length of hospitalization revealed that the average hospitalization for the members of the narrative therapy group had been reduced from 35 to 14 days, while the actual number of days had increased for the control group.

Seymour and Epston (1989) reported on a clinical evaluation of 45 children involved in stealing. Treatment entailed the child, along with the family, restorying the child from "stealer" to "honest person." Treatment lasted an average of 3.3 sessions plus follow-up letters and phone calls. The results revealed that families had a high level of engagement in treatment and that stealing behavior subsided. A follow-up phone call to parents six to 12 months after completion of treatment showed that 80% of the children had not been stealing at all or had substantially reduced rates of stealing.

A more recent study has been conducted using a quantitative single-system design (Besa, 1994). Although this study has some limitations, it represents an innovative effort to empirically evaluate the effectiveness of narrative methods. Besa found dramatic (88–98%) improvement in five out of six families studied and attributed this to the narrative methods used. Using nonpathologizing dependent measures and concisely addressing epistemological issues, Besa has successfully launched narrative methods into the realm of empirical investigation. The future of narrative therapy may rest in the hands of empirical investigators to further examine the effectiveness of the method using ideographic methods (Neimeyer, 1995).

Application to Families Functioning on Other Levels

The narrative approach has been used with a wide variety of individual and family problems such as

Couple/relationship therapy (Hudson & O'Hanlon, 1991)
Sexual offenders, adolescent (Jenkins, 1987)
Substance abuse (Anoretic & Anoretic, 1991)
Schizophrenia (White, 1987)
AIDS (White & Epston, 1991; Dean, 1995)
Male batterers (Jenkins, 1990)
Learning disabilities diagnoses (Stewart & Nodrick, 1990)
Temper problems within a family (M. Epston, 1989)
Anorexia/bulimia (Epston, 1993a; Epston, Morris, & Maisel, 1995)
Grief (White, Spring 1989; McQuaide, 1995)
Residential psychiatric treatment (Menses & Anoretic, 1987)

Summary

The narrative approach to therapy is a postmodern, eclectic approach to individual and family therapy that uses the literary metaphors of story and writing. It is rooted in social constructionism and sociological and linguistic epistemologies. A reaction against the normalizing and restraining effects of culture, the narrative model stresses that the therapeutic relationship should be collaborative, as the client and therapist cocreate differences, new stories, and new realities.

Problems are investigated in terms of their meanings, rather than their causes. Assessment/intervention occurs through the enactment of stories, and as strengths and exceptions emerge that deconstruct and challenge the problem-saturated story. Through a process of interventive interviewing involving questions, problems are externalized, and the relative influence of the problem upon the person is examined.

The influence of the person upon the problem takes center stage. Exceptions to problematic situations are uncovered and their significance highlighted. Curious, gentle, respectful questions can be raised about these exceptions, involving the exception's history, significance, and its spectators/audience (e.g., how did you accomplish it, what does it mean, and who noticed?).

Setbacks can be anticipated and plans made to deal with them. If possible, a reflecting team can provide new descriptions and previously unnoticed exceptions. Letters, certificates, and celebrations can amplify and provide continuity to what has been accomplished between and after sessions.

Discussion Questions

1. In the narrative perspective, what is reality assumed to be?
2. Why does narrative therapy emphasize the meaning of problems rather than their causes?

3. What words, phrases, and metaphors best describe the role of the narrative therapist?
4. What is meant by the phrase "problem-saturated story"?
5. What is the role of assessment in narrative therapy?
6. What is meant by the phrase "the problem is the problem"?
7. To what extent is narrative therapy goal-oriented, as contrasted with process-oriented?
8. What are some of the key ideas that narrative therapists rely on to increase the likelihood that therapy is a process of cocreation rather than therapist-directed?
9. What role do oppression and power play in the life of a person's problem?
10. What role can externalization of the problem play in deescalating the oppressive story of the problem?
11. Why is it important to examine both the influence of the problem on the person and person on the problem? What are some questions a therapist can ask to help the individual and family to explore these influences?
12. What is meant by "looking for exceptions" to the problem? What role can exceptions play in helping to re-author a person's story?
13. What value do letters, celebrations, and reflecting teams have in narrative therapy?
14. To what extent has narrative therapy been evaluated and found to be effective?
15. What are some of the individual and family problems for which narrative therapy has been used?
16. How can the narrative approach be used with families that are perceived to be functioning at each of the four levels?
17. How respectful is the narrative approach of cultural and ethnic differences?
18. How does the narrative approach differ from other approaches in this book?
19. What is your reaction to the assumptions, principles, and techniques of narrative therapy? To what extent is this an approach that you would feel comfortable trying to use with clients?
20. If you used the narrative perspective, how would the way in which you see yourself working with families be different from the way it is now? What effect might your use of narrative ideas have on you and your relationships with families?

Suggested Readings

Andersen, T. (Ed.). (1991). *The reflecting team: Dialogues and dialogues about the dialogues.* New York: Norton.

> *The development of a new strategy in therapy is presented, in which professionals and clients trade places, exchange conversations, and open up new possibilities for change. Dialogues are exchanged in collaborative discussions among family, therapist, and reflecting team, and result in the dissolving of traditional therapeutic boundaries.*

Anoretic, M., & Epston, D. (1989). The taming of temper. *Dulwich Centre Newsletter* (Special ed.), 3–26.

> *Articles are included by Anoretic ("Temper taming: An approach to children's temper problems—Revisited") and Epston ("Temper tantrum parties: Saving face, losing face, or going off your face!"). Anoretic's article discusses temper and behavior problems from a narrative viewpoint, and the development of his ideas in dealing with these issues. Epston's article presents a method for dealing with out-of-control temper in children or adults. The approach is simple, economical, and amusing for all concerned as it teaches individuals to substitute self-control for the control of others.*

Anoretic, M., & Kowalski, K. (1990). Overcoming the effects of sexual abuse: Developing a self-perception of competence. In M. Anoretic & C. White (Eds.), *Ideas for therapy with sexual abuse.* Adelaide, S. Australia: Dulwich Centre.

Drawing from both the narrative approach and from the model of brief solution-focused therapy, the authors approach the issue of sexual abuse as qualitatively not unlike other issues in therapy. They propose a framework for enhancing the perception of self as competent rather than as victim.

Elms, R. (1990). Hostility, apathy, silence and denial: Inviting abusive adolescents to argue for change. In M. Anoretic & C. White (Eds.), *Ideas for therapy with sexual abuse.* Adelaide, S. Australia: Dulwich Centre.

The author describes the narrative model as applied to adolescents who have been abused, and focuses in particular on ideas for engaging them in the process of therapy. The author emphasizes adolescents' understanding the impact of the abuse, and the importance of their developing respectful relationships and a sense of responsibility. The author draws on many ideas of Alan Jenkins and Michael White.

Freedman, J., & Combs, G. (1996). *Narrative therapies: The special construction of preferred realities.* New York: Norton.

Drawing from the narrative approach, the authors present practical information to the clinician intent on learning about the method. Issues of practice, power, sociocultural context, and ethics are addressed in this acclaimed book.

Gilligan, S., & Price, R. (Eds.). (1993). *Therapeutic conversations.* New York: Norton.

Emerging from a conference in Tulsa (June, 1992), the book's contributors are well known in the narrative family therapy tradition, the solution-focused tradition, and conversational therapies. Chapter authors respond to one another's positions and perspectives. Contributors include John Weakland, David Epston, Michael White, Steve de Shazer, Karl Tomm, and Michele Weiner-Davis.

Metcalf, L. (1991). Therapy with parent-adolescent conflict: Creating a climate in which clients can figure what to do differently. *Family Therapy Case Studies, 6*(2), 25–34.

Responsibility and protection are contrasted with freedom and independence as conflicting needs of parents and adolescents. As conflicts increase, guilt and blame often result. Two case examples demonstrate a climate in which families can decide on alternative behaviors and resolve their conflicts. Ideas are used from both the brief, solution-focused model and from the narrative approach.

O'Neill, M., & Stockell, G. (1991). Worthy of discussion: Collaborative group therapy. *Australian–New Zealand Journal of Family Therapy, 12*(4), 201–206.

A narrative approach to group therapy for individuals with schizophrenia is presented. The approach moves from a restrictive view of mental illness toward alternative self-knowledge and empowerment. New ethnographic methodology has been used to measure both process and outcome of the group therapy.

Tomm, K. (1988). Interventive interviewing: Part III. Intending to ask lineal, circular, strategic, or reflexive questions? *Family Process, 27,* 1–15.

This article and the two preceding it ("Interventive interviewing I and II," Family Process, 26, 3–13; 167–183) discuss questions based on circular rather than lineal assumptions. A framework is offered that distinguishes four major groups of questions, with guidelines to their use. Lineal assumptions lead to lineal and strategic questions; circular assumptions lead to circular and reflexive questions. The categories of questions are discussed regarding their effects on families and on therapists.

White, M. (1986). Negative explanation, restraint, and double description: A template for family therapy. *Family Process, 25*(2), 169–184.

> An approach to therapy and the discovery of new solutions is derived from G. Bateson's ideas of double description, restraint, and negative explanation. The family's and therapist's contributions to new discoveries are discussed. Case examples include obsessive-compulsive behavior and childhood fears.

White, M. (1991). Deconstruction and therapy. *Dulwich Centre Newsletter, 3,* 21–40.

> White presents theory and case examples illustrating externalization of the problem and relative influence questioning. He explains deconstruction and the place of meaning in narrative. The article includes discussion of issues of power, the influence of Michel Foucault. It relates discussion of power back to case examples. White challenges therapists to question the notion of "expert power" in therapeutic situations.

White, M., & Epston, D. (1990). *Narrative means to therapeutic ends.* New York: Norton.

> Letters, documents, and certificates become a respectful and often playful means to encourage the restorying of experience. The narrative approach is explained. Many examples are offered, suitable for children, adolescents, and adults, of narrative means that document progress and often defeat of externalized problems. In addition, the restraints of power and the political implications inherent in therapy are discussed.

References

Andersen, T. (Ed.). (1991). *The reflecting team: Dialogues and dialogues about the dialogues.* New York: Norton.

Anoretic, M. (1989, Autumn). Temper taming: An approach to children's temper problems—revisited. *Dulwich Centre Newsletter,* 3–11.

Anoretic, M., & Anoretic, D. (1991). Michael White's cybernetic approach. In Todd & Selekman (Eds.), *Family therapy approaches with adolescent substance abusers.* Boston: Allyn & Bacon.

Bateson, G. (1972). *Steps to an ecology of mind.* New York: Ballantine.

Bateson, G. (1979). *Mind and nature: A necessary unity.* London: Wildwood House.

Besa, D. (1994, July). Narrative family therapy: A multiple baseline outcome study including collateral effects on verbal behavior. *Research on Social Work Practice, 4*(3), 309–325.

Bruner, E. (1986). Experience and its expression. In V. Turner & E. Bruner (Eds.), *The anthropology of experience.* Chicago: University of Illinois Press.

Bruner, J. (1990). *Acts of meaning.* Cambridge, MA: Harvard University Press.

Chang, J., & Phillips, M. (1993). Michael White and Steve de Shazer: New directions in family therapy. In S. Gilligan & R. Price (Eds.), *Therapeutic conversations.* New York: Norton.

Dean, R. G. (1995). Stories of AIDS: The use of the narrative as an approach to understanding in an AIDS support group. *Clinical Social Work Journal, 23*(3), 287–304.

Epston, D. (1984). Guest address: Fourth Australian family therapy conference, Brisbane, September 24th, 1983. *Australian Journal of Family Therapy, 5,* 11–16.

Epston, D. (1992). "I am a Bear": Discovering discoveries. In D. Epston and M. White (Eds.), *Experience contradiction narrative and imagination* (pp. 173–188). Adelaide, South Australia: Dulwich Centre Publications.

Epston, D. (1993a). Workshop on anorexia. Charter-Peachford Hospital, Atlanta, GA.

Epston, D. (1993b). *The approach of the Anti-Anorexia (Bulimia) League.* Auckland, New Zealand: Family Therapy Centre.

Epston, D., Morris, F., & Maisel, R. (1995). A narrative approach to so-called anorexia/bulimia. *Journal of Feminist Family Therapy, 7(1/2),* 69–96.

Epston, M. (1989, Autumn). Temper tantrum parties: Saving face, losing face, or going off your face! *Dulwich Centre Newsletter,* 12–26.

Esler, I. (1987). Winning over worry. *Family Therapy Case Studies, 2,* 15–23.

Fish, V. (1993). Poststructuralism in family therapy: Interrogating the narrative/conversational mode. *Journal of Marital and Family Therapy, 19(3),* 221–232.

Foucault, M. (1979). *Discipline and punish: The birth of the prison.* London: Peregrine.

Foucault, M. (1980). *Power/knowledge: Selected interviews and other writings.* New York: Pantheon.

Hafner, J. (1987). *The Glenside Hospital Family Therapy Unit: An evaluation study.* Unpublished manuscript. Adelaide, South Australia.

Hart, B. (1995). Re-authoring the stories we work by: Situating the narrative approach in the presence of the family of therapists. *Australian and New Zealand Journal of Family Therapy, 16(4),* 181–189.

Hewson, D. (1991). From laboratory to therapy room: Prediction questions for reconstructing the "new-old" story. *Dulwich Centre Newsletter, 3,* 5–12.

Hoffman, L. (1985). Beyond power and control: Toward a "second order" family systems therapy. *Family Systems Medicine, 3(4),* 381–396.

Hoffman, L. (1990). Constructing realities: An art of lenses. *Family Process, 29(1),* 1–12.

Hudson, P. O., & O'Hanlon, W. H. (1991). *Rewriting love stories.* New York: Norton.

Jenkins, A. (1987). Engaging the adolescent sexual abuser. Unpublished workshop notes.

Jenkins, A. (1990). *Invitations to responsibility: The therapeutic engagement of men who are violent and abusive.* Adelaide, South Australia: Dulwich Centre Publications.

Joyce, T. A., & Taylor, V. L. (1990). Mastering words and managing conversations: Therapy as dialogue. *Journal of Strategic and Systematic Therapies, 9(4),* 21–28.

Madigan, S. (1991). Discursive restraints in therapist practice: Situating therapist questions in the presence of the family. *Dulwich Centre Newsletter, 3,* 13–20.

McQuaide, S. (1995). Storying the suicide of one's child. *Clinical Social Work Journal, 23(4),* 417–428.

Menses, G., & Anoretic, M. (1987). Contextual residential care: The application of the principles of cybernetic therapy to the residential treatment of irresponsible adolescents and their families. *Journal of Strategic and Systemic Therapies, 6(2),* 3–15.

Neimeyer, R. A. (1993a). An appraisal of constructivist psychotherapies. *Journal of Consulting and Clinical Psychology, 61(2),* 221–234.

Neimeyer, R. A. (1993b). Constructivist psychotherapy. In K. T. Kuehlwein & H. Rosen (Eds.), *Cognitive therapies in action: Evolving innovative practice.* San Francisco: Jossey-Bass.

Neimeyer, R. A. (1995). Constructing more workable realities and revising our personal stories, or vice-versa. In R. A. Neimeyer & M. J. Mahoney (Eds.), *Constructivism in psychotherapy.* Washington, DC: American Psychological Association.

Seymour, F. W., & Epston, D. (1989). An approach to childhood stealing with evaluation of 45 cases. *Australian–New Zealand Journal of Family Therapy, 10(3),* 49–65.

Sluzki, C. E. (1992). Transformations: A blueprint for narrative changes in therapy. *Family Process, 31(3),* 217–230.

Stewart, B., & Nodrick, B. (1990). The learning disabled lifestyle: From reification to liberation. *Family Therapy Case Studies, 5,* 61–73.

Tandy, C., & Gallant, J. P. (1993). *Narrative therapy: A case study.* Unpublished manuscript. University of Georgia, School of Social Work, Athens, GA.

Tomm, K. (1987). Interventive interviewing: Part I. Strategizing as a fourth guideline for the therapist. *Family Process, 26,* 3–13.

Tomm, K. (1988). Interventive interviewing: Part III. Intending to ask lineal, circular, strategic, or reflexive questions? *Family Process, 27,* 1–15.

Tomm, K. (1993). The courage to protest: A commentary on Michael White's work. In S. Gilligan & R. Price (Eds.), *Therapeutic conversations.* New York: Norton.

White, M. (1986a). Negative explanation, restraint, and double description: A template for family therapy. *Family Process, 25*(2), 169–184.

White, M. (1986b). Family escape from trouble. *Family Therapy Case Studies, 1,* 29–33.

White, M. (1987, Spring). Family therapy and schizophrenia: Addressing the "in-the-corner" lifestyle. *Dulwich Centre Newsletter,* 14–21.

White, M. (1988/1989, Summer). The externalizing of the problem and the re-authoring of lives and relationships. *Dulwich Centre Newsletter,* 3–21.

White, M. (1989, Spring). Saying hullo again: The reincorporation of the lost relationship in the resolution of grief. *Dulwich Centre Newsletter,* 7–11.

White, M. (1989, Summer). Family therapy training and supervision in a world of experience and narrative. *Dulwich Centre Newsletter,* 27–38.

White, M. (1991). Deconstruction and therapy. *Dulwich Centre Newsletter, 3,* 21–40.

White, M. (1993). Deconstruction and therapy. In S. Gilligan & R. Price (Eds.), *Therapeutic conversations* (pp. 22–61). New York: Norton.

White, M., & Epston, D. (1990). *Narrative means to therapeutic ends.* New York: Norton.

White, M., & Epston, D. (1991). A conversation about AIDS and dying. *Dulwich Centre Newsletter, 2,* 5–16.

Chapter 12

Object Relations
Family Interventions

ALLIE C. KILPATRICK, Ph.D., and EBB G. KILPATRICK, JR., S.T.M.

Object relations family therapy is a relatively new model of family treatment. Its origins are in two separate schools of thought whose streams have merged into a dynamic body that is having a major impact on family therapy today. Not unlike the mighty milky white Amazon where it merges with the black waters of the Negro River, but remains separate before finally mingling, psychoanalysis and family therapy have run together and commingled before finally merging to form object relations family therapy.

Object relations theory is considered to be the bridge between psychoanalysis—the study of individuals, and family theory—the study of social relationships. It may be defined as

> *the psychoanalytic study of the origin and nature of interpersonal relationships, and of the intrapsychic structures which grew out of past relationships and remain to influence present interpersonal relations. The emphasis is on those mental structures that preserve early interpersonal experiences in the form of* self *and* object-images. *(Nichols, 1984, p. 183)*

Object relations theory is an existing general framework in psychoanalysis and psychiatry that provides the means for understanding the earliest developmental phases of childhood. It studies attachment to and differentiation from others—a process that is of much importance not only for the personality functioning of the individual, but also for families and social adaptation. The lack of differentiation of family members has become one of the cornerstones of Murray Bowen's work (1978) in understanding families, as well as Helm Stierlin's work (1976) in studying larger social group functioning (Slipp, 1984).

Family Problems

Object relations can be used to understand a vast array of needs, behaviors, problem areas, and symptomatology. However, the judgment as to whether or not object relations family interventions (ORFI) is the most effective approach to use in any given situation can be informed by previous studies and experiences. A family approach seems to be indicated when the family plays a significant role in aggravating or perpetuating the client's problems. These problems may include lack of differentiation, splitting and projective identification, little autonomy, inability to maintain self-esteem and identity, and excessive vulnerability to the influence of the family.

Object relations concepts relate to attachment, connectedness, bonding, caring, love, and responsibility in relationships. They provide an understanding of the deeper reasons for the three most common complaints in marriage: lack of communication, constant arguments, and unmet emotional needs. Such complaints can be seen as resulting from the failure of relatedness, of deficiencies in self-object functioning, and of conflicts between relationship goals and individual goals (Finkelstein, 1987).

Object relations family interventions deal with shared, unconscious, internalized object relations. Focusing on the interaction and interdependence of individual dynamics and family-system functioning is crucial in the application of an integrated understanding to family interventions. The family is not perceived as a set of individuals, but as a system comprising sets of relationships that function in ways unique to that specific family. The immediate goal is not symptom resolution, but a progression through the current developmental phase of family life with an improved ability to work as a group and to differentiate among and meet the individual member's needs. Thus, this model is especially relevant for Level IV families.

In regard to whether or not ORFI is indicated for a specific family, we must remember that psychological maturity is not necessarily related to socioeconomic status. Applegate (1990) explored aspects of object relations theory within the sociocultural context of family constellations, child-rearing practices, race, and ethnicity. The interrelationship of the internal world of object relations and the external world of multiculturalism is offered as a clinically useful way of examining issues arising from ethnic differences. Slipp (1988) observes that ethnicity alone has not been found to be an issue in ORFI's relevance. Although there are differences between ethnic and racial groups, if the clinician is sensitive and skilled, these can be worked through in treatment. In regard to sexual orientation, therapists generally use the same treatment methods with traditional and same-sex couples (Parker, 1996). One must remember, however, that lack of societal supports and resources, as well as societal sanctions imposed by the dominant culture, must be addressed within the therapeutic dialogue. Families that are functioning at Level IV may come to the clinician with problems described as internal or interpersonal conflicts, anger, blaming, lack of communication, desire for growth and greater intimacy, loss of confidence in self and/or spouse, depression, loneliness, or isolation. These families generally want an understanding of these situations and are reflective. The next section presents a case where ORFI is an effective explanatory and interventive method.

Family Case Assessment

Sam and Sally were seen together and without the children for the beginning sessions. The Sumpters' presenting problem was Sam's desire to understand and do something about his own level of anger. They were both concerned because of a recent event that had triggered Sam's anger. He was afraid that he might lose control, and wanted to assure mastery over this aspect of his life before it could lead to problems at work and in interpersonal relationships. He was especially concerned that his anger, which at times was directed at her, might be unleashed at Sally. Sally felt that she must be doing something wrong to bring out his anger. She wanted help in learning how not to enrage him, as his anger was devastating to her. They both desired more intimacy in the marriage, and felt that control of the anger was an important step in that direction.

Sam kept wondering where his intense feelings came from and how they could be controlled. There did not seem to be any particular transition or cluster stress from a life-cycle-stage perspective at that point in time. This was the first time they had sought professional help. Sam and Sally had met in college and married soon afterward while he was in graduate school. They had similar backgrounds and much in common. Sam was three years older than Sally. At the time they came to the family practitioner, their son was eight and their daughter six.

Family history taking revealed that Sam had been born prematurely; there had been concern as to whether he would survive or not. Sam's impressions were that his mother had not wanted the pregnancy at that time. His premature birth and stay in the incubator had likely created considerable anxiety and guilt in his mother, which caused her to be overly indulgent at times and somewhat cold and indifferent at other times. Sam gave examples of how she continued to express her ambivalence toward him in various ways throughout his childhood. These experiences with his mother had a profound impact on the formulation of Sam's personality. He felt extremely close and loving to his mother at some times, while at other times he felt very angry with her and had difficulty controlling his rage. This pattern was somewhat perpetuated in his marriage. Either the relationship was extremely good with much closeness, love, and sexual compatibility, or there was anger, distance, coldness, and aloofness toward his wife. Often, Sam's mother would threaten to leave. His dad would then send Sam to beg her to stay. Thus, the threat of a loved one's leaving was a toxic issue. Sam identified with his father in that he entered the same profession.

Sally's early experiences were quite different. While Sam was the oldest of two boys, Sally was the fourth of five children, the four youngest being girls. She spent a great deal of time and energy trying to get her parents' attention, especially her father's. She did this by excelling in school, in sports, and in her work on the farm. She idolized her father and tried both consciously and unconsciously to win his affirmation and approval. The emotional atmosphere in her family was calm and consistent, with very little anger expressed. As a result, she had great difficulty handling Sam's changes in affect. Sally's mother was a professional woman and was a good role model for handling a career and a family. Sally entered the same profession of teaching.

From this brief summary of the intake information, we see what each individual brought to the marital relationship. Both brought the patterns and processes from their families of origin plus unresolved issues. These unresolved issues obviously began to surface in the marital relationship, and had the potential of leading to marital and family conflict. Interventions were designed to help sort out many of the issues that each individual brought to the marriage. In this family situation, the underlying processes of splitting, introjection, projective identification, and collusion (defined later in this chapter) as they are demonstrated in Sam and Sally's relationship need to be addressed within the context of a therapeutic holding environment. The defenses of denial and projection are used by Sam, and Sally has transferred her dependency on her parents to Sam. Both need to work on differentiation of self from the other. Neither is overly dependent on the families of origin, and they have an autonomous family unit with intact, though permeable, boundaries. They are able to problem-solve through negotiation on issues involving the children, money, in-laws, and sex, and seem to have a caring relationship where humor often is used to ease tensions.

Treatment Goals

The first goal of intervention always is to assure a safe environment. If there is a fear for one's own personal well-being, then this must be resolved before other interpersonal issues can be addressed. In this family situation safety has not been a problem. The issue is more of prevention and growth as Sam seeks to control his anger more effectively so that each one can feel in control.

A second goal is for each partner to look at family-of-origin issues. In this situation, the multigenerational transmission process must be interrupted so that the dysfunctional elements are not projected onto the next generation. Issues and conflicts in Sam and Sally's own marital relationship are related to unresolved conflicts coming out of each one's family of origin. Then the steps in the interactive projection-collusion process are identified and the potentially destructive cycle broken. Each person assumes responsibility for his or her own family-of-origin dynamics and the way that they are projected into and played out in the marriage arena.

Intervention Approach: Theory Base and Major Tenets

Object relations family intervention comes from the application of object relations theory to family systems. Object relations theory and its therapeutic approach regard the individual's inner world and external family as components of an open system. It can be used to develop typologies of family interaction and treatment that take into consideration the intrapsychic influences on family patterns, which in turn affect the client's personality. Thus, psychoanalysis and family treatment complement each other to enhance the theoretical understanding in both fields and to foster an intervention approach that is dependent not on the theoretical orientation of the clinician but on the needs of the client family.

On the historical formulation of ORFI, Freud (1940) must be acknowledged as the father of psychoanalysis, and for his contribution to the psychoanalytic study of family life and its foundation for ORFI. Freud does associate his libido concept with object-seeking. In psychoanalytic literature, **object** refers to persons or things that are significant in one's psychic life, especially the early parental figure. The phrase **object relations** refers to the individual's attitude and behavior toward such objects. Freud influenced many theorists who added to his work and later deviated from it. Some of those who had a part in the early development of object relations theory and treatment have included Ferenczi (1920), Klein (1946), Fairbairn (1954), and others in the British school.

Although the basic tenets of ORFI are based on psychoanalysis, they continue to be modified. Specific historical tenets and concepts are now presented as they are currently used in assessment and interventions.

Freud (1940) originally mentioned **splitting** as a defense mechanism of the ego, and defined it as a lifelong coexistence of two contradictory dispositions that do not influence each other. Kernberg (1972), in tracing the process of splitting through developmental stages, states that splitting of the "all good" (organized around pleasurable mother-child interactions) and "all bad" (derived from painful and frustrating interactions) self-images, object images, and their affective links occurs from two to eight months. The separation of the self from object representations occurs from eight to 36 months. Splitting into good and bad persists, and this is seen as the fixation point for borderline patients. (For example, Sam incorporated his mother's good and bad images, but split them into two parts. He then could see his mother as all good but his self as bad. Later, the bad images were projected on Sally at an unconscious level.) Following the splitting is the integration of the good and bad emotional images so that the separate self and object representations are each both good and bad. It is at this point that the ego, superego, and id become firmly established as intrapsychic structures and that the defenses of splitting are replaced by repression. Slipp (1984) sees this stage as the fixation point for neurotic pathology. In the last stage, internalized object representations are reshaped through actual current experiences with real people. A goal of ORFI is to assist in the development of this integration and reshaping.

Introjection is a crude, global form of taking in, as if those fragments of self–other interactions are swallowed whole. It is the earliest, most primitive form of the internalization of object relations, starting on a relatively crude level and becoming more sophisticated as the child grows (Nichols, 1984). The child reproduces and fixates its interactions with significant others by organizing memory traces that include images of the object, the self interacting with the object, and the associated affect. Good and bad internal objects are included, each with images of the object and the self. For example, if the parent yells, images of a bad parent and an unworthy self are stored. Klein (1946) states that introjection of bad objects, like an empty breast or angry face, generates fear and anxiety that lead the baby into the paranoid position.

Projective identification is a defense mechanism that operates unconsciously. Unwanted aspects of the self are attributed to another person, and that person is induced to behave in accordance with these projected attitudes and feelings (Nichols, 1984). For instance, in the case example, Sam does not accept his own weaknesses and projects them on to Sally. The concepts of transference (Freud, 1905), scapegoating (Vogel & Bell, 1960), symbiosis (Mahler, 1952), trading of dissociations (Wynne, 1965), merging (Boszormenyi-Nagy, 1967), irrational role assignments (Framo, 1970), and family projective process (Bowen, 1965) are all variants of Klein's (1946) concept of projective identification.

Collusion is an integral part of projective identification. The recipient of the split-off part of the partner does not disown the projection but acts on the conscious or unconscious message (Stewart, Peters, Marsh, & Peters, 1975). For example, the need for a "weak" woman requires that both partners agree to the assigned roles. Each spouse's ego identity (which includes both good and bad objects) is preserved by having one or more bad objects split off onto the partner. Thus, each partner disowns his or her bad-object introjects and needs the other to accept the projection of these introjects in a collusive manner (Piercy et al., 1986). Dicks (1963) believes that this collusive process continues because both spouses hope for integration of lost introjects by finding them in each other. Clinicians using object relations theory attempt in various ways to help couples own their introjects and begin seeing their spouses for the people they really are, not projected parts of themselves. In the case of Sam and Sally, Sam projects his bad introjects from his mother to Sally, who colludes and accepts these bad images instead of rejecting them.

Winnicott (1958) builds on his notion of good-enough mothering to the idea of a holding environment. If the good-enough mother (or primary nurturing person) provides a holding environment that is safe, secure, responsive, nurturing, nonretaliating, and supportive of separation-individuation, the child can achieve a firm sense of identity and a lifelong capacity for developing nonsymbiotic object relations.

Scharff and Scharff (1987) develop this concept further by defining the role of the father (or secondary nurturing person) as supporting the holding of the mother physically, financially, and emotionally; the father holds the mother as she holds the baby. This contextual holding provides an environmental extension of the mother's presence that later extends outward to grandparents and family, neighbors, and others. Feminist-informed object relations theory additionally considers the influence of gender on the holding environment. Sex role differentiation and shifting sex role mores are considered to affect the holding environment that is created within the couple, marital, and family settings (Juni & Grimm, 1994). Traditional concepts of masculine and feminine roles are challenged with the emergence of new realities that defy gender specification. A holding environment that typifies excessive power imbalances between partners may be understood within the context of early object relations (Silverstein, 1994). The need for dominance and power, particularly in the area of sexual arousal and pleasure, has been suggested to evolve from excessive control/coercion by a powerful parental object during early psychosexual development.

These concepts of the holding environment also apply to working with families. The clinician needs to provide a holding environment for the family by providing safety, competence, and concern for the whole family, and by engaging with the central issues of the family, being caring, interactive, and understanding. Within this therapeutic "envelope," Sam and Sally could own their introjects and accept each other as different people.

As to the current status of ORFI, there is no overall integrated theory. Various theorists have developed their own perspectives over the years, and others have made attempts at integration. One is Framo (1972), who calls his approach a transactional one. It leans heavily on the notion of projective identification as applied to a family system, and offers a new way of presenting transference. He builds on Fairbairn's notion of the fundamental need for a satisfying object relationship. When a child interprets the parents' behavior as rejection or desertion and cannot give up the parent, it internalizes the loved but hated parent in the inner world of self as an introject (as if swallowed whole) or a psychological representation. In the course of time, as the person begins to force close relationships into fitting this internal role model, these split-off or divided introjects become important. Framo sees the introject of the parent as a critical issue in family therapy, and one that is much neglected. Framo tries to put together a basically intrapsychic concept, introjects, with a system concept. In doing so, he draws out the implications in Bowen's (1978) formulation of family theory for object relations theory.

Boszormenyi-Nagy and Spark (1973) are also concerned about introjects and object relations. They see family pathology as a specialized multiperson organization of shared fantasies and complementary need gratification patterns that are maintained for the purpose of handling past object loss experience.

Monumental groundbreaking work has been done by D. Scharff (1982), J. Scharff (1989), Scharff and Scharff (1987), and Slipp (1984, 1988). For Scharff and Scharff (1987), ORFI derives from the psychoanalytic principles of listening, responding to unconscious material, interpreting, developing insight, and working in the transference and countertransference toward understanding and growth. The immediate goal is not symptom resolution, but progression through the current developmental phase of family life with improved ability to work as a group and to differentiate among and meet the individual member's needs. Slipp (1984, 1988) studied diverse patient populations and their families to explore the interaction and interdependence of individual dynamics and family system functioning. His ultimate goal is to apply an integrated understanding to family treatment.

ORFI's basic tenet is that treatment of the individual and treatment of the family are theoretically and therapeutically consistent with each other, and both are parts of an open system. The two levels of the intrapersonal and the interpersonal are in a constantly dynamic relationship with each other. An assumption is that resolving problems in the relationships in the client's current family necessitates intrapsychic exploration and resolution of those unconscious object relationships that were internalized from early parent-child relationships. Another assumption is that these early influences affect and explain the nature of present interpersonal problems.

Application to Families on Level IV

Families who have needs on Level IV are generally introspective and reflective, and yearn to be more self-actualizing. There may be problems of inner conflict or difficulties with intimacy. Although we may still be treating symptomatic people, our goals have to do with the development of an inner "richness"—insight, more sensitive awareness of the relational world, an understanding of legacies and heritage. In all cases we would hope to deepen awareness of the inner world and to improve understanding of history, style, and unmet yearnings. A very important aspect is the spiritual therapies that help families discover the transcendent aspects of their beings.

In ORFI, the therapeutic environment is established by the therapist's encouragement of open dialogue in a safe, mutually helpful atmosphere. The family practitioner generally maintains a neutral stance that respects each member's autonomy. The practitioner avoids assuming a directive approach but attends to other material produced in the session as described by Slipp (1988). The past is linked to the present through interpretation of the transference, particularly the ways it is acted out interpersonally in the ongoing family relationships. In order to facilitate the acceptance of these interpretations, the therapist needs to join the family empathetically, and to create a safe and secure holding environment where space for understanding is provided. In the research of Sampson and Weiss (1977), creating such a holding environment has been found to be the most crucial element for change and growth. The practitioner's stance with the family is one that reflects an awareness that he or she affects and is affected by the family (Slipp, 1988). ORFI fosters the kind of meaningful shared intimacy with respect for one another's individuality that the philosopher Martin Buber (1958) so aptly described as the "I–thou relationship."

These types of interventions are well suited for those families who have needs on Level IV. Their lives are in good-enough order that this kind of finishing experience makes sense, and they are living in a stable enough way to benefit. Although many of our most highly valued interventions are appropriate for families whose needs are on Level IV, many, if not most, of the families seen by helping professionals such as social workers have more basic needs.

On the other hand, family practitioners who have not experienced Level IV work may be unprepared to deal with clients for whom meaning, awareness, and spiritual growth are issues. Some practitioners would not acknowledge the importance, or even the existence, of an inner world. If such practitioners encounter families who have Level IV needs, referral to a more existentially oriented practitioner would seem appropriate.

Interventions and Techniques

In ORFI, a vital part of the practitioner's role and function is assessment. Scharff and Scharff (1987, p. 155) cite six major tasks to achieve in the assessment phase to determine if ORFI would be effective:

1. The provision of therapeutic space, which includes trust and openness.
2. Assessment of developmental phase and level to determine tasks to be accomplished.
3. Demonstration of defensive functioning to determine ego strength.
4. Exploration of unconscious assumptions and underlying anxiety to determine intervention needs.
5. Testing of the response to interpretation and assessment format to see if they are ready for understanding and insight.
6. Making an assessment formulation, recommendation, and treatment plan.

These major tasks may be accomplished in a more structured assessment phase. Slipp (1984, pp. 204–205) reviews the steps in such an assessment process; see Table 12.1.

In addition to the ethnic differences or conflicts mentioned earlier, attention must also be given to other sociocultural–environmental factors that influence the family. Impacts of the entire ecosystem must be considered in the assessment process.

There are some specific techniques that ORFI uses in the beginning, middle, and last phases of treatment, which Slipp (1988, pp. 199–200) has outlined as a guide for clinicians; see Table 12.2.

Areas of Differentiation
There are specific techniques that differentiate the object relations approach from other treatment approaches. Stewart et al. (1975, pp. 176–177) give six areas of differentiation; see Table 12.3. These highlight overall techniques used in ORFI and discriminate this approach further.

Evaluation of Effectiveness

Because symptom reduction is not the goal of this model, it cannot serve as the measure of effectiveness. The presence or absence of unconscious conflict, because it is not apparent to family members or outside observers, is difficult to measure. Therefore, assessment of effectiveness depends on the subjective clinical judgment of the therapist and on the family's reactions. With the current emphasis on scientific evidence and cost effectiveness, would these measures be considered sufficient? Clinicians would answer yes, as they consider the clinician's observations to be entirely valid as a means of evaluating theory and treatment. Blanck and Blanck (1972, 1987), discussing Mahler's methods and model, state that clinicians who employ Mahler's theories technically do not question the methodology or the findings, for

TABLE 12.1   Assessment Process in Object Relations Family Therapy

- **Explore the Presenting Problem** of patient and its background.
  - (1) Does it seem related to overall family functioning and/or to stress from a family life cycle stage?
  - (2) What has been done so far to remedy the problem?

- **Establish an Individual Diagnosis** for each family member including a judgment concerning the level of differentiation and the use of primitive or mature defenses.
  - (1) Gather data on the client and family development.
  - (2) Note any ethnic differences or conflicts.

- **Evaluate Family Constancy** to determine if parents can maintain their own narcissistic equilibrium, or if patient is needed to sustain their self-esteem and survival.
  - (1) Does a rigid homeostasis or defensive equilibrium exist that binds and prevents the patient from individuating and separating?
  - (2) Is there pressure for personality compliance within the family, or social achievement outside the family?
  - (3) What affiliative, oppositional, and alienated attitudes exist?

- **Explore Precipitating Stress** and its relation to a loss or other traumatic event (negative or positive) or a transitional point in the family life cycle that has disrupted homeostasis.

- **Define Individual Boundaries** for members. These may be rigidly too open (a symbiotically close relationship) or too closed (an emotionally divorced and distant relationship).
  - (1) Are **Generational Boundaries** intact, or are there parent–child coalitions?
  - (2) Are the parental coalition, the subsystems, and authority hierarchy intact?

- **Define the Family Boundary** to see if it is too open (symbiotic relations persist with family of origin) or too closed (family is isolated from community without social support system).

- **Determine the ability to negotiate differences and problem solve** through verbal dialogue involving respect for one's own and others' views, opinions, and motivations versus an egocentric controlling viewpoint resulting in coercion and manipulation.

- **Observe** communication patterns for evidence of spontaneous versus rigid stereotyping, distancing, or obfuscating; level of initiative versus passivity; rigidity of family rules; and the **power-role structure.**

- **Evaluate the loving and caring feelings** amongst members that allow for separateness (rather than acceptance only by conformity) and provide warmth, support, and comfort.

- **Define the treatment goals** in terms of difficulties that have been uncovered, and present the frame or boundaries of the treatment process.

Slipp, 1984, pp. 204–205.

they can confirm them clinically. This is a form of validation that meets as closely as possible the experimentalist's insistence upon replication as criterion of the scientific method. Along these same lines, Langs (1982) posits that the ultimate test of a therapist's formulation is in the use of these impressions as a basis for intervention. He states further that the patient's reactions, conscious and unconscious, constitute

TABLE 12.2   Phases of Treatment in Object Relations Family Therapy

- **During the beginning phase of treatment the techniques are to:**

    1. Develop a safe holding environment through empathy, evenhandedness, and containment; an environment that facilitates trust, lowers defensiveness, and allows aggression to be worked with constructively.

    2. Interpret the circular positive or negative systemic interaction in a sequential nonblaming manner by:

    a. defining its origin

    b. defining what was hoped to be gained

    c. describing its effects

- **During the middle phase of treatment, the techniques are to:**

    1. Interpret projective identification by:

    a. reframing its purpose to give it a positive aim

    b. linking it with a genetic reconstruction

    c. clarifying why an aspect of the self needs to be disowned and projected

    This process diminishes defensiveness, enhances the therapeutic alliance, and facilitates continued work with the reowned projective identification.

    2. Use the objective countertransference as a tool to understand the transferences and to provide material for interpreting projective identification.

- **During the last phase of treatment, the techniques are to:**

    1. Work through individual conflicts and developmental arrests in the intrapsychic sphere. This process is gradual and may continue in individual therapy after the family treatment terminates.

    2. Terminate treatment.

Slipp, 1988, pp. 199–200

the ultimate litmus test of these interventions, and that true validation involves both cognitive and interpersonal responses from the patient.

The views held by current, eminent object relations family therapists are similar. Slipp (1988) holds that meeting the goals of treatment is the criterion that both the family and therapist use to consider ending treatment. These general goals do not lend themselves to empirical measurement, but to subjective assessments by therapists and families. Scharff and Scharff (1987) state that at termination, the family can provide the holding environment for the members that is so necessary for attachment and growth. The family is able to return to or reach an appropriate developmental level so that they fit with the individuals' developmental needs for intimacy and autonomy. Slipp (1988) describes the end result as the restructuring of the internal world of object relations with resultant modification of the family's interpersonal relations. Each individual self is experienced as separate, and less dependent on external objects to sustain self-esteem and identity. The family will be able to function as a group in a more intimate and adaptive fashion that meets each member's needs.

Although outcome studies have been, primarily, uncontrolled case studies, Dicks (1967) reported on a survey of the outcome of couples therapy at the Tavis-

TABLE 12.3 Object Relations Therapy Approach Differentiated from Other Marital/Family Approaches

- While many marital partners may seem quite different, it soon becomes apparent that their psychic structures are very similar. Although they may behaviorally manifest these intrapsychic processes differently through collusion, projective identification, shared fantasy, etc., the similarities should be discussed and made explicit to the couple.

- The ORFI approach goes beyond countertransference usage in allowing the partner to "put into" the therapist disowned or split-off parts of himself. The more classical analytic approach considers the therapist's reactions as irrational countertransference phenomena. This approach regards such material as a valid, legitimate statement of issues with which the patient is struggling.

- When therapists split up a couple to see each of them individually, the emotional exchanges between the therapists will be similar to and/or mirror the affective transactions between the partners in the marital dyad.

- This ORFI approach provides a way of understanding family problems when a child is presented as the identified patient. The child becomes a carrier or container of the split-off, unacceptable impulses of the parent. The child may be idealized just as he may be denigrated.

- The more classical approach focuses on interpreting the patient's perception in terms of internal processes based on early experiences. This system considers the perception to be based on a need to solve an internal conflict through the use of external objects as carriers. There is an active invitation to other people to fulfill these roles.

- In classical analytical theory, the focus is upon individual psychotherapy and pathological involvement. Behaviorally oriented approaches also emphasize individual functioning. In contrast, object relations theory offers a perspective of the individual as a unit in which even the more pathological traits have a healthy reparative aspect. Consequently, the marital dyad continues to function in defiance of apparent breakdown and irreconcilable differences and conflicts. Awareness of the reciprocal, pathological, and subtle attempts to carry out ego repair generates a greater understanding in the therapist of the durability and maintenance of the marital dyad.

Stewart, Peters, Marsh, & Peters, 1975, pp. 176–177. Reprinted by permission of *Family Process*, Inc.

tock Clinic. He rated 73% of a random sample of cases as having been successfully treated. Others have investigated specific tenets of the ORFI theory and provided further empirical evidence of their existence (Slipp, 1984).

Application to Families Functioning on Other Levels

As discussed previously, object relations theory is very useful in understanding a vast array of needs behaviors, problem areas, and symptomatology. This understanding can be applied to families that have needs on any level. Although object relations theory has been utilized extensively to study and treat borderline and narcissistic personality disorders, it is now being used to understand and treat diverse populations and families.

As Slipp (1988) has stated, although ORFI is appropriate for families who desire and can tolerate intensity and closeness, it is certainly not restricted to only those families. As families develop trust and become closer in the intervention process, the treatment itself can serve as a model for more open and intimate relationships among family members. Thus, the growth produced could enable the family to move to a higher level of relating.

A significant, though not the only, variable in selecting the most suitable type of family therapy for a specific family's level of need is the family's socioeconomic level. Clients who have Level I needs with overriding poverty and social problems want help that is more immediate and less abstract. Slipp's (1988) study showed that the ORFI approach is particularly fitting for and effective with middle-class families, as well as a blue-collar population. These families would typically have Level II, III, and IV needs. On the basis of his study findings, ORFI with lower socioeconomic families is least effective and not recommended.

Scharff and Scharff (1987), however, caution clinicians that it should not be assumed that the poor, or culturally or intellectually disadvantaged, cannot benefit from ORFI. Some families will fit cultural stereotypes of concrete thinking and dependency on directives and gratification, but others will take to a more reflective approach. Although this type of intervention is not for all families, it is for those that demonstrate an interest in understanding, not just in symptom relief.

Summary

Object relations family treatment can be effective with families who have their basic physical and nurturant needs met, are capable of abstract thinking and insight, and are interested in understanding and changing destructive patterns of behavior, achieving greater intimacy and commitment, reworking meanings, and rewriting their life stories. These patterns may involve poor communication, conflict, lack of differentiation, weak personal and intergenerational boundaries, inconsistent family structure, and rules. Therefore, ORFI is ideally suited for many Level IV families, and can be very effective with Level II and III families. It is generally not recommended for Level I families.

Discussion Questions

1. What are ORFI's basic tenets, and how do they apply to the case example given?
2. What are the similarities and differences of introjection, projective identification, and collusion?
3. Do ethnicity and gender issues impact the use of ORFI?
4. How are family object relations interventions different from those of individual object relations interventions?
5. From your own practice, identify an individual or family that demonstrates "splitting." Briefly explain why the defense mechanism is evidenced in the person(s) behavior. Can you find projective identification and collusion as well?
6. What is the "holding environment," and how can it be developed and utilized in applying the techniques of ORFI?
7. How is the pain of Level IV families different from that of Level I, II, and III families in view of object relations theory?

Suggested Readings

Applegate, J. S. (1990). Theory, culture and behavior: Object relations in context. *Child and Adolescent Social Work Journal, 7*(2), 85–100.

> *Aspects of object relations theory are explored within the sociocultural context of family constellations, child-rearing practices, race, and ethnicity.*

Fairbairn, W. R. D. (1954). *An object-relations theory of the personality.* New York: Basic Books.

> *A seminal work in object relations theory that has had a significant influence on the later work of Dicks, Bowen, Framo, and others. Required reading for those interested in the role of object relations in psychopathology.*

Finkelstein, L. (1987). Toward an object-relations approach in psychoanalytic marital therapy. *Journal of Marital and Family Therapy, 13*(3), 287–298.

> *Describes the features that distinguish psychoanalytic marital therapy from other forms of marital therapy, describes how object-relations theories can be applied to psychoanalytic marital therapy, and indicates certain directions for further study.*

Scharff, D. E., & Scharff, J. S. (1987). *Object relations family therapy.* Northvale, NJ: Jason Aronson.

> *Represents the Scharffs' efforts to develop a psychoanalytic object relations approach to families and family therapy. The Scharffs demonstrate that object relations theory provides the theoretical framework for understanding, and the language for working with the dynamics of both the individual and the family system.*

Silverstein, J. L. (1994). Power and sexuality: Influence of early object relations. *Psychoanalytic Psychology, 11,* 33-46.

> *This article challenges traditional concepts of masculine and feminine roles with the emergence of new realities that defy gender specification.*

Slipp, S. (1988). *The technique and practice of object relations family therapy.* Northvale, NJ: Jason Aronson.

> *This book extends the clinical application of object relations family therapy that Slipp began in an earlier book. He further develops the application of his family typology to the treatment process with specific attention to techniques and process.*

References

Applegate, J. S. (1990). Theory, culture and behavior: Object relations in context. *Child and Adolescent Social Work Journal, 7*(2), 85–100.

Blanck, G., & Blanck, R. (1972). Toward a psychoanalytic developmental psychology. *Journal of the American Psychoanalytic Association, 20,* 68–710.

Blanck, G., & Blanck, R. (1987). Developmental object relations theory. *Clinical Social Work Journal, 15,* 318–327.

Boszormenyi-Nagy, I. (1967). Relational modes and meaning. In G. H. Zuk & I. Boszormenyi-Nagy (Eds.), *Family therapy and disturbed families.* Palo Alto, CA: Science and Behavior Books.

Boszormenyi-Nagy, I., & Spark, G. (1973). *Invisible loyalties.* New York: Harper & Row.

Bowen, M. (1965). Family psychotherapy with schizophrenia in the hospital and in private practice. *Comprehensive Psychiatry, 7,* 345–374.

Bowen, M. (1978). *Family theory in clinical practice.* New York: Jason Aronson.

Buber, M. (1958). *I and thou.* New York: Scribner.

Dicks, H. V. (1963). Object relations theory and marital studies. *British Journal of Medical Psychology, 36,* 125–129.

Dicks, H. V. (1967). *Marital tensions.* New York: Basic Books.

Fairbairn, W. R. D. (1954). *An object-relations theory of personality.* New York: Basic Books.

Ferenczi, S. (1920). The further development of an active therapy in psychoanalysis. In *Further contributions to the theory and technique of psychoanalysis.* London: Hogarth Press.

Finkelstein, L. (1987). Toward an object-relations approach in psychoanalytic marital therapy. *Journal of Marital and Family Therapy, 13*(3), 287–298.

Framo, J. L. (1970). Symptoms from a family transactional viewpoint. In N. W. Ackerman (Ed.), *Family therapy in transition.* Boston: Little, Brown.

Framo, J. L. (1972). Symptoms from a family transactional viewpoint. In N. W. Ackerman, N. Lielg, & J. Pearce (Eds.), *Family therapy in transition.* New York: Springer.

Freud, S. (1905). *Fragment of an analysis of a case of hysteria. Collected papers.* New York: Basic Books.

Freud, S. (1940). An outline of psychoanalysis. *Standard Edition, 23,* 139–171.

Juni, S., & Grimm, D. W. (1994). Sex roles as factors in defense mechanisms and object relations. *Journal of Genetic Psychology, 155,* 99–106.

Kernberg, O. F. (1972). Early ego integration and object relations. *Annals of the New York Academy of Science, 193,* 233–247.

Klein, M. (1946). Notes on some schizoid mechanisms. *International Journal of Psycho-Analysis, 27,* 99–110.

Langs, R. (1982). *Psychotherapy: A basic text.* New York: Jason Aronson.

Mahler, M. S. (1952). On child psychosis and schizophrenia: Autistic and symbiotic infantile psychoses. *Psychoanalytic Study of the Child,* Volume 7.

Nichols, M. (1984). *Family therapy: Concepts and methods.* New York: Gardner Press.

Parker, G. (1996). Personal Communication with A. Kilpatrick.

Piercy, F. P., Sprenkle, D. H., et al. (1986). *Family therapy sourcebook.* New York: Guilford Press.

Sampson, H., & Weiss, J. (1977). Research on the psychoanalytic process: An overview. *The Psychotherapy Research Group,* Bulletin No. 2 (March), Department of Psychiatry, Mt. Zion Hospital and Medical Center.

Scharff, D. E. (1982). *The sexual relationship: An object relations view of sex and the family.* Boston: Routledge & Kegan Paul.

Scharff, D. E., & Scharff, J. S. (1987). *Object relations family therapy.* Northvale, NJ: Jason Aronson.

Scharff, J. S. (Ed.). (1989). *Foundations of object relations family therapy.* Northvale, NJ: Jason Aronson.

Silverstein, J. L. (1994). Power and sexuality: Influence of early object relations. *Psychoanalytic Psychology, 11,* 33–46.

Slipp, S. (1984). *Object relations: A dynamic bridge between individual and family treatment.* New York: Jason Aronson.

Slipp, S. (1988). *The technique and practice of object relations family therapy.* Northvale, NJ: Jason Aronson.

Stewart, R. H., Peters, T. C., Marsh, S., & Peters, M. J. (June 1975). An object-relations approach to psychotherapy with marital couples, families and children. *Family Process, 14*(2), 161–178.

Stierlin, H. (1976). The dynamics of owning and disowning: Psychoanalytic and family perspectives. *Family Process, 15*(3), 277–288.

Vogel, E. F., & Bell, N. W. (1960). The emotionally disturbed as the family scapegoat. In N. W. Bell & E. F. Vogel (Eds.), *The family.* Glencoe, IL: Free Press.

Winnicott, D. W. (1958). *Collected papers: Through pediatrics to psycho-analysis.* London: Hogarth Press.

Wynne, L. C. (1965). Some indications and contraindications for exploratory family therapy. In I. Boszormenyi-Nagy & J. L. Franco (Eds.), *Intensive family therapy.* New York: Hoeber.

The Family in the Community: Ecosystem Implications

Throughout this book we have been working within the overall metatheories of ecological systems and social constructionism as the philosophical and theoretical base for working with families on four levels of family need. Each type of family intervention for each level of need includes ecological and system implications. As discussed in Chapter 2, the ecological system includes the microsystem, mesosystem, exosystem, and macrosystem. Many of these levels of ecosystems are included in the interventions in the various chapters. However, this concluding section serves to bring these all together with a focus on the community and the total socio-cultural environment within which the family functions and has their needs met—or not met. This concluding section integrates the theoretical and philosophical underpinning from Part I and the microsystem level interventions from Parts II through V with the ecosystem implications of working with families at the macro-system level. It helps the practitioner to see the larger contextual issues when working with individual families.

In Chapter 13, MacNair emphasizes the community as "replete with opportunities for self-empowerment and enrichment" and, at the same time, "fraught with dangers with impediments to self-fulfillment." He examines the community as the broader context in which families can thrive, survive, or break down. A primary goal is to eliminate the barriers and impediments that prevent family practitioners from becoming involved with larger community issues that impact on family functioning at all levels.

Chapter 13

The Family in the Community

RAY H. MacNAIR, Ph.D.

This chapter examines the community as the broader context in which families survive, thrive, or break down. The ecological perspective on the community touches on aspects that have been emphasized by demographers, sociologists, and geographers, as well as social workers. The fundamentals of physical space and economic survival are presented here as an encouragement to family practitioners to recognize the highly pragmatic issues that families face in their local communities. Emphasis is directed to (1) identifying and analyzing the functional forms of sustenance that the community represents to any given family, through family and community interdependencies; (2) the objective variations in community structure that may affect the subjective sense of efficacy experienced by families and practitioners in the form of optimism or pessimism about the client family's life chances; and (3) a holistic and integrative analysis of patterns of human service networking that are intended to overcome the fragmentation found in many community service systems. Finally, a model of integrated family service networking systems is presented.

The Ecological Perspective on Communities

Foremost among the many perspectives on families in the community is ecosystems theory. At the community level, this approach emphasizes place or locality and is close to the intuitive understanding that many people hold regarding their community. Community is the place where things happen in people's lives, where various forces and opportunities converge to define their life chances and the quality of their well-being.

Sociocultural classes are components of any community. People in the same cultural class tend to share similar lifestyles and values that shape a sense of common identity and mutual sentiments. However, while these lifestyles diverge from those of other cultural classes, they nevertheless share interdependencies. People who do not enjoy each other's company in social gatherings nevertheless affect each other's survival and life chances, sense of personal efficacy, and ability to achieve the level of pride and self-realization they may be seeking.

These broader interdependencies are often overlooked in examinations of communities. The ecological perspective includes cultural classes as components, thus allowing attention to be given to the bonds that people feel among their "own kind." The emphasis, however, is extended to the relationships across classes of people, particularly those whose resources are exchanged and shared when the community is functioning well.

The Definition of Human Ecology

Human ecology defines the community as

> *a local population which is organized to exchange resources with its environment at a given level of technology. (Hawley, 1950; Spengler & Duncan, 1956)*

This definition can be broken down into its four parts:

Population

The shape of a local population may be described demographically, referencing age cohorts, varying levels of education, distributions of occupations, and family incomes. For example, when cohorts of children and the aged outweigh the middle cohorts who are economically active, resources may not be available to adequately meet the needs of the young and the old. Similarly, the levels of education and their distribution in a local population affect the community's ability to modernize its economic activities. This problem is circular, as families who attempt to upgrade themselves may find their life chances limited by a depressed economy (Blakely, 1989).

Organization

Many authors have described communities in terms of their ability to govern themselves and solve problems, or their ability to involve various sectors of the population in decision making (Warren, 1978). Economic functioning is, of course, highly affected by resources and their management, as are regulatory functions, education, health, family services, or other human services. Community studies have shown that economic development is in some measure affected by the ability of economic and governmental leaders to organize a consensus for the development of those resources (F. Hunter, 1980; Blakely, 1979). Community human services systems, likewise, are greatly affected by the ability of governmental and human service leaders to formulate positive roles for coordinating bodies (Buell, 1952; Project SHARE, 1972–1981; Lauffer, 1978). Much attention has been given, of course, to the ability of population sectors or consumer groups to organize themselves into self-help organizations, neighborhood organizations, or community action groups, either to negotiate their own internal resources or press for external resources or policies on their behalf (Cox, Erlich, Rothman, & Tropman, 1974; Roberts & Taylor, 1985; Warren, 1962, 1978).

Environment

In the past, much has been made of the effects of the physical context of a community. Placement on a river, isolated mountain area, oceanside port, arctic or desert climate, or plains each make its mark on community life and the exigencies of family life there. Modernization, however, has been characterized by the leveling of these influences with technologies such as irrigation, trucking, air transportation, air conditioning, and cyberspace, all of which shape the availability and use of resources. "Think globally and act locally" is not just an environmental slogan. National and international marketers and governments have made great inroads into the control of local catastrophes and deprivations. On the other hand, the social environments of communities are still highly divergent. Regional differences are well documented in the degree of attention to such issues as education and health services for the disadvantaged. State policies make a great deal of difference, as do regional attitudes concerning the needs of the mentally ill, addicted, or economically dependent.

Technology

Local populations must be organized to make use of available technologies in order to mitigate or direct environmental influences upon the well-being of families. Access to the resources of community transportation systems, personal automobiles, and modern housing are vital factors in the lives of families seeking to develop their standing as self-supporting members of their communities. Increasingly, access to computer technologies is likely to differentiate between those families that have a sense of personal efficacy and those lacking in it. Technology is available to those who understand and possess the skills, and can afford to raise children with knowledge of their uses. Communities will be increasingly challenged to distribute such resources throughout their populations. Likewise, human service organizations are increasingly expected to link themselves to the centers of knowledge and power through computerized technical and professional networks.

If a community is a local population organized to exchange resources from its environment at a given level of technology, then clearly it is an ecosystem, with intricate mutual dependencies among each of these components.

The Basics of the Community Ecosystem

A community is a local population organized to exchange resources in the provision of daily sustenance at various levels of living. It is the larger society that provides protection for communities and the framework for their longer range economic activities. Communities, on the other hand, offer daily access to productive work and income, places of distribution for consumer goods and services (shopping), and places of residence (the family's consumer center). This triangle of sustenance activities is fundamental to all human needs and to the ways in which we meet them. All sustenance activities are placed in communities geographically. However, while geography is not everything, it is involved in everything. In addressing all human needs, places of work, distribution, and residence must somehow be connected. Connections and transportation, therefore, are basic to community life. Their importance is foremost in the minds of all community planners, as well as city and county administrators.

Human service planners and administrators, on the other hand, have been slow to address the transportation needs of their consumers. Often, in modern cities, some limited public transportation is made available. In rural locations, the lack of transportation is a great barrier to utilization of services. Clients may struggle with it every day, and it may be a major impediment in meeting the needs of Levels I and II families.

The ecological conception of community includes much more than geographic connection as a basic issue. To broaden this perspective, we refer to five ways of describing the sustenance functions (Warren, 1978). They are economic activity, regulation, education, sociability, and mutual support. Correspondingly, the resources required for sustenance are goods and services, authoritative approval, career-building knowledge, affiliation, and health and human services. Families cannot survive without these sustenance resources. Attention to them must be included as a part of any family assessment.

The next section examines these functions and corresponding family resources. We then explore the community as a context for optimism or pessimism concerning the resolution of social problems. Following that section we will examine community human service network systems in the resolution of problems.

Assessment of Families in Community

Each of the function–resources has a bearing on the sense of personal efficacy and optimism or pessimism of the family. This section explores each function with reference to the ecological niche occupied by the family, discussed in Chapter 2.

The Economic Function

It is important to attend to individual or family economics. What kind of jobs do the family members have? What are they qualified for? What training resources are available to them, starting with basic education, job readiness training, skill training, and occupational or professional education programs? Can confidence-building educational groups be developed? What is the employment market for them, and what are the levels of unemployment? What sociocultural stigmas do they have that are barriers to education or employment? What can be done to overcome those barriers? Again, social workers can be involved in community development efforts to make such programs available if they do not already exist (Chilman & Nunnaly, 1988).

The social constructionist perspective is also pertinent here. If programs are to be developed or strengthened, advocacy to overcome sociocultural barriers is needed. Family members cannot be pushed into levels of aspiration that they assume are above their ability to pursue. The family's niche in the community offers a function and an identity, but it may also exercise a conservative influence on family members. Niches can be altered and raised by changes in the family's interpretation of its strengths and capabilities. Raising aspirations will succeed only when family members desire such a change and are ready to pursue it. A change in the occupational niche of the family members, for example, can have a major impact on family well-being, but only when they recognize their own strength to handle the training, and when they pursue additional skills and resources.

Personal economics includes the notion of frugality in shopping and consumption, and the idea that lower prices must be accessed. Convenience shopping is usually expensive; buying on credit often means paying much more for the commodity. On the other hand, bulk purchases are useful only if goods are not wasted. Many tips for frugal shopping can be given, which, in the long run, can mean major differences in lifestyle. Hence, consumer economics is another vital area of concern to the family.

Housing, residential location, and neighborhood relations may also be under-emphasized among some family practitioners. Social workers have long understood the need to collect enough dollars to stave off an eviction, thereby avoiding the sinkhole of homelessness. The importance of cohesion among neighbors must not be overlooked.

The benefits of neighborhood supports against crime and delinquency, for mutual child care, or joint action to demand services from local government, must also not be overlooked. Public housing authorities have increasingly recognized the benefits and have assigned staff to facilitate the organizing efforts.

Regulation

Local and state governments function jointly to administer standards that both limit behavior and offer opportunity for improvement in community conditions for families. Traffic control and driver licensing, law enforcement, recreation, zoning, public housing, business licensing, child-care standards, child and adult protective services, labor department tests, and other community-based regulatory standards all require approval from public authorities in order for families to go about their daily business.

Other regulations affecting families are administered by private business, such as loan departments of financial institutions, credit bureaus, private housing developments, employer tests, labor union tests, or professional and semiprofessional standards. In many cases, these authorities act under governmental standards for administering their regulations.

In all cases, family behavior and resources are involved in meeting the standards required by the service. The ability to maneuver within bureaucracies is essential. "Bureau assertiveness" is a family strength that must be assessed and fostered, particularly among Level I and II families. On the other hand, sociocultural labeling by the bureaucracy may be a barrier to the approvals that are needed. Sometimes the authorities must be goaded into overcoming their own biases. At the same time, family members must be helped to overcome their own sense of worthlessness in the face of a history of rejection. This challenge is a major concern of the social constructionist perspective on family practice.

The problems of bias and labeling are compounded in communities with limited resources for transportation. Cultural definitions of "here" and "there" are barriers to access of services that must be overcome if they are to benefit families (Suttles, 1968). Level I families who feel uncomfortable going "there" to "their turf" are doubly hindered, especially if transportation is difficult. Again, it is vital to acknowledge the experience of family unease in unfamiliar or inaccessible environments, and work with them and others to overcome such barriers (Suttles, 1968).

Education

One of the major challenges for families at all levels is to foster the desire and the discipline necessary for learning. Early intervention programs, preschool education, and K–12 education programs that reinforce the efforts of the family are becoming increasingly accessible to Level I and II families. They are seen by the prevention professionals as the most effective forces that exist in communities against substance abuse, delinquency, and teen pregnancy. They represent the most effective broad-based strategies to produce a sense of personal efficacy among children who otherwise may feel worthless and rejected by normative authorities.

Our secondary schools are the institutions most equivalent to the "training corps for rites of passage" observed by anthropologists among hunting and gathering societies (Hultkrantz & Vorren, 1982; Cohen, 1964). They attempt to prepare puberty-age cohorts for adult roles by putting them through skill training and confidence-building exercises and then conferring a final certificate of accomplishment. In the process, it is assumed that students will be acculturated and bound to the community's normative values and standards.

They fall short of this goal, often for a variety of reasons. With large, unvaried programs, many individuals find their preparation inadequate to meet the specific opportunities available to them. Both skill- and confidence-building exercises may miss the mark. Also, given the specialized profession of education, teachers as role models often appear to be irrelevant to the anticipated adult roles of some students. Finally, teachers may appear more as bureaucratized functionaries than respected authorities; hence, they are not seen by some as worthy of consideration or emulation.

Given such situations, young people may accept a culture of rebellion, which, through peer groups, offers opportunities for status and strength and its own brand of acculturation and role-modeling. Family life, then, may come to seem irrelevant to one's life chances in the community, and such youth is subject to a condition of "anomie" or rootlessness. Expectations for independence from the family may become out of tune with external realities. As a result, these youths enter the early adult years without a clear sense of identity and without a realistic grounding for a career, within the law, that will produce the anticipated income.

Such conditions can persist over time, and unsettled youth become unsettled parents. The function of intervention becomes, then, one of searching for new self-definitions and skills, including career-building opportunities for parents, while connecting parents to career-building activities in school for their children. When professionals appear to be irrelevant as resources in such efforts, these tasks are daunting indeed.

When appropriate, basic education programs for young adults and parents are pertinent. Questions of location and sociocultural compatibility must be acknowledged and resolved when planning for these programs. School bus transportation may be demeaning, for example. White-collar middle-class teachers may be unprepared to relate meaningfully to children from Level I and II families. Apprenticeship experiences may well be more effective approaches, though such programs are rare and expensive. Our communities have much work ahead to bridge these gaps. Again, practitioners can be advocates for the development of suitable programs.

Sociability

The function of sociability and its resultant sense of affiliation and emotional support are increasingly recognized as important resources for all families. The well-known correlation between social isolation and family violence underscores this point (Hansen & Harway, 1993). Through social constructionist interventions, families can come to recognize the strength they receive from friendships and other social groupings, and they can begin to seek them out more effectively. Avenues of affiliation include routine-oriented or safety-conscious as well as action- or risk-oriented affiliations (Gans, 1962). The former bespeaks dependability; the latter danger and getting into trouble. Clearly, practitioners would prefer their clients to pursue affiliations that reinforce safer alternatives.

Typical social outlets include peer groups, occupational cadres, neighborhood friends, social clubs (however informal they may be), sporting teams (including coaching activities), and entertainment and recreation outings. Consumer marketing specialists and researchers have long recognized the importance of these activities, which proffer an identity and style of life on members of the family (Weiss, 1988). Religious organizations also provide many with a sense of identity and self-confidence. Family practitioners should recognize such resources, and attend to their possibilities as well as limitations (Wilkinson, 1993; Walsh, 1993).

American society has a way of proffering these opportunities and then undercutting them. Religious conflict is rife (J. Hunter, 1991). Peer groups and neighborhood friends are fluid; occupational cadres fall away whenever jobs are lost or shifted or retirement takes place. Injury may remove the sports club affiliation. When a family is evicted from its housing, they may become isolated from all neighborhood affiliations. Family intervention requires much patience and skill in sifting through the possibilities for reconnections. The family may know what is needed and appropriate for sustaining itself, or it may not understand the importance of social networks or how to sustain them.

Support

When individuals falter or external misfortunes occur, the family's level of living (defined economically and socially) can be drastically reduced. Whether the problem is a bank failure, a factory closing, a natural disaster, an illness in the family, an emotional breakdown, substance abuse, a criminal conviction, or some form of violence, supports are needed to keep the family from falling apart or losing its sustenance and pride. The first line of defense in most communities is usually some form of insurance, social security, unemployment compensation, hospital or health maintenance service, home health care, or other personal services in the private sector. Professional and informal personal guides may be consulted in order to ferret out such resources.

The decision to pursue professional or bureaucratic help may be born of total despair, or it may be a result of sociocultural understandings of the role of such agencies. These understandings may have built up over many years, even generations of experience and hearsay. Agency reputations are seen differently by different social groups because of differing previous treatment, or because of subcultural values of independence, professionalism, or fatalism. Studies have shown a clear preference among lower socioeconomic classes for physical health professionals, while upper-middle-class individuals are more likely to seek the help of a psychologically oriented service (Freidson, 1961; Harwood, 1981).

What happens as a result of seeking help from an agency or professional is a matter of perception. Tangible forms of support may be available, but when despair is potent and complex, such help may be insufficient. Family fatalism persists, and even practitioners can succumb to a sense of hopelessness. Optimism and pessimism and a sense of personal efficacy are functions of both the client's and the professional's anticipations.

The next section explores the possibility that the community as a social system may actually foster this pessimism or optimism through the culture of its social agency networks.

The Community as a Source of Pessimism or Optimism: A Sense of Collective Efficacy

Every community has a unique character. The more one becomes involved in community life, the more one realizes there can be moods of optimism about the future, or negative feelings that things are unlikely to get better. In pessimistic communities, young people tend to feel that they have little good to anticipate, and they frequently wish to leave in order to improve their lives. Problems seem intractable, and agreement about action to be taken eludes community leaders. On the other hand, the optimistic community, while it may have troubles, feels that improvements are coming; collective forethought and decision making will produce action for the better.

At least two types of explanation can be given for such differences: economic and sociocultural. The economic explanation points at economic resources, productivity, and the distribution of wealth as sources of optimism. The sociocultural explanation indicates that racial or ethnic divisions may paralyze community leaders and render positive action impossible, on the one hand, and cultural norms and values that favor diversity may encourage positive action, on the other. First, we review the economic explanation.

The Economy

Simple community economics suggests that when jobs are scarce, two optional responses are available. Capital can move to the labor market, such as it is, or labor can move to the centers of capital. In the latter strategy, people simply move away to seek a better life. The loss of stability and social supports in such a move may be rending to the community and the family. In the former strategy, the community must attract investment from other centers into the community; and labor pools must be prepared for the levels of technology that are required to provide manpower for the new forms of productivity. This strategy, in some instances, will require a level of coordination between educational and training programs and business development that is very demanding (Blakely, 1989; Shaffer, 1989; Rubin & Rubin, 1992). Decision makers across the community must be optimistic, consensual, and well coordinated. Family practitioners can be supportive of this process.

A simplified typology of communities will clarify this point further. Typically, communities are either (1) commercial–agricultural centers; (2) one-company towns; (3) one-industry communities, with a number of companies; (4) multi-industry, blue-collar communities; (5) multi-industry and professional, white-collar centers; and (6) multi-industry, professional, and financial centers.

A brief description (see Table 13.1) and the assumed consequences for the community's optimism or pessimism are provided here:

1. Commercial–agricultural centers are typical rural towns with very little industrial or professional activity. Agricultural businesses and commercial trade are mixed with small processing plants and warehouses. Leadership is provided by commercial trade businessmen of long-standing reputations. Efforts to attract industry are made, but inertia in the technology and educational arenas renders such efforts weak and rarely successful (Ady, 1986; Bradshaw & Blakely, 1979). On the other hand, churches can be sources of positive change, especially when they have optimistic leadership.

2. One-company towns, such as mill towns, are historically cohesive communities under the paternalistic guidance of company executives. Company workers tend to be paid low wages, and they are beholden to the company for buying on credit. They are generally cared for, but at a low standard of living. Educational

TABLE 13.1   Types of Communities and Their Climates

Type	Organizational Character	Resources	Leadership	Climate for Human Services
Rural commercial	Static	Weak	Reputational leaders	Negative—people should take care of themselves
One-company town	Constrained	Weak to moderate	Patrons	Negative—we take care of our own
Single-industry community	Focused	Variable	Monolithic	Variable but minimized
Single industry— absentee owned	Commensalistic	Variable	Vacuum– charisma	Variable— sometimes optimized
Multiple industries— blue-collar	Complex commensalistic	Strong	Pluralistic	Favorable
Multiple industries; including service sector	Symbiotic	Strong	Pluralistic	Favorable—inventive
Financial center	Complex symbioses	Super	Mega- consensual	Favorable—magnetic

programs that might raise the aspirations of workers' families are discouraged. Little or no change takes place as long as the one company remains the key employer in town. In recent years, economic forces have destabilized these communities, and they have become increasingly pessimistic in outlook (Fuguitt, 1989).

3. Communities with a number of one-industry companies tend to be somewhat more optimistic, because workers have, in principle, more choices for employment. Their choices of occupation are still somewhat limited, however, and industry leaders are quite capable of blocking change through informal, consensual decision making behind the scenes. Again, larger economic changes can affect such an industry unfavorably, and the vulnerability of such a community exacerbates their pessimistic tendencies. Efforts to modernize the educational system and human services may be somewhat more effective, but they struggle against the odds (Tyson, 1989).

4. Multi-industry, blue-collar communities offer their labor force much more opportunity. The blue-collar nature of the community leads, in this context, to greater self-confidence among workers to organize on their own behalf and bargain for consideration. They may also be able to elect political leaders who cater to their needs. Education, health, and human service programs are much more likely to receive favorable attention in this context. Efforts to address social problems may be somewhat routine and unimaginative, but the level of optimism can be much higher than in the previous types of community (Sternleib & Listokin, 1981).

5. Multi-industry and professional, white-collar centers may have major employers of white-collar, professional workers in addition to the blue-collar labor force of the typical industry-diverse community just described. Government, hospital, or university centers are cases in point. These communities include in their volun-

teer and professional agency workforces highly talented people who are willing to address the need to develop effective programs. They are more likely to be risk takers and develop imaginative programs. Optimism concerning the opportunities to resolve problems tends to be relatively high, especially when economic conditions are favorable (Sternleib & Listokin, 1981).

6. Multi-industry, professional, and financial centers, such as New York, Chicago, or San Francisco, contain all the advantages described in item 5. In addition, they have access to financial decision makers who typically have influence in governmental and private foundation circles. The tax base is stronger than that of smaller communities. On the other hand, social problems are also typically enormous. Talent and wealth combine to produce inventiveness and optimism, which are tempered only by the enormity of problems to be addressed. Resources abound, but they may well be inadequate to the task. Many human-service planners and providers work under favorable conditions, although many do not because of the very large caseloads.

The Sociocultural Perspective

The sociocultural perspective focuses attention on ethnic and racial divisions that the economic view tends to ignore. The effect of racial and ethnic division in a community is well known and reasonably well understood. Frequently, it is debilitating to the process of making positive decisions to address social problems. The key ingredient is fear or anxiety that "those people" will waste precious resources and nothing good will happen. On the other side stand the advocates for empowerment of disadvantaged people. The trust that this approach requires, however, is difficult to build in an environment fraught with fear and anxiety.

In this context, practitioners may be the fulcrum that can nurture trust and coalition building. Insofar as practitioners are the object of trust, they can develop programs with community support. One approach would be to support programs of family empowerment (Haynes & Singh, 1993) in the context of objectives that the public will support, including self-sufficiency, employment, effective child rearing, and economic self-help.

If it is true that practitioners and agency leaders are a part of the total sociocultural mix, how can they offer the public the accountability that they require while combining forces to offer families the resources they need to pull themselves together and develop their "self-empowerment" capabilities?

First, they can recognize the collectivist world view of many peoples of color. They can build an organizing model based on the strengths of families, extended families, and networks of friends and neighbors. Cultural celebration, multicultural facilitation, and a humble supportive role among practitioners will serve to position the practitioner to ask family members and neighbors for help in identifying programs in family development centers (Guitterez, Alvarez, Nemon, & Lewis, 1996; Gaudin, Wodarski, Arkinson, & Avery, 1990–1991).

Practitioners and agency leaders are a part of the total sociocultural mix. They must be accountable to the community and offer families the resources they need to pull themselves together and develop their "self-empowerment" capabilities.

We now address patterns of human service networking as they reflect the community's optimism or pessimism and sense of collective efficacy.

Patterns of Human Service Networking

In the late 1940s, Bradley Buell (1952) observed the migrations of rural southerners into northern cities and the difficulties they experienced. They lacked the educational and organizational skills needed to understand what to do when family supports fell away as a result of the migration. They seemed to feel like aliens in a maze of human service and health agencies, and they distrusted the formality they encountered in bureaucracies that presumably had been designed to serve them. Buell conducted a tracking study in Minneapolis of families as they entered the network and stumbled through it in their efforts to survive.

Buell found (1) gaps in needed services; (2) duplication of services, each of which was inadequate by itself; (3) contradictory advice given by agencies, which should have been coordinated; (4) fragmentation, or the practitioner's view that one partial approach to a complex of problems would be sufficient to solve all problems; (5) bias against people in poverty as unworthy of the agency's time and energy; and (6) bureaucratic barriers to referral, including transportation, waiting lists, and repetitive paperwork. Much has been done nationwide in the ensuing years to address these problems and build coordinated networking systems. However, much resistance and inertia remain, and the problems of fragmentation persist. Many families today fail to wade through from one needed service to another. Much of the service that is rendered is wasted, because complementary services that would reinforce the gains made initially are not rendered.

The federal government, state governments, and foundations have taken up the banner of "integrated services" in a variety of ways. Resources and mandates for coordination have been offered and then revoked. Many pilot "integrated systems" have been tested, and that process continues in the 1990s.

Each community responds in its own way under varied state mandates and creative support by foundations. Within each community, a culture that engenders coordination emerges in varying degrees. A variety of styles can be identified, which result from and affect the optimism or pessimism of the agencies' collective network. They are (MacNair, 1981):

1. An authoritative style, which requires a command response to assigned coordinators. This style appears to result from a cynical view that providers will not consistently participate in networking systems unless they are commanded to participate. The command style invokes resentment and resistance by providers, with the result that a "turf-guarding" pattern emerges, sometimes with a vengeance. The pessimistic basis for the authoritarian style, in other words, provokes further pessimism.

2. A formalist style, based on the idea that providers do not have time and means to talk to each other, and have established a paperwork system of referrals that avoids talking altogether. Again, much resistance and inertia is produced,

related to the impersonal basis of the system. On the other hand, the possibility of generating highly efficient computerized networks is currently being pursued in some locations. We predict that they may produce a receptive provider response to the extent that providers feel the system is easy to operate and seems to be designed for their benefit.

3. The universalist style, based on an overly optimistic managerial assumption that *all* providers are equally able and willing to make *all* appropriate referrals for *all* clients who need them. Failing to recognize the thorough training and supervision such an assumption requires, this style generates confusion and a sense of inadequacy, resulting in cynicism.

4. The humanistic style, which relies on self-generated interpersonal networks and personalized connections. This style is grounded in an optimism about human relationships among providers. It can regenerate its own optimism if it is fostered carefully throughout the agency network. On the other hand, it may be biased and somewhat inconsistent.

5. The professional style, in which individual providers throughout the agency network are assigned to coordinating roles and trained accordingly. "Dedicated" case managers work with a professional level of knowledge of families with complex and intractable social problems. They have the knowledge of the agency network required to utilize it thoroughly. This approach is grounded in both optimism and realism. It can still lead to resentment by individual providers in agencies of the special status of professional case managers, unless it is tempered with a touch of humanism and guided teamwork. The result can be highly optimistic.

6. An inventive style, resulting from a sense that new, creative forms of networking and somewhat charismatic leadership will generate an enthusiasm for client change and an appreciation for coordinating roles that is contagious. Inventions are frequently sponsored by outside bodies and offer special resources. Hence, they are born of optimism and are expected to generate optimism and a sense of efficacy within the network. Examples are the historic "case finding" programs that put outreach workers on the street to discover hidden but responsive clients; and the evolving family preservation programs, which place practitioners in the home to render both case management and therapy services along with guided family building exercises (see Chapter 5).

None of these styles addresses the problem of the midlevel managers who are frequently left out of the design and implementation of networking systems. Often, cynical by virtue of their position, middle managers are capable of undermining the best-designed system. Thus, we suggest it is advisable to engage middle managers in the design and implementation of integrative systems. Teamwork at their level is just as vital as it is at the level of service provision.

Indeed, top managers, middle managers, service providers, and families themselves should all be involved in designing and implementing a networking system that engenders optimism and a sense of efficacy.

The next section proposes a model of a goal-directed community human service system.

A Model of a Community Human Services Networking System

This goal-directed model is based on the assumption that there are at least three types of human service: those directed at survival (Level I families), those focused on self-empowerment (Level II and III families), and those geared for self-realization and prevention (Level III and IV families). Examples of survival-oriented services are unemployment compensation, food stamps, Temporary Assistance to Needy Families (TANF, formerly AFDC), homeless shelters, psychiatric hospitals, youth detention centers, runaway shelters, and detoxification facilities. Corresponding self-empowerment services are training and job placement services, public housing in which rent is paid, outpatient mental health, youth home placement or family preservation service, and addiction treatment and support groups.

Self-realization and prevention services are career development programs, housing subsidies through Section 8 of the U.S. Housing Act, individual or family therapy, education for child rearing, and preventive action systems. The term "preventive actions systems" refers to inventive self-help organizing and empowerment activities that pull together at-risk populations prior to the outbreak of problems, such as teen pregnancy or teen drug addiction. For example, teen councils have been known to organize preventive actions systems of volunteers to mentor younger people, clean up neighborhoods, or offer community services.

For too long American society has been content to offer minimal survival services, or less, to Level I families. Self-empowerment has often been an espoused objective, but often the optimism and sense of professional efficacy required for success have been lacking. Limited resources and clearly documented effectiveness have been barriers to the development and maintenance of self-empowerment and self-realization/prevention services.

Nevertheless, an array of programs at all three levels is available in most urban communities. It is the goal-directed interconnection that is often missing. If survival, self-empowerment, and self-realization/prevention programs were clearly linked, a sense of effectiveness would be more likely. Each program should be designed to demonstrate achievement at one level, readiness to go to the next level, and preparation to receive families from previous levels. Practitioners should be prepared to guide families at Levels I and II from one set of goals to the other when their progress warrants the connection. A goal-directed human services networking system will demonstrate its eagerness to prepare families for the next level and receive them at the next. Documentation of progress should be used to account to the public for the achievements being made. A model of the three types of goals and their interconnections can be offered visually, as in Figure 13.1.

The model suggests that community-wide policies be established that encourage agencies to link with each other through information systems and goal setting

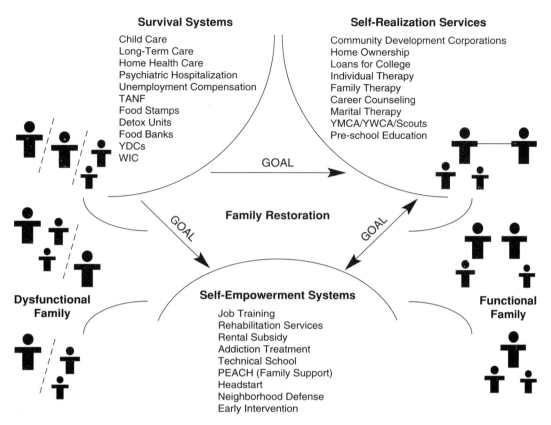

Survival Systems

Child Care
Long-Term Care
Home Health Care
Psychiatric Hospitalization
Unemployment Compensation
TANF
Food Stamps
Detox Units
Food Banks
YDCs
WIC

Self-Realization Services

Community Development Corporations
Home Ownership
Loans for College
Individual Therapy
Family Therapy
Career Counseling
Marital Therapy
YMCA/YWCA/Scouts
Pre-school Education

GOAL

Family Restoration

GOAL

GOAL

Dysfunctional Family

Functional Family

Self-Empowerment Systems

Job Training
Rehabilitation Services
Rental Subsidy
Addiction Treatment
Technical School
PEACH (Family Support)
Headstart
Neighborhood Defense
Early Intervention

FIGURE 13.1   **Community human service networking systems, linking policies, programs, and practices.**

with clients. Resources would be expected to follow clients through their connections within the networking system. Connections between programs are thus established that link TANF with child care, education, job training programs, and employment services. Finally, family practitioners will be primed for a networking practice through community workshops that focus on an awareness of the availability of program connections and the policies that guide those connections. A sense of optimism can thus be generated among families that the service system is set up to work for them.

The challenge for community human service networks is threefold: (1) to promote a culture among providers, middle managers, and top managers that they are part of a broader system of accountability; (2) to focus on the perception of client family members of their own readiness for different kinds of services; and (3) to structure a networking system that honors the specialized problems of individual family members, and at the same time integrates the service plan together with the family as a whole. Family practitioners could participate in such a system with a greater sense of confidence that their efforts will receive recognition as they move families forward.

Summary

The model of family practice that is suggested here is one that emphasizes the community as replete with opportunities for self-empowerment and enrichment. At the same time, it is fraught with dangers and with impediments to self-fulfillment. It recognizes the differences between communities in the level of positive and optimistic organizing that takes place among disadvantaged (Level I and II) families and on behalf of such families.

In addition to recognizing the variations in community attitudes and behavior, it is suggested that family practitioners participate in community development and prevention activities that have the potential for expanding opportunities and reducing self-defeating forms of pessimistic behavior. Individual family practice must be distinguished from group, neighborhood, or community-level activities. The social constructivist practitioner can, however, encourage individual participation when an assessment shows a readiness for it. This approach is consistent with the "Family Empowerment and Social Justice" model proposed by Haynes and Singh (1993).

The practitioner may also wish to refer to Gaudin's (1984) concept of "social work roles"; Kruzich's (1988) chapter in Chilman, Cox, and Nunnaly, "Helping Families with Income Problems"; and finally, Parsons, Hernandez, and Jorgensen's (1988) generalized practice model, "Integrated Practice: A Framework for Problem Solving." These models merge an individualistic model of family practice with models that focus on the collective activities of education groups, neighborhood organization, self-help, community planning, and legislative action. Clearly, these models reduce or eliminate the division and cleavage that are felt between clinical practitioners and macro-level practitioners. This is the major thrust of the multi-level view of families and family practice.

Discussion Questions

1. What does it mean to have an "ecological perspective?" What is included in the "ecosystem"?
2. Can you identify in your own words the functional framework for assessment of families in the community? Can you use that framework to analyze creatively individual, neighborhood, communitywide, and legislative policy issues pertinent to families?
3. How does the economic structure of a community affect its optimism or pessimism regarding its capacity to take effective action against community social problems?
4. How does the cultural mix of a community affect the level of trust required in community building?
5. In performing an assessment of community human-service networks, what features of network structure and function would you look for? What kinds of networks work best in the long run?

6. If you could design a community human-services networking system for families, what would it look like?

Suggested Readings

Buell, B. (1952). *Community planning for human services.* New York: Columbia University Press.

> *This research report is based on a tracking study of over one hundred families with multiple prob-lems and a sense of being lost in the community network of agencies. It is the first to document the fragmentation of services and establish the need for integrative practices among agencies. It is a landmark study.*

Chilman, C., Cox, F., & Nunnaly, E. (Eds.). (1988). *Employment and economic problems: Families in trouble series, Volume I.* Beverly Hills, CA: Sage.

> *The editors present a compilation of articles on the issues families face with the threat of unem-ployment and loss of income, subjects that family practitioners must address if they are to deal with social justice issues on the individual and family levels. The articles are seminal.*

Gans, H. J. (1962). *The urban villagers: Groups and class in the life of Italian-Americans.* New York: Free Press of Glencoe.

> *The author conducted an anthropology-style study of an Italian neighborhood in Boston that was scheduled for "removal" in an urban redevelopment project. Attention is given to family struc-ture and culture, religion and politics, street-level recreational behavior, and relationships with the "caregivers" in social agencies. For the first time, a vivid portrayal is presented of the way a population of tenuous status views the people who pose as their guardians of social betterment.*

Gaudin, J., Wodarski, J., Arkinson, N., & Avery, L. (1990–1991). Remedying child neglect: Effectiveness of social work interventions. *Journal of applied social sciences, 15*(1), 97–123.

> *The author describes a networking intervention study with neglectful families. The intervention consisted of personal networking, volunteer linking, employing neighborhood helpers, and social skills training. A variety of measures were used to assess the results of the intervention.*

Guitterez, L., Alvarez, A., Nemon, H., & Lewis, E. (1996). Multicultural organizing: A strat-egy for change. *Social Work, 41*(5), 501–508.

> *Concepts of community organizing are developed that take into account issues of cultural com-petence, social justice, family, and neighborhood empowerment. The role of the social worker is differentiated by virtue of degrees of identity with the ethnicities of the family and neighborhood.*

Litwak, E., & Meyer, H. (1974). *School, family, and neighborhood: The theory and practice of school-community relations.* New York: Columbia University Press.

> *A framework is developed for ways to organize reaching families who are culturally and socially distant from or at odds with human-service providers. The neighborhood school is the focus of the presentation, but the framework is applicable to a variety of social agencies.*

Parsons, R., Hernandez, S., & Jorgensen, J. (1988, September/October). Integrated practice: A framework for problem solving. *Social Work,* 417–421.

> *A generalist concept of social work practice is formulated that integrates the individual level of intervention, group habilitation, collective community levels of intervention, and social policy and legislative levels. Concepts of competence, empowerment, and management are viewed within a collectivist frame.*

Suttles, G. D. (1968). *The social order of the slum: Ethnicity and territory in the inner city.* Chicago: University of Chicago Press.

> *The author conducts a mix of forms of study in three types of neighborhoods in Chicago: Hispanic, African-American, and Italian. Each neighborhood formulates its own subjective (social constructionist in the present language) sense of ownership of its territory versus other people's territory. The concept of a "defensive" neighborhood is developed in which outsiders, including officials of all kinds, are fed incomplete forms of information and insiders are protected.*

Weiss, M. (1988). *The clustering of America.* New York: Harper & Row.

> *This is a compilation of business marketing data on various types of neighborhoods in American society. The family forms, consumer tastes and patterns, lifestyles, and forms of expression are identified for 40 types of neighborhoods. These types are somewhat useful in providing orientation for practitioners to the culture and expectations of families in their contexts.*

References

Ady, R. (1986). Criteria used for facility location. In N. Walzer & D. Chicoine (Eds.), *Financing economic development in the 1980s.* New York: Praeger.

Blakely, E. J. (Ed.). (1979). *Community development research: Concepts, issues, and strategies.* New York: Human Sciences Press.

Blakely, E. J. (1989). *Planning local economic development: Theory and practice.* Beverly Hills, CA: Sage.

Bradshaw, T., & Blakely, E. (1979). *Rural communities in advanced industrial society: Development and developers.* New York: Praeger.

Buell, B. (1952). *Community planning for human services.* New York: Columbia University Press.

Cohen, Y. A. (1964). *The transition from childhood to adolescence.* Chicago: Aldine.

Cox, F. M., Erlich, J., Rothman, J., & Tropman, J. (Eds.). (1974). *Strategies of community organization: A book of readings.* Itasca, IL: Peacock.

Freidson, E. (1961). *Patients' use of medical practice: A study of subscribers to a prepaid medical plan in the Bronx.* New York: Russell Sage Foundation.

Fuguitt, G. (1989). *Rural and small town America.* New York: Russell Sage Foundation.

Gans, H. J. (1962). *The urban villagers: Groups and Class in the Life of Italian-Americans.* New York: Free Press of Glencoe.

Gaudin, J. (1984, May). Social work roles and tasks with incarcerated mothers. *Social Casework, 279–286.*

Gaudin, J., Wodarski, J., Arkinson, N., & Avery, L. (1990–1991). Remedying child neglect: Effectiveness of social work interventions. *Journal of Applied Social Sciences, 15*(1), 97–123.

Guitterez, L., Alvarez, A., Nemon, H., & Lewis, E. (1996). Multicultural organizing: A strategy for change. *Social Work, 41*(5), 501–508.

Hansen, M., & Harway, M. (Eds.). (1993). *Battering and family therapy: A feminist perspective.* Newbury Park, CA: Sage.

Harwood, A. (1981). *Ethnicity and medical care.* Cambridge, MA: Harvard University Press.

Hawley, A. (1950). *Human ecology: A theory of government structure.* New York: Ronald Press.

Haynes, A. W., & Singh, R. N. (1993). Helping families in developing countries: A model based on family empowerment and social justice. *Social Development Issues, 15*(1), 27–37.

Hultkrantz, A., & Vorren, O. (1982). *The hunters: Their culture and way of life.* Tromso, Germany: Universitetsforlaget.

Hunter, F. (1980). *Community power succession: Atlanta's policy-makers.* Chapel Hill: University of North Carolina.

Hunter, J. (1991). *The culture wars: The struggle to define American society.* New York: Basic Books.

Kruzich, J. (1988). Helping families with income problems. In C. Chilman, F. Cox, & E. Nunnaly (Eds.), *Employment and economic problems: Families in trouble series, Volume I.* Newbury Park, CA: Sage.

Lauffer, A. (1978). *Social planning at the community level.* Englewood Cliffs, NJ: Prentice Hall.

MacNair, R. (1981). *Case coordination: Designing interagency teamwork.* Athens: Institute of Community and Area Development, University of Georgia.

Parsons, R., Hernandez, S., & Jorgensen, J. (1988, September/October). Integrated practice: A framework for problem solving. *Social Work,* 417–421.

Project SHARE. (1972–1981). U.S.H.E.W. Government Printing Office.

Roberts, R., & Taylor, S. (1985). *Theory and practice of community social work.* New York: Columbia University Press.

Rubin, H., & Rubin, I. (1992). *Community organizing and development.* New York: Macmillan.

Shaffer, R. (1989). *Community economics: Economic structure and change in smaller communities.* Ames: Iowa State University Press.

Spengler, J. J., & Duncan, O. (1956). *Demographic analysis.* Glencoe, IL: Free Press.

Sternleib, G., & Listokin, D. (Eds.). (1981). *New tools for economic development: The enterprise zone, development bank, and RFC.* New Brunswick, NJ: Center for Urban Policy Research.

Suttles, G. D. (1968). *The social order of the slum: Ethnicity and territory in the inner city.* Chicago: University of Chicago Press.

Tyson, T. (1989). *Two sides of the sunbelt: The growing divergence between the rural and urban South.* New York: Praeger.

Walsh, F. (1993). *Normal family processes.* New York: Guilford Press.

Warren, R. L. (1962). *Patterns of community action: A university lecture.* Waltham, MA: Brandeis University.

Warren, R. L. (1978). *The community in America.* Chicago: Rand McNally College.

Weiss, M. J. (1988). *The clustering of America.* New York: Harper & Row.

Wilkinson, I. (1993). *Family assessment: A basic manual for practitioners.* New York: Gardner Press.

Glossary

Note: These definitions are based on how the terms are used in this book.

Accommodation   The process of adjustment of family members to each other in order to coordinate their functioning, or a therapeutic tactic used by practitioners, especially in structural family interventions, to adapt to the family style in order to create a therapeutic alliance.

Attachment Theory   Concepts about the stages that children go through in developing social relationships and the influence of this development on relationships in later life.

Behavior Rehearsal   A technique used in social learning family interventions where the practitioner suggests desired behavior and then encourages the person or family to behave similarly through demonstrations, role plays, or descriptions.

Boundaries   A central concept in family systems theories that utilizes abstract dividers between or among parts of a system such as between individuals and subsystems within a family or between the family and the environment. These boundaries may change over time as the system goes through various developmental stages.

Brief Family Therapy   Short-term interventions that are usually goal-oriented, active, and focused. They emphasize resolving the presenting problem rather than seeing it as a symptom of underlying dysfunction.

Brokerage   A function of case managers to identify, locate, and obtain needed community resources for individuals and families.

Case Management   A procedure for planning, securing, and monitoring services on behalf of a person or family from a variety of relevant agencies and resources.

Circular Causality   The recursive nature of interactions of the family and other systems where the behavior of one component affects the behavior of all others.

Coaching   In Bowen's family theory, the practitioner's role is to be both a role model for individual family members in the differentiation of self-process and a facilitator or coach as they explore their families of origin.

Cognitive Restructuring   Procedures that attempt to modify or restructure disruptive or maladaptive thought patterns that may result in maladaptive behaviors by changing feelings and actions.

Collusion   An integral part of projective identification in object relations theory where the recipient of the split-off part of the partner does not disown the projection but acts on the conscious or unconscious message.

Confidentiality   A principle of ethics where the family practitioner or other professional may not disclose any information about the individual or family without that person's or family's consent. This includes identity, content of verbalizations, or opinions.

Cultural Pluralism   The coexistence and mutual respect for differences and strengths of cultures and groups other than one's own.

Detriangulate   In Bowen's family theory, this intervention consists of pointing out the triangulation process in order to withdraw a person from the buffer or go-between role, usually with parents so as not to be drawn into alliances with one against another. This is many times more helpful than dealing with the presenting issues.

Developmental Transitions   The movement of persons or families from one life stage to another. This is a time of greater stresses, problems, and conflicts as tasks from the previous stage are consolidated, and progress toward the tasks of the next stage is begun.

Differentiation   In family systems theory, this is the psychological separation of intellect and emotion in the differentiation of self, and also the ability of family members to separate their identities, emotions, and thoughts from other family members in terms of autonomy and independence. This is the opposite of fusion or enmeshment.

Eclecticism   The use of many theories together or in sequence, or selected parts of them used in combination. Caution is urged in the selection of theories to use together.

Ecology   A science that studies the relationships that exist between organisms and their environment. In human ecology, it relates to how humans adapt or achieve goodness of fit with the environment.

Ecological Systems Perspective   A metatheory that shows the systemic relatedness of family variables and the environment, and allows for multiple intervention methods and practitioner roles.

Ecomap   A diagram used to show reciprocal influences between a family and their environment. It would include extended family members, relevant social institutions, and environmental influences.

Ecosystem   A concept pertaining to the physical, biological, and social environments of family members and the interaction between every relevant component contained therein.

Effectiveness   Producing a definite or desired result. Research into the effectiveness of different theories can help us determine their validity; however, since many theories are not prescriptions for actions but are about ideas and interpretations, the research findings do not give us all the answers about usefulness.

Empowerment   The process of helping a person or family increase their influence and strength over their own lives and circumstances.

Encopresis   The inability to control one's bowel functions: an elimination disorder.

Enmeshment   In structural family theory, this is where boundaries are blurred between family members, so that there is little autonomy or independent functioning.

Environment   The conditions, circumstances, and influences of ecological or situational forces that affect the development and behavior of individuals or groups in a particular setting.

Equifinality   The premise that the same result may be reached from different beginning points.

Eriksonian theory   Erik Erikson's conceptualization of human psychosocial development through eight stages of life. Each stage has a task to be accomplished before the next stage can be reached. There are conflicts or danger at each stage that could interfere with development.

Ethnic Competence   The ability to behave in a manner that is congruent with expectations of various ethnic groups, thus demonstrating respect for the family's cultural integrity.

Ethnocentrism   The belief that one's own culture or ethnic group is superior to others.

Ethnographic Interviewing   Learning about specific cultures or groups by going into their natural settings, as is done when family preservation workers go into a family's home and community to provide services.

Exosystem   This system represents the social structures, both formal and informal, that influence, limit, or constrain what happens there. Exosystem practice would focus on community-level factors that have an impact on the way people function.

Externalizing Problems   A technique in the narrative approach of getting families to view problems as external to them, thus motivating them to strengthen exceptions to the problems and control them.

Family Preservation   Intensive services based on family strengths that are provided to families where children are at imminent risk of out-of-home placement.

First-Order Change   In systems theory, this is a temporary and superficial change in the family system and the way it functions that leaves the basic structure and functioning of the system unchanged.

Fusion   Fusion occurs where blurred intellectual and emotional functioning within an individual parallels the degree to which that person loses autonomy and differentiation with other family members.

Generic   Relating to more basic universal characteristics or patterns such as those commonly found in all families, such as boundaries and authority.

Genogram   A graphic presentation of a multigenerational relationship system where recurring behavior patterns within the family system can be traced.

Habitat   The place where a person or family lives, including the physical and social setting within cultural contexts.

Holistic   An individual or family is seen as more than the sum of all its parts, and problems are more than specific symptoms. Physical, social, psychological, spiritual, and cultural influences are integrated.

Homeostasis   A dynamic balance or equilibrium in a family or other system where one or more variables are very stable.

Idiographic Research   The study of an individual, couple, or family where baselines are established and repeated measures are used to determine results of interventions. The results may be replicated with other individuals, couples, or groups.

Idiosyncratic   Characteristics that are unique to a particular family with their own expectations, meanings, interactions, and behaviors that would not be representative of other families.

Indigenous Workers   Members of a community who work with helping professionals in providing services such as those used in family preservation.

Introjection   In object relations theory, a primitive form of identification involving a process where an individual takes in the characteristics of other people, which then become part of the individual's own self-image.

Joining   A process whereby the practitioner enters the family system and relates to all members individually and to subsystems, thus developing a therapeutic alliance so that treatment goals may be reached.

Levels of Need   Used specifically in this book to refer to families' specific needs, where lower-level needs must be met before higher-level needs are addressed.

Life Stage Theory   The idea that every period of life, including that of an individual, couple, or family, has certain goals and dangers inherent in it that serve to modify behavior and order priorities. Each higher stage builds on the accomplishments of the previous stage or may be hampered by unfinished tasks.

Macrosystem   The larger system that includes the overall broader context and culture. Macrosystem practice would work toward improvements in the general society through such means as political action or community organization.

Maintenance   An accommodation technique that is supportive of a family's structure as it is. The practitioner may relate to other family members through this structure, as, for example, a parent as the central figure.

Mental Research Institute (MRI)   The original developer of "brief therapy," this institute is in Palo Alto, California, and the model is based on the work of Gregory Bateson. MRI involves a cybernetic systems approach to working with families, which focuses on observable behavioral interactions and the interventions that alter the system.

Mesosystem   The system that incorporates the interactions of individuals, families, and groups within the person's microsystem. Mesosystem practice would focus on interpersonal relationships within these systems.

Metaphor   A figure of speech containing an implied comparison, where a word or phrase ordinarily used for one thing is applied to another to express feelings, imagination, or objective reality.

Metatheory   A comprehensive system of thought that covers a wide area of practice and that would accept the inclusion of other perspectives and methods.

Microsystem   This system represents the individual in family and group settings that incorporate the day-to-day environment. Microsystem practice would focus on interventions on a case-by-case basis to deal with the problems faced by individuals and families.

Mimesis   A therapeutic tactic used especially by structural family practitioners as an accommodation technique, where the practitioner imitates or mirrors a family's style and communication and behavioral patterns in order to gain acceptance and accomplish goals.

Modeling   Used in social learning theory to encourage the imitation and acquisition of behaviors observed in others that have led to more desirable outcomes.

Multiculturalism   Understanding, appreciating, and valuing cultures other than one's own with their own uniquenesses and strengths.

Narrative   A story created by a person or family where objective and subjective experiences are selectively arranged, which serve to organize and give meaning to the person or family.

Niche   The particular role or status of an individual or family in its community and environment resulting from accommodation to this environment.

Normalizing   A therapeutic technique that depathologizes problems in a way that changes perceptions of the situation, gives relief to the family, and deemphasizes the problem.

Object Relations Theory   An interactional systems theory that views the basic human motivation as the search for satisfying interpersonal relationships. It is based upon early parent–child interpersonal relationships, which the child internalizes and which become the model for later interpersonal relations in the family of origin, mate selection, family of procreation, and other intimate relationships.

Oppression   When a group, institution, or government places severe restrictions on or withholds power from other groups or institutions.

Premack Principle   A social learning principle that requires the completion of a desired activity or low-probability behavior before doing a preferred activity or high-probability behavior. Also known as "Grandma's law."

Presuppositional Questioning   In solution-focused interventions, a family is led to believe that a solution will be achieved by implying the occurrence of a specific event or selecting a specific verb tense. For example, saying "What good things happened since last session?" instead of "Did anything good happen since last session?"

Projective Identification   An unconscious defense mechanism and interactional style of families where unwanted aspects of the self are attributed to another person, thus inducing that person to act according to these projected feelings and attitudes in an act of collusion.

Relabeling   A therapeutic intervention that involves reframing a problem in more positive terms so that it is perceived differently and so that the person or family can respond to it differently and in a healthier way.

Resilience   The ability to withstand and rebound from crises and adversities.

Restructuring   The process of producing change in a family system through changing its structure, for example, strengthening the boundaries around the spousal subsystem.

Second-Order Change   In systems theory, this is a basic and lasting change in the structure and functioning of a family.

Self-Help Organizations   These are formally structured groups, such as Parents Without Partners or Alcoholics Anonymous, that provide mutual assistance for the group participants who have a common problem with which some of the members have coped successfully.

Service Networks   The linking of formal or informal persons, agencies, or organizations on behalf of a person or family in order to make the services available, accessible, and needs-satisfying.

Shaping   A procedure used especially in behavioral therapy where an area of competence or desired behavior is acknowledged and reinforced.

Social Constructionism   A metatheory where behaviors and relationships are seen in terms of organized efforts to create meaning out of personal experiences. Reality is seen as constructed by the person or family, family functioning is based upon shared meanings, and the family practitioner becomes a coauthor of a living story with them.

Social Learning Theory   This theory focuses on reciprocal relationships and uses principles from social and developmental psychology and learning theory for understanding and treating behavior.

Solution-Focused Intervention   A style of intervention that emphasizes solutions or exceptions that families have already developed for their problems rather than the problems themselves.

Splitting   In object relations theory, a primitive defense process where a person separates the good from the bad in an external object and then internalizes this split perception. These splits can then be projected upon other people.

Strategic Family Interventions   A therapeutic approach where the practitioner designs interventions to resolve specific problems that will, at the same time, require the family system to modify other interactions. The focus is on second-order change and breaking the recursive sequence that seems to be maintaining the problem.

Symbiosis   An intense emotional attachment where the boundaries between individuals become indistinct, and they react as one as in an undifferentiated ego mass.

Tarasoff Decision   A 1976 ruling by the Supreme Court of California in the case of *Tarasoff v. Regents of the University of California*, stating that, under certain circumstances, psychotherapists whose clients tell them that they intend to harm someone are obliged to warn the intended victim.

Therapeutic Alliance   The capacity of the practitioner and family systems to mutually invest in and work together toward their goals.

Therapeutic Contract   The agreement that the family and the practitioner have worked out together concerning what the problem is and how they will work on it. Goals, methods, mutual obligations, and timetables may be a part of the formal or informal agreement.

Triangle   In family systems theory, this is a three-person system that results when a dyad under stress pulls in a third person to dilute the stress and maintain the system. The triangle is considered to be the smallest stable emotional system.

Triangulation   In family systems theory, it can refer to any triangle where the conflict of two persons pulls in a third person and immobilizes this third person in a loyalty conflict. Most commonly it involves two parents and a child.

Author Index

AAMFT Code of Ethics, 56–57
Adams, J. F., 151
Adnopoz, D. J., 67, 68
Ady, R., 219
Ainsworth, M. D. S., 71
Alvarez, A., 221
Ambrosina, R., 20
Andersen, T., 183
Anderson, D. A., 59
Anderson, H., 143
Anoretic, D., 176–179, 186
Anoretic, M., 176–179, 186
Aponte, H., 8, 58, 78
Applegate, J. S., 193
Arkinson, N., 221
Arthur, J., 126
Assagioli, T., 58
Avery, L., 221

Baker, L., 117, 156
Baldwin, L. M., 4, 150
Bardill, D. R., 59
Barth, R., 71
Baruth, L. G., 52
Bateson, G., 173, 176
Beavers, W. R., 4, 9, 155, 156,
    161–162, 165
Beavin, J. H., 19
Bebbington, P., 92
Becvar, D. S., 51, 59
Becvar, R. J., 51
Bell, N. W., 197
Bennett-Alexander, D., 40
Berg, I. K., 151
Berger, P., 23
Bergin, A. E., 117
Bergman, J. S., 155, 156, 161, 162
Berman, M., 166
Bertsche, V. A., 89

Besa, D., 176, 185
Biegel, D. E., 71
Biestek, F. P., 38, 39
Bishop, D. S., 4, 150
Blakely, E. J., 212, 219
Blanck, G., 200
Blanck, R., 200
Booth, C., 71, 72
Boss, P. G., 51, 52
Boszormenyi-Nagy, I., 197, 198
Bowen, M., 160, 161, 163, 165, 192,
    197, 198
Bowlby, J., 18, 71
Bradshaw, T., 219
Bray, J. H., 52
Breunlin, D. C., 16
Broderick, C. B., 43
Brower, A. M., 17
Bruner, E., 177
Bruner, J., 177
Buber, M., 38, 199
Buell, B., 212, 222
Bumberry, W. M., 27, 28
Burden, S. L., 156
Bushorn, R. J., 6, 8, 68

Calhoun, G., 126
Campbell, J., 57, 58
Canda, E., 58
Cantor, M., 89
Caragonne, P., 89
Carkhuff, R. R., 38
Carter, B., 107, 109, 160, 163
Carter, G. W., 93
Catherall, D. R., 38–39, 40
Caust, B. L., 43
Center for the Study of Social Policy,
    73
Chang, J., 175, 177

Chau, K. L., 41, 42
Chilman, C., 214
Cleveland, P. H., 5, 21
Cobb, S., 18
Cohen, Y. A., 216
Colapinto, J., 117
Cole, E., 72
Combs, G., 165
Condon, M., 45
Congress, E. P., 43
Cooklin, A., 104
Corisglia, V., 144
Cornett, C., 58
Cox, F. M., 213
Craig-Van Grack, 77

Dattalo, P., 85, 86, 91, 93, 94
Davatz, U., 38
Davis, K. E., 26
Dean, R. G., 186
Derrida, J., 26
de Shazer, S., 139–140, 142, 144, 148,
    149
Devore, W., 40
Dicks, H. V., 197, 202
Doherty, W. J., 51, 52
Dore, M. M., 71
Duncan, O., 212
Duva, J., 72

Efran, J. A., 50
Ellenberg, D. B., 165
Ephross, P. H., 22, 90
Epstein, N. B., 4, 150
Epston, D., 28, 32, 173, 174, 176–178,
    183–186
Epston, M., 186
Erlich, J., 213
Esler, I., 172

Fadden, G., 92
Fairbairn, W. R. D., 196
Falicov, C. J., 83
Faraci, A., 118
Fay, L. F., 156
Ferenczi, S., 196
Finkelstein, L., 193
Fish, V., 176
Fishman, H. C., 103, 107, 113
Fleischman, M., 126
Fleming, M., 85
Foucault, M., 175
Fox, M., 57
Framo, J. L., 197, 198
Freedman, J., 165
Freidson, E., 218
Freud, A., 67
Freud, S., 196, 197
Fuguitt, G., 220

Gadamer, H. G., 26
Gale, J. E., 144
Gallant, J. P., 180
Gans, H. J., 217
Garfield, S. L., 117
Gaudin, J. M., 4, 18, 221, 226
Geertz, C., 25
Geismar, L. L., 67
Gelber, J., 25
Gendlin, E. T., 38
Gergen, K. J., 25–28
Germain, C. B., 17–20, 32
Gillette, D., 44
Giordano, J., 41, 162
Gitterman, A., 17, 19, 20, 32
Glaser, B. A., 126, 132
Goldenberg, H., 19, 83, 95
Goldenberg, I., 19, 83, 95
Goldstein, A., 38
Goldstein, H., 24, 29
Goldstein, J., 67, 70
Goolishian, H. A., 143
Gordon, E. M., 106
Green, S. L., 51
Greene, R. R., 22, 83, 87, 88, 90, 92–94
Grigsby, R. K., 67, 71
Grimm, D. W., 197
Groze, V., 83
Guerin, P. J., 106, 156, 159–161, 165
Guerney, B. G., 103
Guitterez, L., 221

Haapala, D., 72
Hafner, J., 185
Hampson, R. B., 4, 155, 156, 161–162, 165
Hansen, J. C., 51
Hansen, M., 217
Hardy, K. V., 42–43
Harris, S. M., 165

Hart, B., 176, 177
Hartman, A., 4, 8, 20, 32, 89, 90
Harway, M., 217
Harwood, A., 218
Hawley, A., 212
Haynes, A. W., 221, 226
Hays, J. R., 52
Hearn, G., 88
Hefferman, J., 20
Held, B. S., 29
Hernandez, S., 226
Hervsi, O., 118
Hewson, D., 172, 173
Hines, P. M., 41
Ho, K. H., 83
Hoffman, L., 23, 44, 172, 173
Holland, T. P., 24, 53, 58, 59
Holle, M. C., 17
Horejsi, C. R., 89
Horne, A. M., 126, 132
Hsu, J., 83
Huber, C. H., 52
Hudson, P. O., 186
Hulgus, Y. F., 4
Hultkrantz, A., 216
Hunter, F., 212
Hunter, J., 217

Jackson, D. D., 19
Jenkins, A., 186
Jones, M. A., 76
Jorgensen, J., 226
Joyce, T. A., 172
Juni, S., 197
Jurich, J. A., 151

Kaplan, L., 67
Kaplan, M., 82
Karrer, B. M., 83
Kautto, J. G., 156
Keen, S., 44
Keller, J. F., 58
Kelly, P., 165
Kelly, T., 84
Kernberg, O. F., 196
Kiesler, D. L., 38
Kilpatrick, A. C., 4, 5, 21, 53, 58, 59
Kinney, J., 71, 72
Kisthardt, W. E., 86, 87
Klein, M., 196, 197
Kropf, N. P., 84, 87
Kruzich, J., 226
Kuhn, A., 86
Kuhn, D. R., 83
Kuipers, L., 92
Kune-Karrer, B. M., 16
Kurtines, W., 118

Laird, J., 4, 8, 20, 32, 89
Langs, R., 201

Lasorte, M. A., 67
Lauffer, A., 212
Lazarus, R. S., 17, 18
Leavitt, S., 72
Lee, E., 41
Leiby, J., 59
Leupnitz, D. A., 117
Levin, V. S., 75
Levine, I. S., 85
Lewis, E., 221
Libow, J. A., 43
Link, R. J., 28
Listokin, D., 220, 221
Littell, J. H., 71
Long, D. D., 17
Luckmann, T., 23
Lukens, M. D., 50
Lukens, R., 50

MacNair, R., 222
Madigan, S., 176
Magura, S., 76
Mahler, M. S., 197
Maisel, R., 186
Maluccio, A. N., 32
Marsh, S., 197, 203
Maslow, A., 3
Mattaini, M. A., 20
May, G., 59
McGehee, E., 57
McGoldrick, M., 41, 83, 107, 109, 160, 162–165
McNamee, S., 27, 28
McQuiade, S., 186
Menses, G., 186
Meyer, C. H., 17, 32
Miller, S. D., 151
Minahan, A., 89
Minuchin, S., 8, 38, 83, 103–107, 110–113, 116–118, 156
Molanar, A., 142, 148, 149
Montalvo, B., 103
Moore, R., 44
Moore, S. T., 89
Morris, F., 186
Morris, P. W., 130
Morris, S. B., 126, 132
Moses, B. S., 76
Mount, B., 85
Moyers, B., 57, 58
Mucucci, J. A., 165

Nagler, S. F., 67
National Association of Social Workers, 56, 89, 92
National Opinion Research Project, 45, 46
Neimeyer, R. A., 172, 179, 185
Nelson, G. M., 89
Nelson, H., 71

Nelson, K. E., 71
Nemon, H., 221
Nichols, M., 19, 20, 29, 103–105, 112, 116, 192, 196, 197
Nodrick, B., 186
Nunnaly, E., 214
Nyland, D., 144

O'Hanlon, W. H., 24, 28, 32, 139, 142–150, 186
Ooms, T., 45, 46

Paquin, G. W., 6, 8, 68
Parker, G., 193
Parsons, R., 226
Passmore, J. L., 126, 132
Payne, M., 16, 30
Pearce, J. K., 41, 162
Peck, M. S., 59
The People of Color Leadership Institute, 41–42
Peters, M. J., 197, 203
Peters, T. C., 197, 203
Pharis, M. E., 75
Phillips, M., 175, 177
Piercy, F. P., 151, 197
Pincus, A., 89
Pinsof, W. F., 11, 38–40
Polansky, N. A., 4, 18
Polkinghorne, D. E., 25
Prest, L. A., 58
Preto, N. G., 41
Project SHARE, 212

Quinton, D., 68

Rapp, C., 86
Raskin, P. A., 43
Reed, H., 57
Rehr, H., 89
Rhodes, S. L., 83
Richmond, M., 89
Ricoeur, P., 25
Rivest, M., 71
Roberts, R., 213
Roberts-DeGennaro, M., 88
Robin, A., 130
Rogers, C., 38
Rolls, J. A., 165
Rose, S., 87
Rosen, H., 32
Rosenblatt, P., 166
Rosenthal, J. A., 83
Rosman, B. L., 103, 117, 156
Rothman, J., 85, 213
Rubin, A., 88, 89
Rubin, H., 219

Rubin, I., 219
Rutter, M., 68
Rzepnicki, T., 71, 76

Sachs, P. R., 165
Saleebey, D., 72, 86
Sampson, H., 199
Sarbin, T. R., 23
Sawhill, I. V., 45
Sayger, T. V., 126, 132, 133
Scharff, D. E., 197, 198, 200, 202, 204
Scharff, J. S., 197, 198, 200, 202, 204
Schlesinger, E. G., 40
Schneider, M., 130
Schneider, R. L., 87
Schrader, S. S., 43
Schuerman, J. R., 71
Schumer, F., 103
Schwartz, M., 57
Schwartz, R. C., 16, 19, 20, 29, 103
Scott, D., 24
Seaberg, J. R., 76
Selekman, M., 151
Selig, A. L., 68
Seymour, F. W., 185
Shafer, C. M., 90
Shaffer, R., 219
Shepherd, J. N., 52
Shilton, P., 4
Shulman, L., 45
Shuttlesworth, G., 20
Silverstein, J. L., 198
Simon, F. B., 19, 20, 27
Simon, G., 113
Singh, R. N., 221, 226
Siporin, M., 59
Slipp, S., 192, 193, 196, 198–204
Sluzki, C. E., 178
Smalley, R. E., 71
Smith, A. R., 57
Solnit, A. J., 67
Spark, G., 198
Specter, P. D., 25
Spengler, J. J., 212
Stanton, M. D., 117
Stein, T., 76
Steinberg, R. M., 93
Sternlieb, G., 220, 221
Stewart, B., 186
Stewart, R. H., 197, 200, 203
Stierlin, H., 19, 192
Structural Family Systems Ratings, 118
Sudweeks, C., 126, 132, 133
Sullivan, M., 28

Suttles, G. D., 216
Szapocnki, J., 118
Szykula, S. A., 126, 132, 133

Tandy, C., 180
Taylor, S., 213
Taylor, V. L., 172
Thyer, B., 76–77
Todd, T. C., 117
Tomm, K., 176, 178, 182
Towle, C., 3
Tracy, E. M., 71
Tropman, J., 213
Trotz, V., 89
Truax, C. B., 38
Tseng, W. S., 83
Tyson, T., 220

Van Ness, P., 57
Vogel, E. F., 197
Von Bertalanffy, L., 17, 19
Von Glasersfeld, E., 23
Vorren, O., 216
Vourlekis, B. S., 88

Wakefield, J. C., 23
Walker, J. M., 126, 132
Walsh, F., 217
Warren, R. L., 212–214
Watzlawick, P., 19
Webster, D., 151
Weil, M., 89
Weiner-Davis, M., 24, 28, 32, 139, 142–150
Weiss, J., 199
Weiss, M. J., 217
Weiss, R. S., 18
Wells, K., 71
Weltner, J. S., 4, 8–9, 67, 68, 73, 77, 78, 104, 118, 140, 152, 155, 158
Weston, K., 83
Whitaker, C. A., 27, 28
White, M., 27, 28, 32, 173, 176–179, 181–184, 186
Whittaker, J. K., 71
Wilkinson, I., 217
Winnicott, D. W., 197
Wodarski, J., 221
Wolin, S., 5
Wolin, S. J., 5
Woody, J. D., 53, 54
Worthen, D., 59
Wynne, L., 19, 197

Yuan, Y. T., 71

Zwernik, K., 85

Subject Index

AAMFT Code of Ethics, 56–57
Abuse, ethical issues of, 51
Accommodation, 109–110, 111–112
Actualization
    Level IV families and, 10
    in structural interventions,
        113–116
Adaptations, in ecosystems
    metatheory, 18–19
Advocacy
    in case management, 93–94
    Level I families and, 75–76
Affiliations, as family resource,
    217–218
AIDS
    case management and, 90
    narrative interventions and, 186
Alcohol abuse, in Level III families,
    156
Alliances. *See* Coalitions
American Association of Marriage
    and Family Therapy, 56–57
Anger, narrative interventions and,
    186
Anomie, youth and, 216–217
Anorexia nervosa, 156, 186
Apprenticeship programs, 217
Asian Americans, solution-focused
    interventions and, 151
Assessment
    in case management, 83–84, 92
    in ecosystems metatheory, 20–22
    in family systems interventions,
        156–158
    of Level I families, 4, 7*t*, 68–70,
        83–84
    of Level II families, 6, 7*t*, 124–126
    of Level III families, 7*t*, 8–9, 141,
        156–158

of Level IV families, 7*t*, 9–10,
    194–195
in narrative interventions,
    173–174
in object relations interventions,
    200, 201*t*
Audiotapes, in narrative
    interventions, 183–184
Authority. *See also* Executive
    systems; Leadership
    in human service networking, 222
    in Level II families, 104
Awareness, Level IV families and,
    199

Beavers Family Competence Scale, 4
Beavers Interactional Competence
    Scale, 9
Behavior
    deviant, 176
    social constructionism and, 24–25
    social learning interventions and,
        127
    solution-focused interventions
        and, 142, 143
Behavioral interventions, 8, 11
Bias
    bureaucracies and, 216
    spirituality and, 58
Blue collar communities, climate of,
    220
Borderline personality, 196
Boundaries
    in Level III families, 155, 160
    in relationships, 109–110
    in structural interventions,
        114–115
Boundary-spanning approach, 88
Bulimia, 186

Bureaucracies, effects on families,
    215–216

Caretaker/child relationship, 67
Case management
    advocacy in, 93–94
    assessment in, 83–84, 92
    building relationships in, 91–92
    evaluation in, 94–95
    family-centered practice and, 89
    family needs and, 91, 95
    interventions, 91–94
    key features of, 82, 86–88
    Level I family problems and, 82
    systems theory and, 90
    treatment goals, 84–85
    treatment models, 85–86
Case management team, 86
Case managers, roles of, 89, 91, 95
Case plans, 92
Causality, 20, 177
Celebrations, in narrative
    interventions, 183–184
Certificates, in narrative
    interventions, 183–184
Change
    enhancing, in narrative
        interventions, 181
    family capacity for, 105, 106
    solution-focused interventions
        and, 139, 140, 142–143
    theory of, 177–178
Charity Organization Societies, 89
Children
    caretaker relationship and, 67
    disciplinary strategies, 130–131
    in Level I families, 76
    in Level II families, 6
    in Level III families, 155–156

narrative interventions and, 178, 185
poverty and, 45–46
safety and, 76
self-control strategies, 130
in single-parent families, 46
structural interventions and, 117
in triangulation, 161
Chores. *See* Tasks
Chronic anxiety, 160
Church-related counseling, 10
Client-helper relationship, 74–75
Clients
  interactions with problems, 179–181
  linking to services, 93
Client systems
  evaluation of, 94–95
  in therapeutic alliance, 39–40
Coaching, 163–165
Coalitions
  family practitioners and, 115–116
  in Level II families, 7–8
Codes of ethics, 54*t*, 55–57
Coercion, in treatment, 52
Cognitive restructuring, 127–128, 129
Colleagues, unethical behavior and, 56
Commercial-agriculture communities, climate of, 219
Commonalities, in family practice, 37–40
Communication skills training, 131–132
Communities
  basic characteristics of, 213–214
  ecosystems theory and, 211–214
  human service networking in, 222–223
  local economics and, 218–221
  sociocultural composition and, 221
  spirituality and, 59
  sustenance resources in, 214–218
Community workers, engagement of Level I families and, 73
Competence, reinforcement of, 116
Complaint pattern intervention, 149
Complaints. *See* Problems
Compliments, in solution-focused interventions, 148
Computer technology, communities and, 213
Conceptualization, in spirituality, 58
Confidentiality, 52
Conflict, ecosystems metatheory and, 23

Conflict resolution
  Level I families and, 75
  Level II families and, 77
Consequences, in child disciplinary strategies, 131
Consumer economics, family skills in, 215
Context pattern intervention, 149
Continuum of care, 86
Control
  in Level III families, 155
  in social constructionism, 26–27
Convenience shopping, 215
Conversation, in solution-focused interventions, 143–144, 145
Cooperation, in solution-focused interventions, 144–145
Coping, 8–9, 18, 128
Couples therapy, 186
Courts, confidentiality and, 52
Creativity, in human service networking, 223
Credit purchasing, 215
Crisis intervention theory, 71
Critical thinking, in ethics, 54*t*
Cross-cultural marriages, 41
Cross-cultural practice model, 41, 42*f*
Culturagram, 43
Cultural competency, 41–43
Cultural genogram, 43
Culture. *See also* Sociocultural conditions
  social constructionism and, 26
  story patterns and, 25
Cutoff, in Level III families, 160

Deception, by practitioners, 52
Decision making, guides for, 53–55
Demographics, Level II families and, 123
Denial, 29
Depathologizing problems, 147–148
Detector function, in case management process, 86, 87*f*
Detriangling, 164
Development, needs and, 3
Developmental patterns, 83
Deviant behavior, 176
Diagnosis
  in solution-focused interventions, 139
  in structural interventions, 105–108, 112
Differentiation
  in family members, 192
  in Level III families, 9
  of self, 159–160
Dilemmas, in narrative interventions, 181

Dimensions of clinical judgment model, 53–55
Disciplinary strategies, for children, 130–131
Discrimination, social constructionism and, 29
Diversity issues, in family practice, 40–46
Dominance, 198
  in Level III families, 9
  social constructionism and, 29
"Dual perspective," in ethnic sensitive practice, 40–41

Eastern Europe, medical ethics in, 51
Eating disorders, 156
Ecological systems metatheory. *See* Ecosystems theory
Ecomaps, 92
Economic resources
  availability and use of, 214–215
  in communities, 212
  Level I families and, 68
  oppression and, 45
Economics, effects on community climate, 219–221
Ecosystems, separating interventions from, 51
Ecosystems theory, 16–23, 24*t*
  applications to family practice, 20–22
  communities and, 211–214
  compared with social constructionism, 30–32
  intensive family preservation services and, 71
  major concepts in, 17–19
  problems with, 22–23
  systems theory and, 19–20
Education
  communities and, 212
  problems in, 216–217
Effector element, in case management process, 86, 87*f*
Elderly, advocacy and, 93–94
Empathy, 38
Empowerment, 221, 224, 225*f*
Enactment, 113
Encopresis, narrative interventions and, 173–175
Engagement
  of Level I families, 73–74
  of Level III families, 161–163
Enmeshment, in Level III families, 160
Environment
  adaptations and, 18–19
  communities and, 213
  in ecosystems metatheory, 20
Equifinality, 19
Ericksonian techniques, 150

Ethics
 codes, 54t, 55–57
 decision making and, 53–55
 issues in family practice, 50–53
Ethnic division, effects on
  community climate, 221
Ethnic sensitive practice, 40–43
Ethnographic interviewing, 74
Evaluation, in case management,
  94–95
Exceptions, solution-focused
  interventions and, 145–146
Exceptions questions, 182
Executive systems. *See also*
  Authority; Leadership
 in Level I families, 67, 68
 in Level II families, 77
Exosystems, 20, 21f, 22
Experience-of-experience
  questions, 182–183
Experiential interventions, 11
Externalization, in narrative
  interventions, 176, 178–179

Faith, 58
Families of the Slums (Minuchin), 117
Family. *See also* Level I families;
   Level II families; Level III
   families; Level IV families
 advocacy and, 93–94
 bureaucracies and, 215–216
 consumer skills, 215
 defined, 30
 developmental patterns, 83
 differentiation in, 192
 flexibility in, 105, 106
 life cycle of, 83
 modern stresses and, 122
 restructuring, 113–116
 sculpting, 10
 sensitivity in, 106, 107
 sociability and, 217–218
Family Assessment Device, 150–151
"Family Empowerment and Social
  Justice" model, 226
Family history, 104, 105
Family life context, 106, 107
Family map, 112
Family-of-origin issues, 195
Family practice
 commonalities and, 37–40
 diversity issues and, 40–46
 ecosystems metatheory and,
   20–22, 30–32
 social constructionism and, 27–28,
   30–32
Family practitioners. *See also*
   Therapeutic alliance;
   Therapeutic contract
 feminist, 43

helping relationship and, 37–40
 in human services networking,
   225, 226
 influence on community climate,
   221
 intervention choice points and,
   11–12
 Level I families and, 74–75
 Level III families and, 155,
   161–165, 166
 in metatheories, 20, 22, 23, 31
 in narrative interventions, 173
 in object relations interventions,
   199, 200–203
 in social learning interventions,
   128–129
 spirituality and, 59
 in structural interventions,
   110–116
Family Preservation and Support
  Services Act (1993), 71
Family preservation service models,
  72
Family structure
 diversity in, 46
 in family diagnosis, 105, 106
 in Level II families, 126
Family systems interventions
 assessment in, 156–158
 evaluations of, 165–166
 intervention techniques, 161–165
 theoretical bases, 159–161
 treatment goals, 158–159
Family systems theory, 19–20, 24t
 in family case management, 90
 intensive family preservation
   services and, 71
 object relations interventions and,
   192, 195–196
 structural interventions and, 103
Family welfare, *versus* individual
  welfare, 51
Feedback, in systems theory, 19
Feminism, 43–44
 solution-focused interventions
   and, 151
 welfare issues and, 51
Flexibility, in families, 105, 106
Formalism, in human service
  networking, 222–223
"Formula first session task," 149, 151
Foucault, Michel, 175–176
Fragmentation, in human service
  networking, 222
Functional theory, intensive family
  preservation services and, 71

Gender, holding environment and,
  197
Gender issues, 43–44

Generalist case management model,
  85, 86
Generic structure, 107–108
Genograms, 157, 157f, 163, 166
 cultural, 43
 Level I families and, 74
 Level IV families and, 10
Genuineness, 38
Goal-directed model, in human
  service networking, 224–226
Goals. *See* Treatment goals
Godparents, 74
"Grandma's law," 131
Grief, 186

Habitat, in ecosystems metatheory, 18
Harvard Medical School, 57
Helping relationship, 37–40
Historical interventions, 11
History of exception questions, 182
Holding environment, 197–198, 199,
  202
Home-based services, 71. *See also*
   Intensive family preservation
   services
Homelessness, 46
 ecosystems model of, 21f, 22
Homeostasis
 ecosystems metatheory and, 23
 feedback and, 19
Homosexual couples, 103
Hope, spirituality and, 58–59
Housing, 46
Human ecology. *See* Ecosystems
   theory
Humanism, in human service
   networking, 223
Human service leaders, influence on
   community climate, 221
Human service networks
 evaluation of, 94–95
 goal-directed model, 224–226
 patterns in, 222–223
Human services
 in communities, 212–213, 218–221
 evaluation of, 94–95
 linking clients to, 93

Idiographic design, 76
Idiosyncratic structure, 107–108
Illness, Level I families and, 82
Imagery, 130
Income inequality, 45
Individual boundaries, 114
Individual welfare, *versus* family
   welfare, 51
Individuation, 9
Inequality, in income, 45
Informed consent, 52
Inner world, 199

Institutional racism, 45
"Integrated Practice" model, 226
Intensive family preservation
  services
    application to Level I families,
      72–73
    core values, 72–73
    interventions and techniques in,
      73–76
    theoretical base of, 71–72
Interactional interventions, 11
Intergenerational models. *See*
    Family systems interventions
Interpersonal processes, 20
Interpretation
    in ecosystems metatheory, 31
    in social constructionism, 26, 27,
      31
Interventions
    in case management, 91–94
    choice points, 10–13
    in ecosystems metatheory, 20–22,
      31
    Level I families, 4–6, 7*t*, 71–76
    Level II families, 6–8, 77, 110–116,
      127–132
    Level III families, 7*t*, 9, 78,
      144–150, 161–165
    Level IV families, 7*t*, 10, 78,
      178–185
    in object relations interventions,
      199, 200, 202*t*, 203*t*
    separating from larger
      ecosystems, 51
    in social constructionism, 31
Interviewing, of Level I families, 74
Introjection, 196–197, 198
Intuitive thinking, in ethics, 54*t*
Inventiveness, in human service
    networking, 223
Inventories, of strengths, 74
Isolation, violence and, 217
"I-Thou" relationship, 38, 199

Joining
    Level III families and, 162–163
    in solution-focused interventions,
      144–145
    in structural interventions,
      111–112
Judeo-Christian tradition,
    community awareness and,
      59
Judiciary, confidentiality and, 52

Knowledge, in ecosystems and
    social constructionism, 32

Labeling, bureaucracies and, 216
Laxatives, abuse of, 156

Leadership, 4, 220*t*. *See also*
    Authority; Executive systems
Learning disabilities, narrative
    interventions and, 186
Learning environment, 128
Letters, in narrative interventions,
    183–184
Level I families, 4–6, 7, 152
    assessments, 68–70, 83–84
    bureaucracies and, 215–216
    case management and, 82–95
    compared to Level II families, 77
    educational issues and, 216, 217
    genograms and, 166
    interventions, 71–76, 91–94
    object relations model and, 204
    parental system in, 118
    social learning model and, 133
    structural model and, 118
    treatment goals, 70–71, 84–85
    typical examples of, 68
Level II families, 6–8
    assessments, 104–108, 124–126
    case management and, 91, 95
    compared to Level I families, 77
    coping with bureaucracies and,
      215–216
    educational issues and, 216, 217
    genograms and, 166
    interventions, 110–116, 127–132
    social learning model and,
      126–132
    solution-focused model and, 152
    structural model and, 104–118
    treatment goals, 108–109, 124–126
    typical problems in, 104, 122–124
Level III families, 7*t*, 8–9
    assessments, 141, 156–158, 174
    case management and, 95
    family practitioners and, 155,
      161–165, 166
    family systems model and,
      155–166
    interventions, 144–150, 161–165
    narrative model and, 173–175
    oppression and, 45
    parental system in, 118
    social learning model and, 133
    solution-focused model and,
      140–152
    structural model and, 118
    treatment goals, 158–159, 174–175
    typical problems in, 140–141,
      155–156
Level IV families, 7*t*, 9–10, 118
    assessments, 174, 194–195
    case management and, 95
    genograms and, 166
    interventions, 178–185
    narrative model and, 171–186

object relations model and,
    193–204
oppression and, 45
social learning model and, 133
solution-focused model and, 152
typical problems in, 171–174, 199
Libido, 196
Life cycles, 83
Life stress. *See* Stress
Life transitions, 20

Macrosystems, 20, 21*f*, 22
Maintenance, in structural
    interventions, 112
Male batterers, 186
Managers, in human service
    networking, 223
Manipulation, by practitioners, 52
Marital conflict
    in Level II families, 6
    in Level III families, 156
    object relations interventions and,
      193
Masculinity, critiques of, 44
McMaster Family Assessment
    Device, 150–151
Meaning
    Level IV families and, 199
    in narrative interventions,
      172–173
    social constructionism and, 27, 29
    stories and, 23, 25–27
Medicine, spirituality and, 57
Men's movement, 44
Mental illness
    case management and, 84–85
    implications for relationship
      building, 92
    strengths perspective and, 87
Mesosystems, 20, 21*f*, 22
Microsystems, 20, 21*f*, 22
Middle managers, in human service
    networking, 223
Migrants, human service
    networking and, 222
Mimesis, in structural interventions,
    112
Minorities, poverty and, 45–46
Minuchin, Salvador, 103
Mother-blaming, structural
    interventions and, 117
Mothers, single. *See* Single parents
Multiculturalism, 40, 193
Multigenerational transmission,
    195. *See also* Family systems
    interventions
Multi-industry communities,
    climate of, 220–221
"Multiproblem families." *See* Level I
    families

Narrative interventions, 32, 172–174
assessment in, 173–174
evaluations of, 185
intervention techniques, 178–185
Level IV families and, 10
stories in, 171
theoretical base, 175–178
theory of change in, 177–178
theory of power and oppression
in, 175–176
theory of problems in, 176–177
treatment goals, 174–175
Narratives. *See* Narrative
interventions; Stories
NASW Code of Ethics, 56
National Association of Social
Workers. *See* NASW Code of
Ethics
National Commission on Children,
45–46
Needs. *See also* Problems
in development, 3
distinguished from pathology, 68
levels of ("house analogy"), 4–10
Negative feedback, 19
Neurosis, 196
Niche, in ecosystems metatheory, 18
Normalizing, in solution-focused
interventions, 147–148
Norms, ecosystems metatheory and,
23
Nuclear family, life cycle of, 83
Nursing values, solution-focused
interventions and, 151
Nurturance, 74–75

Object relations family interventions
assessment in, 194–195, 200, 201*t*
evaluations of, 200–203
family needs and, 193–194,
203–204
intervention techniques, 199, 200,
202*t*, 203*t*
Level IV families and, 199
origins of, 192
theory base and major tenets,
195–199
treatment goals, 195
Object relations theory, 192, 196
Older families, advocacy and,
93–94
One-company communities, climate
of, 219–220
Oppression, 44–45
giving attention to, 40
theory of, 175–176
Optimism
in communities, influences on,
218–224
spirituality and, 58–59

Organization, in definition of
community, 212–213

Paradoxical interventions, 165
Parenting
accommodation and boundary
making in, 110
in Level I families, 4, 67, 68, 118
in Level II families, 6, 123
in Level III families, 118
Parents, single, 4, 45, 46, 83
Passivity, 162
Pathology
distinguished from need, 68
as dysfunctional interactions, 110
Patriarchy, critiques of, 44
Perceptions, solution-focused
interventions and, 142, 143
Personal meaning. *See* Meaning
Personal well-being, 156
Persons with AIDS
case management and, 90
narrative interventions and, 186
Person-to-person contact, 164
Pessimism, in communities,
influences on, 218–224
Physical settings. *See* Habitat
Physiological needs, 3
Plots, in social constructionism,
25–26
Population, defined, 212
Positive feedback, 19
Positive imagery, 130
Positive reframing, 130
Postmodernism, 172, 175
Poverty, 45–46, 68
Power, 198
social constructionism and, 29
theory of, 175–176
Prejudice, 29
Premack principle, 131
Premorbid state of the family, 160
Presuppositional questioning,
143–144
Prevention services, 224
Privileges, in child disciplinary
strategies, 131
Problem-focused strategic
treatment, 141–142
Problem focused structural-strategic
intervention, 151
Problems. *See also* Needs
depathologizing, 147–148
effects of, 179
externalization of, 178–179
influences on, 179–181
solution-focused interventions
and, 139–140, 142–143,
147–148
theory of, 176–177

Problem-solving skills training, 128,
132
Productivity, Level III families and,
156
Professional communities, climate
of, 221
Professionalism, in human service
networking, 223
Projective identification, 197
Psychiatric treatment, narrative
interventions and, 186
Psychoanalysis, object relations
interventions and, 192, 196
Psychosomatic symptoms, 117
Public policy, poverty and, 45
PWAs. *See* Persons with AIDS

Questions
in narrative interventions, 178,
182–183
in solution-focused interventions,
143–144

Racism, 45, 221
Reality. *See* Relativism
Rebellion, role of schools in, 216–217
Reciprocal exchange, 17
Reconnecting, in family systems
interventions, 164–165
Reflecting team, 183
Reframing, 130
Regulation, effects on families,
215–216
Relatedness, in ecosystems
metatheory, 18
Relationships
accommodation and boundary
making in, 109–110
caretaker/child, 67
client-helper, 74–75
in family case management,
91–92
helping, 37–40
implications of mental illness in,
92
"I-Thou," 38, 199
in Level III families, 156
needs and, 3
therapeutic, 128–129
triangulation and, 160–161
Relationship therapy, 186
Relative Influence Scale, 180
Relativism
in narrative interventions,
172–173, 175
in social constructionism, 25, 29
Relaxation training, 130
Religious organizations, 10, 217
Resilience, in Level I families, 4–5
Resistance, 31, 144

Resolution, 140
Resources
 inventory, 74
 Level I families and, 68–70
 solution-focused interventions and, 139, 142
Respect, in helping relationship, 38
Restlessness, 216–217
Restructuring, 113–116
Reversals, in family systems interventions, 164
Rights, niches and, 18
Risk assessment, in Level I families, 76
Role modeling, 75, 77
Rural communities, climate of, 219
Rural migrants, 222

Safety, 195
 of children, 76
Schizophrenia, 159, 185, 186
Schools, problems in, 216–217
Secular spirituality, 57
Selector function, in case management process, 86, 87f
Self, differentiation of, 159–160
Self-actualization, 59
Self-control training, 129–131
Self-empowerment services, 224, 225f
Sensitivity. *See also* Ethnic sensitive practice
 in families, 106, 107
Service plans, in case management, 92
Services. *See* Human services
Sessions, practitioner's control of, 165
Setbacks, in narrative interventions, 181
Sex roles, holding environment and, 197
Sexual orientation, object relations interventions and, 193
Sexual therapy, 186
Shopping, family skills in, 215
Significance questions, 182
Single-case design, 76, 77
Single parents, 4, 45, 46, 83
Single-system design, 185
Sociability, as family resource, 217–218
Social attachment theory, 71
Social constructionism, 23–30
 applications to family practice, 27–28
 assumptions about control in, 26–27
 compared with ecosystems metatheory, 30–32

family economic resources and, 215
gender issues and, 44
narrative interventions and, 172
personal meaning in, 25–27
problems with, 29
relativism and, 25, 26
solution-focused interventions and, 142
Social justice, 59
Social learning family interventions, 126–132
 effectiveness of, 126
 evaluations of, 132–133
 intervention techniques, 127–132
 theoretical base, 126–127
Social learning theory, 71
Social needs, human development and, 3
Social network maps, 74
Social norms, ecosystems metatheory and, 23
Social systems model, in case management, 86, 87f
Social work, history of, 89
"Social work roles," 226
Sociocultural conditions, communities and, 211–213
Socioeconomic level
 family support preferences and, 218
 object relations interventions and, 204
Solution-focused family interventions
 assumptions in, 139–140
 basic tenets of, 142–143
 evaluations of, 150–152
 interventions, 144–150
 narrative model and, 175
 problem-focused strategic treatment and, 141–142
 treatment goals, 143–144
"Solution-focused hypnosis," 150
Space, manipulation of, 114
Spectator questions, 182–183
Spiritual growth, 50, 57–60, 199
"Spirituality and Healing in Medicine Conference," 57
Splitting, 196
Status quo, ecosystems metatheory and, 23
Stories, 171. *See also* Narrative interventions
 cultural themes and, 25
 in family systems interventions, 165
 personal meaning and, 25–27
 in social constructionism, 23–25
 theory of change and, 177–178

Strength
 Level I families and, 4–5, 68–70, 72, 74
 Level II families and, 77
 perspective, in case management, 86–87
 social constructionism and, 28
 solution-focused interventions and, 139, 142
Stress
 coping and, 18
 in ecosystems metatheory, 17, 18
 in Level II families, 106, 107, 123
 in Level III families, 160
 modern, 122
 redirecting, 115
Structural family interventions
 assessment in, 104–108
 assumptions and goals of, 103
 evaluations of, 117–118
 interventions, 110–116
 in Level II families, 7–8
 theoretical base, 109–110
 treatment goals in, 108–109
Structural Family Systems Ratings, 118
Subjectivity, spirituality and, 58
Substance abuse, 186
Subsystems, in structural interventions, 114–115
Success, restructuring families for, 127–128, 129
Support
 availability in communities, 218
 inventory, 74
 in Level II families, 106, 107
Supportive care case management, 86
"Surprise task," 149–150
Survival-oriented services, 4, 12. *See also* Level I families
 in communities, 214–218
 in human services networking, 224, 225f
Symptoms
 functionality, 177
 relabeling of, 116
Systems. *See also* Family systems interventions
 in therapeutic alliance, 39–40
Systems theory, 19–20. *See also* Family systems theory

Talk, in solution-focused interventions, 143–144, 145
Tasks
 assigned by family practitioner, 116
 assigning to children, 131

Tasks *(continued)*
  in solution-focused interventions, 149–150, 151
Technology, communities and, 213
Teenagers, in Level II families, 6
Teen councils, 224
Temper problems, 186
Texts. *See* Stories
Themes, in social constructionism, 25–26
Therapeutic alliance, 37–40, 128–129. *See also* Family practitioners
Therapeutic contract, 112–113. *See also* Family practitioners
Therapist case management, 86
Therapy, dominance and, 165, 176
"Think break," 143, 148
Time, 30–31
  collapsing, in narrative interventions, 181
Time-outs, 130–131
Transactional patterns
  in Level II families, 106, 107
  in structural interventions, 113–116

Transportation systems, communities and, 213
Treatment goals, 31
  case management, 84–85
  family systems interventions, 158–159
  Level I families, 70–71, 84–85
  Level II families, 108–109, 124–126
  Level III families, 158–159, 174–175
  narrative interventions, 174–175
  object relations interventions, 195
  solution-focused interventions, 140, 143–144
  structural interventions, 108–109
Triangulation
  detriangling, 164
  in Level III families, 160–161

Unethical behavior, reporting, 56
Unique account questions, 182
Unique outcome questions, 182
Unique redescriptions questions, 182

Universalism, in human service networking, 223

Values
  ethnic sensitive practice and, 41
  in social constructionism, 25–26
  in spirituality, 58f
Violence
  family isolation and, 217
  Level II families and, 6

Warmth, in helping relationship, 38
Welfare benefits, 45
Well-being, 4. *See also* Level I families
White collar communities, climate of, 220–221
Wholeness, in systems theory, 19
Wives, in Level III families, 9
Women
  "externalizing conversations" and, 176
  life cycle and, 83
Women's movement, 43–44. *See also* Feminism